In Defense of the Bush Doctrine

In Defense

of the

Bush Doctrine

ROBERT G. KAUFMAN

THE UNIVERSITY PRESS OF KENTUCKY

Publication of this volume was made possible in part by a grant
from the National Endowment for the Humanities.

Scholarly publisher for the Commonwealth,
serving Bellarmine University, Berea College, Centre College of Kentucky, Eastern
Kentucky University, The Filson Historical Society, Georgetown College, Kentucky
Historical Society, Kentucky State University, Morehead State University, Murray State
University, Northern Kentucky University, Transylvania University, University
of Kentucky, University of Louisville, and Western Kentucky University.
All rights reserved.

Editorial and Sales Offices: The University Press of Kentucky
663 South Limestone Street, Lexington, Kentucky 40508-4008
www.kentuckypress.com

07 08 09 10 11   6 5 4 3 2

Library of Congress Cataloging-in-Publication Data

Kaufman, Robert Gordon.
In defense of the Bush doctrine / Robert G. Kaufman.
p. cm.
Includes bibliographical references and index.
ISBN-13: 978-0-8131-2434-6 (hardcover : alk. paper)
ISBN-10: 0-8131-2434-4 (hardcover : alk. paper) 1. United States—Foreign relations—
2001– 2. United States—Foreign relations—Philosophy. 3. Bush, George W. (George Walker),
1946– —Political and social views. 4. Terrorism—Government policy—United States.
5. War on terrorism, 2001– 6. Iraq War, 2003– 7. Unilateral acts (International law)
8. Intervention (International law) I. Title.
E902.K385 2007
327.73009'0511—dc22   2006038458

This book is printed on acid-free recycled paper meeting the requirements of the American
National Standard for Permanence in Paper for Printed Library Materials.

Manufactured in the United States of America.

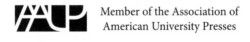

To the memory of Corporal Mark Asher Evnin, USMC

May 18, 1981–April 3, 2003

Killed in action, Al Kut, Iraq

Contents

Acknowledgments

I am immensely grateful to those who made this project possible. Matthew Spalding at the Heritage Foundation planted the seed for systematically developing my ideas about the Bush Doctrine. Under the auspices of Heritage, he hosted my delivering a public lecture on the first principles of American foreign policy in light of the events September 11, 2001. He commented insightfully and sympathetically on several versions of the manuscript. I also benefited greatly from the encouragement of Dean James Wilburn at the Pepperdine School of Public Policy, who provided a stimulating intellectual atmosphere for me to undertake this book. Several friends and colleagues generously took the time to read this manuscript. My warm thanks to Professor James Q. Wilson for his insightful comments and assurances that the manuscript should be published. My warm thanks as well to Michael Warder, Vice Chancellor at Pepperdine, and my dear friend Kelsey Bush Nadeau for their wise and sympathetic editorial suggestions. Vincent Beerman, my research assistant, and Marie Ann Thaler, the administrative assistant for the Pepperdine School of Public Policy, also deserve great credit for their labors on this manuscript and their patience with me.

My special thanks go to the director of the University Press of Kentucky, Steve Wrinn, his assistant, Anne Dean Watkins, and their fine staff, particularly Ann Twombly, my deft and patient copy editor.

As usual, my greatest thanks go to my family: to my parents, who in my childhood cultivated my interest in history, politics, and lively debate, even when they typically disagreed with my ultimate conclusions; to my sister, who is enormously generous and brave; to my daughters, Caroline and Natalie, who indulged their father in so many ways; and above all, to my lovely wife, Anne, who is the anchor of my life.

Introduction

September 11, 2001, marks a pivotal day for American grand strategy. Homicide bombers initiated World War IV by demolishing the Twin Towers of the World Trade Center and destroying part of the Pentagon. This attack shattered the optimistic illusions so prevalent during the tranquil 1990s that American foreign policy had reached the end of history: democracy was triumphant and catastrophic wars were a relic of the past. The Bush administration's bold and ambitious grand strategy for waging the war on terror (the Bush Doctrine) has ignited a passionate debate about the purposes of American power and America's role in the world.

The Bush Doctrine rests on two main pillars. First, the events of September 11 rudely demonstrate the inadequacy of deterrence, containment, or ex post facto responses when dealing with terrorists and rogue regimes bent on acquiring weapons of mass destruction (WMD); hence, the United States cannot rule out the option of using force preemptively rather than reactively. Second, the root cause of 9/11 and similarly inspired aggression is the culture of tyranny in the Middle East, which spawns fanatical, aggressive, secular, and religious despotisms; hence, the United States must promote democratic regime change in that region. Or, in the words of President Bush, "The gravest danger to freedom lies at the perilous crossroad of radicalism and WMD technology."[1] His remedy is "the advance of freedom, especially in the Middle East."[2] The president envisages the achievement of these goals as the work of generations: "The United States is in the early years of a long struggle similar to what our country faced in the early years of the Cold War. The twentieth century witnessed the triumph of freedom over threats of fascism and communism. Yet a new totalitarian ideology now threatens, an ideology grounded not in secular philosophy but in the perversion of a proud religion. Its content may be different from the ide-

1

ologies of the last century, but the means are similar: intolerance, murder, terror, enslavement, and repression."[3] The most scathing criticism of the Bush Doctrine in the United States has come from a formidable coalition of isolationists, realists, and liberal multilateralists.[4] Such discord is the norm in times of peril. In the annals of American history, war often has served as the catalyst for fundamental transformations of American grand strategy.[5] The wars of the French Revolution and Napoleon, lasting from 1792 to 1815, triggered a ferocious debate in America over foreign policy, which eventually culminated in President Washington's dictum of no entangling alliances or commitments outside the Western Hemisphere that entailed the cost or risk of war. This strategy of isolationism, or armed neutrality, reigned supreme in American diplomacy for nearly 150 years; the discredited American intervention in World War I was the exception that proved the rule. It took the Japanese attack on Pearl Harbor on December 7, 1941, and Nazi Germany's declaration of war against the United States days later to convince a generation of American statesmen once and for all that isolationism no longer sufficed to protect American national security in the changing circumstances of the twentieth century.

After World War II the Truman administration devised a new grand strategy of vigilant containment in response to the emergence of the Soviet threat and the advent of nuclear weapons. This strategy aimed to wear down and ultimately defeat Soviet totalitarianism through robust forward deterrence and through the establishment of a worldwide American alliance system, with the democracies of Western Europe and Japan as the linchpins.

During the 1970s the agonizing debate over the Vietnam War generated intense pressure to recast American grand strategy. The unanticipated outcome of this debate was the election of Ronald Reagan, who contributed mightily to winning the Cold War during the 1980s by reviving and intensifying President Truman's original conception of robust containment.

This book offers a vigorous defense of the Bush Doctrine and the principles underlying it, which I call moral democratic realism. It strives to connect the Bush Doctrine and the contemporary debate over American foreign policy to the richer, deeper tradition of American diplomatic history, drawing from the positive lessons as well as the cautionary tales of the past. Two major premises shape this case for moral democratic realism and the Bush Doctrine's conformity to it.

The first is that the fundamental purposes of American foreign policy have remained largely the same since the founding of the United States: to assure the integrity and vitality of a free society, "which is founded upon the dignity and worth of the individual." Or in the timeless words of National Security Council 68 (NSC 68), written in 1950, which laid out the rationale for U.S. strategy for much of the Cold War: "Our determination to maintain the essential freedoms as set forth in the Constitution and the Bill of Rights; our determination to create conditions under which our free and democratic system can live and prosper; and our determination if necessary to defend our way of life, for which as in the Declaration of Independence, with firm reliance on the protection of Divine Providence, we mutually pledge to each other our lives, our Fortunes, and our sacred Honor."[6] The second is that the cardinal virtue of prudence, as St. Thomas Aquinas defined it—"right reason about things to be done"—ought to serve as the standard for evaluating the best practicable American grand strategy.[7] Aquinas's conception of prudence does not correspond to mere caution or Machiavellian cunning. On the contrary, it not only presupposes moral virtue, the choice of right ends, but also the wisdom to choose the right means to achieve them. The eminent Thomist Joseph Pieper aptly expresses Aquinas's conception of prudence that informs this book:

> The pre-eminence of prudence means that so-called "good intentions" and "meaning well" by no means suffice. Realization of the good presupposes that our actions are appropriate to real situations, that is, to the concrete realities that inform the environment of concrete human action; and that we objectively take concrete reality seriously, with clear-eyed objectivity. . . . In the decisions of prudence, which by the very nature of prudence are concerned with things concrete, contingent, and future, there cannot be that certainty which is possible in a theoretical conclusion. . . . Man, then, when he comes to a decision cannot ever be sufficiently prescient nor can he wait until logic affords him absolute certainly. If he waited for that, he would never come to a decision; he would remain in a state inconclusiveness, unless he chose to make a shift with deceptive certitude. The prudent man does not expect certainty where it cannot exist, nor on the other hand does he deceive himself with false certainties.[8]

The requisites for prudence in statecraft include, among other things, the capacity to apply general principles to particular circumstances; a realistic assessment of man's nature and the dynamics of the international environment; discernment about the probable consequences of alternative courses of action; and the ability to reconcile the desirable with the possible.[9]

Employing this standard of prudence, chapters 1 through 4 analyze the inadequacies of major alternative schools of foreign policy that are at odds with the Bush Doctrine: isolationism, neorealism, classical realism, and liberal multilateralism. Chapter 5 lays out the precepts of moral democratic realism and the compelling rationale for it as the best practicable guide for American foreign policy. Moral democratic realism is congenial with but not identical to Charles Krauthammer's democratic realism.[10] Like the neoconservative outlook of William Kristol and Robert Kagan, it incorporates the higher realism that understands why spreading stable, liberal democracy is in the American national interest.[11] Yet moral democratic realism grounds American foreign policy more explicitly in Judeo-Christian ethics than Krauthammer does. It also imposes tighter geopolitical limits on the use of American power to promote democracy than Kristol and Kagan's more unconstrained vision does. For, as George Weigel observes, "Democracy is not simply a matter of procedures; democracy is a matter of ideas, ideals, and moral commitments. . . . Neither skepticism nor relativism by their own logic can give account" for why people should aspire to be free, tolerant, decent, and civil.[12]

Chapter 6 assesses the record of the three major contending approaches to the final two decades of the Cold War: President Nixon's realism; President Carter's liberal multilateralism; and President Reagan's moral democratic realism. This is a critically important case not only because of the intrinsic importance of the Cold War, but because these approaches continue to dominate the current debate over the Bush Doctrine. Chapter 7 argues that the war in Iraq was a correct application of the Bush Doctrine. Chapter 8 weighs the implications of the Bush Doctrine and moral democratic realism for the challenges American foreign policy will face beyond the war on terror, the most daunting of which is the rising power of China.

1

The Imprudence
of Isolationism

Commentators as astute as Charles Krauthammer and Norman Podhoretz have largely dismissed rather than systematically refuted the isolationist tradition in their powerful defenses of President Bush's approach to the war on terror.[1] This is a mistake. As Eugene Rostow has observed more perceptively, public understanding of the American tradition in foreign affairs before World War I—particularly Washington's Farewell Address and the Monroe Doctrine—still has a significant influence on the way in which the nation conceives of its proper role in the world.[2] One must seriously confront contemporary isolationist critics of President Bush, such as Patrick Buchanan, who warn of dire peril for the nation unless we repudiate the policy of democratic globalism. Revisiting the formative period of American foreign policy also refines our facility for making reasonable distinctions between the permanent and the contingent aspects of the Founders' thinking about foreign affairs.[3]

In a series of books, articles, and public commentary, Buchanan has set forth a systematic rehabilitation and defense of an America-first foreign policy that demands the withdrawal of American power and protection from most of the world outside the Western Hemisphere.[4] His main line of argument runs as follows: by piling up open-ended, extravagant, and provocative commitments unrelated to the true interests of the nation, American leaders have "reenacted every folly that brought previous great powers to ruin." Borrowing heavily from the arguments of Paul Kennedy's

1987 *The Rise and Fall of the Great Powers,* Buchanan assails as reckless and unsustainable a foreign policy that commits America to go to war for scores of nations where we have never fought. He warns that the day of reckoning is approaching when American global hegemony is going to be challenged, and our leaders will discover they lack the resources to make good on all the war guarantees they have handed out so frivolously; and the American people, awakened to what it is their statesmen have committed them to do, will declare war themselves, unwilling to pay the price of empire.[5]

Buchanan calls the Bush Doctrine "a prescription for permanent war for permanent peace, though wars are the death of republics." Wisdom, according to Buchanan, yielded again to hubris when the Bush administration committed the United States to extending liberty and freedom in the Middle East. He identifies as the root cause of Islamic hostility toward the United States the massive American presence in the Middle East and what he considers our one-sided support for Israel. We must, Buchanan declares, jettison American commitments that risk our involvement in major conflicts in Europe, Asia, the Middle East, and Latin America. Instead, he advocates a return to isolationism—or in his preferred designation, "the America First Tradition"—which, he claims, governed American foreign policy from 1776 until 1917.

There are, however, several enormous problems in Buchanan's analysis fatal to his project of reviving isolationism as an alternative to President Bush's moral democratic realism.

Washington's Strategy of Non-entanglement Rightly Understood

Americans wisely have repudiated Buchanan's hostility to the notion of exporting the institutions of freedom. From our founding, our great statesmen have always conceived of the United States as an empire of liberty, a beacon for spreading democracy elsewhere; indeed, the Declaration of Independence defines rights not in particular but in universal terms. What Americans have always debated vigorously is not the desirability but the possibility of expanding the zone of democratic peace at tolerable cost and risk.[6] During our formative period in the early nineteenth century, the nation confined its role to promoting freedom by example. The United States was still a fledgling republic, vulnerable to the major powers of a European state system; domestic conditions for establishing liberal democracy abroad remained unpropitious. John Quincy Adams captured the essence of a policy that was surely prudent for the conditions of his time:

> America, in the assembly of nations, since her admission among them, has invariably, though often fruitlessly, held forth to them the hand of honest friendship, of equal freedom, of generous reciprocity. . . . She has abstained from interference in the concerns of others, even when conflict has been for principles to which she clings, as to the last vital drop that visits the heart. . . . Wherever the standard of freedom and independence has been or shall be unfurled, there will her heart, her benedictions and her prayers be. But she goes not abroad, in search of monsters to destroy. She is the well-wisher to the freedom and independence of all. She is the champion and vindicator only of her own.[7]

Thus, when the wars of the French Revolution broke out in 1792, President Washington stoutly and prudentially defied the intense pressure of Secretary of State Thomas Jefferson and Speaker of the House James Madison to construe broadly our obligations to France under the Franco-American Alliance of 1778 and adopt a pro-French orientation that would risk war with Great Britain and Spain. Instead, Washington proclaimed in his seminal Neutrality Proclamation of 1793 American impartiality in the struggle between France and Great Britain. Jefferson, Madison, and the powerful pro-French forces in American politics that they represented construed the French Revolution wrongly as a struggle for well-ordered liberty analogous to the American Revolution rather than the descent into tyranny it was to become.

Washington not only harbored more serious doubts about the trajectory of the French Revolution, but also recognized that the United States was in no position to embark on ideological crusades in any event. Even after the Treaty of Paris of 1783, which ended the Revolutionary War, the American strategic position remained precarious. Spain controlled New Orleans and access to the Mississippi, on which three-eighths of American trade depended. Great Britain continued to occupy military posts in the West, despite its own agreement to evacuate; the British continued to stir up the hostility of Indian tribes toward American settlers.

The international wars stemming from the French Revolution, which consumed the major European powers for more than two decades, posed simultaneously an immense opportunity and potentially grave danger for the nation. By staying neutral, the United States could expand relatively unmolested and settle its frontier problems with Britain in the north and Spain in the south to America's advantage and without war. If the United States became embroiled in the French Revolution, the young nation would become perilously vulnerable to France's British and Spanish enemies sitting athwart its vital flanks.[8]

These strategic circumstances dictated the policy of neutrality Washington pursued during his two administrations and inspired his Farewell Address of September 19, 1796, in which he justified this strategy. "Our detached and distant situation invites and enables us to pursue a different course," counseled Washington.

> If we remain one people ... the period is not very far off, when we may defy material injury from external annoyance ... when belligerent nations, under the impossibility of making acquisitions upon us, will not likely hazard the giving us of provocation; when we may choose between peace and war as our interests, guided by our Justice, shall counsel. ... Why forgo the advantages of so peculiar a situation? —Why quit our own to stand on foreign ground? Why, by interweaving our destiny with that of any part of Europe, entangle our peace and prosperity in the toils of European ambition, Rivalship, Interest, Humor or Caprice? 'Tis our true policy to steer clear of permanent alliances, with any portion of the foreign world. ... Taking care always to keep ourselves by suitable establishments, on a respectable defensive posture, we may safely trust to temporary alliances for extraordinary circumstances.

The principles that Washington set forth in the farewell address—nonentanglement in affairs outside the Western Hemisphere—were not only prudent but necessary in an era of multipolarity: the United States was weak in the world of the strong. In these circumstances the United States had no interest at stake worth the potentially mortal risk of being prematurely immersed in the "vicissitudes, combinations, and collisions" of a European states system.[9] The source of Buchanan's error lies not in his defense of eighteenth- and nineteenth-century isolationism, but in his extension of this policy into a permanent rather than contingent strategy, which the Founders never intended.

Nor does Buchanan grasp how much the efficacy of isolationism presupposed another contingent rather than permanent condition: a self-regulating European balance of power, in which Great Britain operates reliably as the ultimate balancer.[10] Long before Sir Halford Mackinder developed his conception of geopolitics at the beginning of the twentieth century, generations of British statesmen instinctively practiced fundamentals of his geopolitical maxims: if a single hostile power or combination of such powers came to dominate Europe, it would possess the abundance of resources necessary to overcome Great Britain on sea as well as on land. Great Britain therefore had a vital interest in preventing any such powers from achieving this dominance. Winston Churchill wrote:

> For four hundred years the foreign policy of England has been to oppose the strongest, most aggressive, most dominating power on the Continent. . . . Faced by Philip II of Spain, against Louis XIV, . . . against Napoleon, against William II of Germany, it would have been easy and must have been very tempting to join with the stronger and share the fruits of his conquest. However, we always took the harder course, joined with the less strong Powers, and made a combination among them, and thus defeated and frustrated the Continental military tyrant wherever he was, whatever nation he led. Thus we preserve the liberty of Europe. . . . Here is that wonderful unconscious tradition of British foreign policy. . . . I know of nothing which has occurred to alter or weaken the justice, wisdom, valour and prudence upon which our ancestors acted. I know of nothing in military, political, economic, or scientific fact which makes me feel that we are less capable. I know of nothing which makes me feel that we might not, or cannot, march along the same road. . . . Observe that the policy of England takes no account of which nation it is that seeks overlordship of Europe. . . . It is concerned solely with whoever is the strongest or politically dominant tyrant.[11]

During our formative period, 1776–1824, all great American statesmen from Benjamin Franklin to John Quincy Adams paid keen attention to the European balance of power, deftly exploiting the rivalries it spawned: first to win independence for America; then to consolidate the American republic; then vastly to expand the realm of it. The 1778 alliance with France, so decisive for the outcome of the Revolutionary War, came about through our exploitation of the long and bitter rivalry between Great Britain and France. French statesmen regarded the success of the American Revolution as a way of avenging Britain's smashing victory in the French and Indian War.

During the initial phase of the wars of the French Revolution, the Washington administration exploited the distractions of and rivalries between the major powers of Europe to secure two major treaties. Jay's Treaty of 1794 brought the British finally to execute fully the Treaty of Paris of 1783, diminished the American Indian threat in the Northwest, and averted a war with the British over neutral rights for which the United States was woefully unprepared. Pinckney's Treaty of 1795 with Spain secured American access to the entire Mississippi, which was so important for retaining the loyalty of the Western states and expanding across the continent.[12]

Similarly, the great diplomatic historian Samuel Flagg Bemis described the Louisiana Purchase of 1803 as "another magnificent example" of how Europe's distresses worked to America's advantage. It was the impending resumption of war between France and Great Britain that induced Napoleon to sell the Louisiana Territory to the United States for a bargain price: the size of the nation virtually doubled, and the United States was ensured that it would become a vast continental republic rather than a vulnerable coastal state.[13]

Europe's rivalries again worked to America's advantage to produce another great milestone in American diplomacy: the Monroe Doctrine of December 1823 prohibited European powers from restoring to Spain any of its former colonies that had established their independence. Monroe could proclaim this bold doctrine with confidence—in defiance of the Holy Roman Alliance of France, Russia, Prussia, and the Hapsburg Empire—because the Royal Navy silently but effectively underwrote it. Great Britain also opposed the restoration of Spanish colonial rule to newly independent Latin American republics for strategic as well as commercial reasons. As the dominant maritime and commercial power of the day, Britain preferred an independent Latin America open to trade rather than a Spanish empire that restricted it. Hence, Great Britain warned France and other members of the Holy Roman Alliance against interference with the independence of the former Spanish colonies.[14]

With the exception of Thomas Jefferson, who obtusely dismissed the grave danger Napoleon would pose to the United States if France conquered all of continental Europe and Great Britain, virtually all the Founders dreaded the prospect of a single power achieving such dominance, with good reason: the preservation of the European balance of power was vital to the United States as well as to Great Britain. Even Jefferson acknowledged that "it cannot be in our interest that all Europe should be reduced to a single monarchy." He wished for and expected "a salutary balance [that] may be ever maintained among nations."[15]

The American interest in preventing any single hostile hegemon from dominating any of the world's major power centers thus has remained constant since the founding. In the late eighteenth and early nineteenth centuries, the United States had neither the need nor the capacity to maintain a balance of power in Europe; a felicitous combination of technology, prevailing political conditions on the European continent, and foresight of British statesmanship produced an equilibrium among the major powers of Europe that was favorable to American interests. In the second half of the nineteenth century, the prodigious expansion of the American republic coincided with a period of remarkable stability in Europe, and Americans were inclined to take this European equilibrium for granted.[16]

Isolationism's Peril and the Two World Wars

By the beginning of the twentieth century, a convergence of political and technological developments had rendered the strategy of isolationism perilously obsolete. The rise of a united, enormously powerful Germany at the cutting edge of the Industrial Revolution after 1871, and the belated but incipient emergence of Russia into modernity beginning in the late nineteenth century, had radically undermined the equilibrium of the European balance of power, along with Britain's capacity to maintain it.

No one grasped the logic or implications of this transformation better than Halford Mackinder. His prescient theories, first set forth in *Geographical Pivot of History*, published in 1904, have rightly shaped American grand strategy since World War II. Mackinder warned that any single power dominating the resources of Eurasia, "the World Island," as he called it, would have the potential to dominate the world, including the United States. He depicted the history of Eurasia as a perennial struggle between more closed, authoritarian continental empires of the east-central European heartland, preeminent in land power, versus more free and eventually more democratic empires of Western Europe, preeminent in sea power. According to Mackinder, the maritime states enjoyed a significant comparative advantage over their rivals between 1500 and 1900, because of the superior mobility and flexibility of sea versus land power. He warned, however, that the advent of railroads and the internal combustion engine would substantially erode this advantage in the twentieth century. In these new political, technological, and economic conditions, powerful heartland empires could mount a more plausible attempt at world domination than ever before. He ranked Germany, and eventually Russia, as the two most formidable contenders for achieving such domination. As early as 1905, Mackinder advocated an alliance of maritime democracies to contain both of them. He wrote later that such an association might have avoided World War II "if the triple alliance of the United States, Great Britain, and France, negotiated at Versailles, had become operative."[17]

Although one can legitimately quarrel with the particulars of Mackinder's analysis, the main thrust of his argument remains unassailable: the United States cannot remain safe in a world in which a hostile hegemon dominates any or all of the world's power centers, which today include not just Europe but eastern Asia and the Middle East. Nor can Americans prudently ignore the imperative of revising U.S. grand strategy to meet new threats, or pursuing new opportunities that dynamic and changing conditions in world politics may yield.

After 1900 the United States could no longer count on reaping without cost the huge benefits that the balance of power had provided it during the eighteenth and nineteenth centuries. First, Great Britain alone could not maintain the balance against Germany's two hegemonic bids for empire that culminated in World Wars I and II. Nor could the British maintain the balance against the Soviet Union's bid for hegemony during the Cold War. It became necessary for the United States to jettison its isolationism to create what Churchill called an imbalance of power in favor of the Western democracies. The twentieth-century emergence of the United States as an economic superpower made possible what changing strategic conditions made necessary. By 1900 United States generated 25 percent of the world's manufacturing product, a figure nearly twice the size of Great Britain's and Germany's combined total. Tragically, it would require the devastating calamity of the two world wars with Germany to dispel once and for all the illusions to which Buchanan and his isolationist remnant still cling.

Ignoring the recent work of Niall Ferguson, Thomas J. Fleming, and others who offer a more respectable if ultimately unpersuasive case against World War I, Buchanan continues to revive Charles Tansill's old canard that an insidious combination of pro-British sentiment, the interests of Wall Street bankers fearful of Britain's defaulting on its huge loans, Theodore Roosevelt's militarism, and Woodrow Wilson's utopianism dragged the United States into a costly war in defiance of our previous tradition and national interest. Buchanan's historical assumption—that a German victory in World War I would not have posed great danger to the United States—is dubious.[18] Fritz Fischer, David Fromkin, Donald Kagan, and others have demonstrated that Germany aspired to use a conquered Europe as a base for world empire.[19] Consider, most notoriously, the German war plan of October 1914, which set forth war aims mutually exclusive with the legitimate interests of the other European powers and the United States. The British historian Michael Howard conveys aptly what German victory would have entailed: "A German hegemony offered nothing except the rule based on military power exercised by a caste concerned only to preserve and extend its own dominance. . . . Prussianism . . . remained a creed that despised the liberal democracy of the West, elevated service to the state as the highest virtue, and glorified military values above all others. Such sentiments can be found elsewhere in Europe. . . . But nowhere else did they exist in such a ferocious combination."[20]

The geopolitical assumptions of contemporary isolationists are even more dubious than those of the historical ones. It made strategic sense for America to stay out of European conflicts so long as Britain operated as an effective balancer, ensuring that no Continental power achieved a decisive aggregation of power. By 1917, however, Germany was too powerful for Britain to overcome without American intervention.

Theodore Roosevelt is the American statesmen who grasped America's strategic interests more quickly and clearly than any of his contemporaries.[21] He not only played a pivotal role in convincing Americans to enter World War I, but more generally became the most prominent and persuasive advocate of vigilant internationalism and interventionism: "As long as

England succeeds in keeping up the balance of power in Europe, not only in principle but reality, well and good. Should she, however, fail in doing so, the United States should be obliged to step in, at least temporarily, in order to reestablish the balance of power in Europe, never mind against which country or countries our efforts have to be directed. In fact, we are becoming, owing to our strength and geographical situation, more and more the balance of power of the whole globe."[22]

Roosevelt recognized that the United States faced new dangers and the size and strength of American power conferred new responsibilities.[23] He recognized that America's moral and geopolitical interests lay in the victory of the Western democracies over an authoritarian, militarist Germany, whose regime Roosevelt considered the root cause of German aggression that precipitated World War I: "We are going to war with Germany because Germany has bitterly wronged us. But there is much more at stake. We are fighting Germany because under its present government, a government of ruthless and despotic militarism, Germany has become the arch foe of international right and of ordered freedom throughout the world."[24] Though his countrymen assumed complacently that Great Britain would successfully muster a coalition of European states to thwart German ambitions, Roosevelt knew better: He called early and often for the United States to enter the war, not just to maintain freedom of the seas and to make the world safe for democracy, but to prevent a German victory that would topple that balance of power that was in America's national interest to sustain.

There is, of course, much that is legitimate to criticize about the way the United States intervened in World War I in general and about the diplomacy of President Woodrow Wilson in particular: his utopian vision that the United States was fighting a war to end all wars; his unrequited faith in collective security rather than alliances; his obsession with and utopian aspirations for the League of Nations; his role in negotiating the much maligned Treaty of Versailles; and his inability to compromise with Senator Henry Cabot Lodge, which resulted in the rejection not only of the League of Nations, but of the more important forerunner to the North Atlantic Treaty Organization (NATO)—an alliance among the United States, Great Britain, and France to buttress the peace and restrain Germany's discontent from taking a violent path.[25]

Yet all this does not invalidate the powerful case for American entry into World War I. The Treaty of Versailles was flawed, but it was not the punitive peace that Buchanan, echoing John Maynard Keynes, portrays. It was considerably less severe than what the Germans had in mind for Western Europe, judging by their October 1914 war plans, or what they imposed on the defeated Russians with the Treaty of Brest-Litovsk in 1918. The tragedy of World War I was not American intervention, but the failure of the victors, including the United States, to enforce the Versailles Treaty's disarmament provisions when they had the power to do so. By any standard of measure, the America-first policy that Buchanan champions exponentially increased the cost of World War II.[26]

Yet Buchanan defiantly insists that Franklin Delano Roosevelt (FDR) foolishly and deceitfully maneuvered the United States into the war—the same charge he now levels at neoconservatives for the Bush Doctrine and the 2003 war with Iraq. By Buchanan's analysis (a rehash of the historian A. J. P. Taylor's revisionist account that Taylor later had the good sense to disavow), "Hitler had not wanted war with the West. But when the West declared war, he overran France to secure his rear before setting out to conquer the East. . . . Hitler saw the World divided into four spheres: Great Britain holding its Empire; Japan dominant in East Asia; Germany master of Europe; and America Mistress of the Western Hemisphere."[27] Buchanan adds: "If Hitler could not put a soldier in England in the fall of 1940, the notion that he could invade the Western Hemisphere—with no surface ships to engage the United States and British fleets and U.S. airpower dominant in the west Atlantic—was preposterous."[28] Buchanan does not believe that "hundreds of thousands of American boys should have been killed in Europe and Asia fighting Hitler and Tojo," because he does not believe the United States was threatened by Japan's bid for empire in Asia or Nazi Germany's domination over all of Europe.[29]

Buchanan's defense of the morally and geopolitically indefensible violates all standards of strategic prudence. Historians have established beyond reasonable doubt that Hitler strove to dominate not only the entire European continent, but the entire world. Hitler expected eventually to fight the United States when Nazi Germany had the enormous resources of Eurasia at its disposal, and when the United States would have no allies to resist a Nazi onslaught. Would not a conquered Europe have provided Hitler the strength he needed, at least for intimidating the United States into acquiescing to his dominance everywhere else? Would the United States really have reduced the cost and risk of confrontation by waiting even longer?[30]

Although FDR made his share of serious mistakes, his role in over-coming isolationist opposition to American intervention in World War II is not one of them. FDR understood sooner and more clearly than any prominent political figure of the day besides Churchill the mortal threat Nazism posed. That FDR was not more resolute sooner is a more plausible argument than Buchanan's isolationist critique.[31] When World War II began in September 1939, Roosevelt, like most Americans, hoped that American aid to Britain and France would suffice to defeat Hitler. American rearmament began in earnest, and Roosevelt became convinced of the necessity for direct American involvement in the war only belatedly, after the fall of France in June 1940 proved that aid alone was insufficient. The United States entered World War II woefully unprepared and nearly too late, grievous mistakes for which isolationists must bear a large share of responsibility.[32]

Roosevelt's diplomacy toward the Soviet Union was indeed his most dangerous and costly mistake. He badly underestimated the malevolence and ambitions of the Soviet regime. He fatuously believed, in the words of his sympathetic biographer Conrad Black, that "there was susceptibility in Stalin to deal honorably with an American leader who was not a European imperialist." He hoped, Black added, "that Stalin would succumb to the temptation of being a figure for stability and gradually a reliable associate in the governance of the world."[33] In 1940 Roosevelt chose Henry Wallace as his vice president, a man who would run for president in 1948 claiming no containment of the Soviet Union was necessary. One shudders to think how the Cold War would have turned out had Roosevelt died before the 1944 election, when he finally replaced Wallace on the ticket with Harry Truman, or had Eleanor Roosevelt succeeded in her bid to keep Wallace as vice president.

Nevertheless, the policy of isolationism that Buchanan defends and the appeasement of Hitler during the 1930s deserve significantly more blame than Roosevelt's mistakes for Soviet domination of much of Eastern Europe after World War II. An American military presence in Europe after World War I might have stabilized the European continent and deterred the Germans from gambling on Hitler in the first place. The democracies could have stopped Hitler right up until the German remilitarization of the Rhineland in March 1936 without relying on Soviet power, had statesmen ignored Roosevelt's isolationist critics and heeded Churchill's warning about the need for decisive preemptive action to save "much blood, toil, tears, and sweat."

Even as late as the Munich crisis of September 1938, France and Britain together could have defeated Nazi Germany. By 1939, however, the democracies had squandered an enormous material advantage pursuing the morally and strategically bankrupt policy of appeasement.[34] During World War II Roosevelt rightly saw Hitler as a greater danger than Stalin. Limited collaboration with the Soviet Union was, therefore, prudent under the terrible circumstances to avert the greater moral and geopolitical evil of a total Nazi victory.

FDR's sound instincts as a strategist also served, overall, to mitigate some of the more dangerous aspects of his fatuous view of communism. He was right to insist on a cross-channel invasion of France in June 1944, which contributed to containing Soviet influence in Europe far more effectively than Churchill's preferred strategy of invading Europe through the "soft underbelly" of Italy and the Balkans.[35] He and Churchill also were right to insist on the unconditional surrender of Germany and Japan, which paved the way for both vanquished powers to emerge as vital components of a successful democratic alliance system that triumphed over an evil and gravely dangerous Soviet empire.[36]

Yet a more sagacious Roosevelt would have heeded Churchill's advice to push as far into Eastern Europe as possible, which at least would have saved Berlin and most of Czechoslovakia from Soviet control. A less naive Roosevelt would not have repeated Wilson's mistake of embracing pernicious illusions about the efficacy of international organizations and collective security as a substitute for American power and the willingness to use that power.[37]

The Perils of Isolationism during the Cold War

American statesmen after World War II finally learned the lessons that Halford Mackinder and Theodore Roosevelt had sought to impart. First, the United States could not be secure if a single hostile hegemon dominated the major powers of the world—Europe and East Asia because of the intrinsic resources those regions possess, and the Middle East because of its abundance of oil on which the entire world depends. Second, the Soviet Union could mount a plausible bid to achieve such dominance absent muscular American deterrence. Third, Western Europe, Japan, and other key allies in vital geopolitical power centers needed firm, credible, and unambiguous security commitments, because only the United States possessed the resources to contain the Soviet Union in a bipolar world of two superpowers. Fourth, new technologies—most dramatically the advent of nuclear weapons—diminished further the advantage of America's insular geographic position. Fifth, these weapons ruled out the option of totally defeating the Soviet Union by traditional military means.[38]

The strategy of vigilant containment that the Truman administration devised and subsequent Cold War administrations implemented to varying degrees easily meets the standard of prudence that ought to be the measure of any sound strategy. Vigilant containment established the framework for winning the Third World War, a more appropriate name for the Cold War, at tolerable cost and risk, given the enormity and malignancy of the Soviet threat to America's vital interests. Vigilant containment also constituted a vastly more prudent strategy than any of the alternatives, particularly the isolationism that the honorable but mistaken Robert Taft, Republican senator from Ohio, continued to advocate even after the Second World War. Senator Taft opposed American participation in the NATO alliance and vigilant post–World War II internationalism generally; he favored a "Fortress America" concept that would have made the world safe for Stalin and Mao, just as interwar isolationism made the world safe for Hitler, Mussolini, and Tojo.[39]

The Perils of Isolationism Today

Likewise, in the prohibitively unlikely event that the United States ever embraced it, Buchanan's or any other variant of an America-first policy would yield nothing but strategic and moral disaster in today's environment.[40] The imperatives of geopolitics still mandate a strong, activist, global American foreign policy for the reasons Henry Kissinger described: "Geopolitically, America is an island off the shores of a large landmass of Eurasia, whose resources and population far exceed the United States. The domination by a single power of either of Eurasia's two principal spheres—Europe or Asia—remains a good definition of strategic danger for America. . . . For such a grouping would add the capacity to outstrip America economically, and in the end, militarily."[41]

Similarly, the United States still must prevent any hostile entity from dominating the Middle East. The world's need to ensure access to that region's enormous supplies of oil is an important reason but not the only vital one. Such a hegemon would pose an unacceptable strategic danger by having the potential to combine the power emanating from controlling the Middle East's oil reserves with radicalism and the proliferation of weapons of mass destruction (WMD). Especially in a unipolar world, in which the United States is the sole superpower, robust American power and the willingness to use that power remain indispensable to deter hegemonic threats from arising in vital geopolitical regions, or to defeat such bids at the lowest possible cost and risk, should deterrence fail. The diffusion of WMD capabilities has expanded the zone from which grave threats can arise. Now smaller countries can conceivably inflict the type of damage on the United States that in previous eras required a large geopolitical power base even to contemplate. The United States must possess the capabilities and inclination to thwart such threats as well.

Like Buchanan, liberal isolationists such as Eric Nordlinger have it backwards when they advocate maximizing conciliation, disengaging from America's worldwide alliance system, and reassuring dangerous challengers.[42] The best practicable order depends on the United States robustly deterring its adversaries and reassuring its friends by clear and credible commitments to vital geopolitical regions.

Contrary to Nordlinger's and Buchanan's claims, the United States can afford to operate as the ultimate balancer in Europe, East Asia, and the Middle East, now and for some time to come. Even Paul Kennedy has repudiated his earlier warnings about the dangers of American imperial overstretch, from which Buchanan draws so heavily. Writing in the *Financial Times* in February 2002, Kennedy marveled that "nothing has ever existed like the disparity in power" between the United States and the rest of the world—not even the Roman, Muslim, or British empires at their peaks. The United States spends more on deterrence than the next nine countries combined, an asymmetry that will increase as the United States under President Bush continues to raise defense spending substantially. The result is an array of force Kennedy calls "staggering."[43]

Simultaneously, the American share of world economic product steadily expanded from 22 percent in the 1980s to about 30 percent today, as the Russian and Japanese share declined. Since the 1980s growth rates in the European Union also have lagged far behind those of the United States. This trend is likely to continue because of Western Europe's demographic decline, an overgenerous welfare state, the difficulty of assimilating its burgeoning Muslim population, and the inability of Western European governments to muster the will to make their economic systems more competitive.[44]

Even more remarkably, the United States achieved and can sustain its current level of military predominance indefinitely and inexpensively. The United States now spends less than 4 percent of its gross domestic product (GDP) on defense, compared with 13.5 percent in fiscal year (FY) 1953 under President Truman, 8.7 percent in FY 1969 under President Johnson, and 6.0 percent in FY 1986 under President Reagan. The Bush administration's defense spending as a percentage of GDP is just slightly higher than that of the Roosevelt administration on the eve of Pearl Harbor, when the United States remained unprepared and isolationist.[45]

In the long term, China potentially poses the most serious threat to American predominance. Nevertheless, the gravity of this thrust will depend on whether the Chinese economy continues to grow annually at a rate of 9 or 10 percent for the next three decades; and whether the political system averts the cataclysmic convulsions that frequently plunged the nation into chaos. The American economy will remain way ahead of China's, even under the most optimistic scenarios for Chinese economic growth and political stability. Josef Joffe shows why with this highly plausible calculation: assuming China maintains a 7 percent annual growth rate endlessly, and assuming the U.S. economy grows correspondingly at a modest 3 percent a year, the U.S. GDP in 2035 will still exceed China's by a factor of 2.5.[46]

Writing in the March/April 2005 issue of *Foreign Affairs,* David S. Levy and Stuart H. Brown sum up their persuasive refutation of the "overstrech myth" this way:

Despite the persistence and pervasiveness of this doomsday prophecy, U.S. hegemony is in reality solidly grounded: It rests on an economy that is continually extending its lead in the innovation and the application of new technologies, ensuring its continuing appeal for foreign central banks and private investors. The dollar's role as the global monetary standard is not threatened, and the risk to U.S. financial liabilities has been exaggerated. To be sure, the economy will at some point have to adjust to the decline in the dollar and a rise in interest rates. But these trends will at worst slow the growth of U.S. consumers' standard of living, not undermine the United States' role as global pacesetter. If anything, the world's appetite for U.S. assets bolsters U.S. predominance rather than un- dermines it.[47]

The upshot is this: no plausible counterweight to American diplomatic, military, and political power looms on the horizon for many years to come. What the United States has not been able to afford since the beginning of the twenty-first century is the America-first strategy that Pat Buchanan and other contemporary isolationists propound.

2

The Perils of Neorealism

It is best to envisage the distinctions among various schools of thought in American foreign policy on a continuum: isolationism is at one end of it; full-fledged Wilsonian collective security is at the other; and various forms of realism and democratic globalism lie somewhere in between.[1] Many of President Bush's sharpest and most prominent critics come from the realist tradition in American foreign policy, which has two main branches: neorealism and classical realism. This chapter will address the neorealist challenge to the Bush Doctrine.

The Premises of Neorealist Theory

Neorealism draws from classical realist theories, which emphasize the enduring importance of power, geopolitics, and rivalry in international relations, as well as the frequent necessity of war as a means to defend vital interests. It differs, however, from classical realism in one crucial respect: whereas the flawed nature of man is the starting point for classical realists such as George F. Kennan and Hans Morgenthau writing in the American tradition, neorealists claim greater scientific precision by giving primacy to what they call the structure of the international system. This structure ultimately defines how states behave, including the United States. By *international system* neorealists mean the distribution of power among the major states that struggle to survive in conditions of anarchy, that is, with no single overriding authority having the monopoly on the legitimate use of violence. Systems have different dynamics depending on what neorealists call polarity—a system may have one (unipolar), two (bipolar), three (tripolar), or four or more (multipolar) major powers.

Correspondingly, Kenneth Waltz, the father of neorealism, and his leading disciples discount the importance of major powers' regime type or ideology or the individual motives of statesmen for understanding international politics. Their argument is that the dynamics of the international system operate as an invisible hand that impels statesmen to calculate cost and risk essentially the same way—whether the states are tyrannies or democracies; whether the president is Ronald Reagan or Jimmy Carter; whether the leader is Winston Churchill, Neville Chamberlain, Joseph Stalin, or Saddam Hussein. For Waltz and neorealists generally, state behavior varies primarily on the basis of differences of power rather than ideology, internal structure of property relations, or form of government.[2]

Neorealists reject in particular the idea of a democratic peace—that stable, liberal democracies do not fight one another. So they oppose any American foreign policy that identifies regime type as the root cause of aggression or that places great emphasis on the need to defend and expand stable, liberal democracy. This includes Franklin Roosevelt's and Winston Churchill's views of causes of and cures for the threats Nazi Germany and imperial Japan posed; Harry Truman's or Ronald Reagan's version of vigilantly containing Soviet communism with the object of promoting regime change; and the Bush Doctrine today.[3]

Whereas classical realists such as Hans Morgenthau and Henry Kissinger tend to be offensive realists, viewing great powers as inherently aggressive, the leading neorealists, John Mearsheimer excepted, tend to be defensive realists, reluctant to countenance the use of force. These defensive neorealists consider security in international politics as generally plentiful rather than precarious. For they assume that states for the most part seek security rather than hegemony and balance against, rather than bandwagon with, sources of danger that periodically arise.[4]

Neorealism and American Foreign Policy

During the Cold War defensive neorealists criticized what they considered the excessive zeal of American foreign policy and its exaggerated sense of threat; Ronald Reagan was a prime target of their disapproval. In his first book, *The Origins of Alliances*, which propelled him to the pinnacles of academic prominence, Stephen M. Walt, dean of Harvard's Kennedy School of Government, argued that the United States could take a relatively relaxed view of the Soviet threat because balancing is the dominant tendency of international politics. The United States should worry more, according to Walt, "about how it provokes opposition through misplaced belligerence." He concluded that "knee-jerk opposition to leftist forces in the Third World should be abandoned" because Marxist ideology "is a relatively weak cause of alignment."[5]

During the First Gulf War of 1990–1991, many leading neorealists opposed the first Bush administration's use of force to liberate Kuwait after Saddam Hussein's invasion.[6] During the current war on terror, neorealists have assailed President Bush's policy of preemption and democratic globalism, especially the war President Bush launched in 2003 to liberate Iraq. John Mearsheimer pronounced in a *New York Times* editorial published November 4, 2001, that the use of American military power in Afghanistan could not succeed; indeed, it only made "the problem worse."[7] On September 26, 2002, thirty-three scholars, many of them prominent neorealists, published an advertisement in the *New York Times* opposing the invasion of Iraq to remove Saddam. This group proposed instead that "the United States should maintain vigilant containment of Iraq—using its own assets and the assets of the United Nations."[8]

Mearscheimer and Walt laid out the standard neorealist antiwar rationale in the January–February 2003 issue of *Foreign Policy*. An invasion of Iraq was, in their view, more likely to provoke bitter anti-American backlash than trigger democratic reform in the Arab world. Even if such reform succeeded, they discounted its potential effect on American policy. Even if Saddam acquired nuclear weapons, Mearsheimer and Walt assured us, Saddam would pose no extraordinary danger, because he was rational and deterrable. Consequently, they saw "no good reason why the United States cannot contain Iraq, just as it contained the Soviet Union during the Cold War."[9]

More recently, Walt has lamented "how much the United States would have gained" had the it followed his approach: "Had the Bush Administration rejected preventive war in Iraq in March 2003 and chosen instead to continue the UN–mandated inspections process that was underway, it would have scored a resounding diplomatic victory."[10] Instead, Walt predicts, the United States will probably leave Iraq in even worse shape than it was under Saddam Hussein.[11]

Now Walt has published a new book, *Taming American Power: The Global Response to U.S. Primacy,* which has reaped acclaim among academics and liberal critics of the Bush administration. He denounces President Bush's policy of global dominance as a dangerous failure and sets forth a neorealist strategy of "offshore balancing" as an alternative. Under this strategy the United States would repudiate the Bush Doctrine and deploy its power abroad under only two conditions: a direct threat to vital American interests—Europe, industrialized Asia, or the Middle East—and the inability of regional powers to uphold the balance on their own.[12]

The United States, Walt believes, must behave as a more mature great power and avoid the temptation of arrogance if it wants its privileged position to be acceptable to others. "Instead of telling the world what to do and how to live—a temptation that both neoconservative empire builders and liberal internationalists find hard to resist—the United States should lead the world primarily by its example." Walt makes one conspicuous exception from such restraint: democratic Israel. Like Pat Buchanan, Walt blames Israel for many of our troubles in the Middle East; if Israel remains unwilling to grant the Palestinians a viable state—or if it tries to impose an unjust solution unilaterally—then Walt advocates that the United States end its economic and political support. Neither Arafat's tyranny nor the poisonous ideology that sustained it have any bearing, in Walt's view, on assessing the Palestine Liberation Organization's (PLO) ultimate motives or the justice of Israel's response.[13]

The Limits of Neorealism

Neorealism contains elements of truth that American policy makers always ought to ponder. The distribution of power is indeed critical in international politics. In a unipolar age the United States has a broader range of prudential strategic options than in the bipolar era of the Cold War or multipolar world of the nineteenth-century European balance of power. It is sometimes counterproductive, as neorealists claim, to wield American power with what Stephen Walt calls "too many footprints."

Neorealism also offers a set of foreign policy prescriptions that are intuitively appealing. If neorealists such as Walt are right, the United States can pursue a less active foreign policy, saving much bloodshed and terror, while allowing the international system's natural dynamic to provide

American security at much less cost and risk. If, however, neorealists are wrong and American statesmen heed their advice, the United States could find itself in great difficulty, which greater vigilance and dedication to the spread of democracy could have averted.

In an excellent critique of neorealist opposition to the 2003 invasion of Iraq, the Georgetown University political scientist Robert Lieber notes the "mixed record" of neorealist predictions since the end of the Cold War.[14] His assessment is much too generous. The actual historical record demonstrates the opposite of what neorealism claims. The dynamics of the international system do not eliminate powerful states' significant range of choice. Nor do states invariably balance against threats in a timely and effective way. Nor do all states or statesmen behave essentially alike. Regime type, ideology, and the propensities of individual leaders account for substantial variations in how states not only define their interests but pursue them. Contrary to what neorealism maintains, prudence often calls for statesmen to accept the costs of commitments and risks of action sooner to prevent potentially greater dangers from arising later, even when future scenarios are inevitably speculative.[15]

Neorealism and Appeasement

Begin with the dismal failure of the policy of appeasing Nazi Germany and the horrific consequences of it.[16] Stephen Walt claims that the history of the 1930s offers strong evidence in support of his theory and policy prescriptions.[17] This is untenable, to say the least. Does Walt really believe that Great Britain, France, or the other European powers countered Nazi Germany vigilantly or effectively? Massive evidence, including Hitler's own assessment, proves otherwise.[18] Consider Churchill's devastating indictment of the policy of appeasement that Walt defends:

> That we should all have come to this pass makes those responsible, however honorable their motives, blameworthy before history. Look back and see what we had successively accepted and thrown away: a Germany rearmed in violation of a solemn treaty; air superiority or even air parity cast away; the Rhineland forcibly occupied and the Siegfried Line built or building; the Berlin-Rome Axis established; Austria devoured and digested by the Reich; Czecho-

slovakia deserted and ruined by the Munich Pact, its fortress line in German hands; its mighty arsenal of Skoda henceforward making munitions for German armies. . . . The services of thirty-five Czech divisions against a still unripened German army cast away. . . . All gone to the wind.

And now, when every one of those aids had been squandered and thrown away, Great Britain advances, leading France by the hand, to guarantee the integrity of Poland—of that very Poland which with hyena appetite had only six months before joined in the pillage and destruction of the Czech state. . . . History, which we are told is mainly the record of crimes, follies, and miseries of mankind, may be scoured and ransacked to find a parallel of this sudden and complete reversal of five or six years policy of easygoing placatory appeasement, and its transformation overnight into a readiness to accept an obviously imminent war on far worse conditions and on far greater scale.[19]

Indeed, the dominant theme of *The Gathering Storm,* the first volume of Churchill's magisterial history of the Second World War, starkly contradicts neorealism's counsel that democracies assess threats without regard to regime type or the animating ideology of the menacing power: "How the English-speaking peoples through their unwisdom, carelessness, and good nature, allowed the wicked to rearm."[20] The dynamics of domestic politics, misperception, and poor statesmanship all played a vital part in the tragic failure to stop Hitler sooner. The policies of British prime ministers Stanley Baldwin and Neville Chamberlain, which Walt bizarrely characterizes as an effort to balance "that came very close to succeeding," resulted in disaster. The German invasion of Poland on September 1, 1939, unleashed a devastating war that France lost and Great Britain could not win alone. The war also killed sixty million people, including six million Jews whom the Nazis exterminated, and led the Soviet Union into the heart of east central Europe, enslaving its population for the next half century.

Interwar statesmen committed the terrible mistake of appeasing Hitler precisely because of their too-relaxed view of Nazism, and because of their erroneous judgments about the relative gravity and priority of multiple threats. That the appeasers had, in Walt's words, "good reason to think" that Hitler posed only a limited threat does not excuse them from censure or save the flawed theories on which they relied. The appeasers, too, believed that the logic of the international system rather than the nature of the Nazi regime primarily determined German foreign policy. Most considered Hitler not an ideologue but a reasonable man with whom they could do business, someone who calculated risk prudently.

Walt's untenable effort to manipulate history to fit his theory, though vexing, raises less serious questions than his distressing lack of proportion, which casts further doubt on the prudence of relying on either his theory or his prescriptions for American foreign policy today. Compare, most strikingly, his gentle treatment of the appeasers with his strident criticisms of many aspects of American foreign policy during the Cold War and of the Bush Doctrine today. Yet the United States won the Cold War with substantially less cost and risk than the failed policy of appeasement imposed on democracies during the interwar years. Contrast, for example, the absence of war in Europe during the past sixty years with the carnage of the first forty-five years of this century. Note, too, that the most robust versions of containment neorealists criticize most severely—President Truman's and President Reagan's—succeeded far better than the softer alternatives more congenial to neorealist thinking, which the United States actually pursued with poor results during the decade of the 1970s.

Neorealism and the Cold War

The Cold War reveals emblematically the imperative of taking regime type and ideology into account in devising a prudential grand strategy. Unlike neorealists, American Cold War statesmen with the greatest foresight recognized that more than the international environment strongly affected the conduct of states. Unlike neorealists, they recognized an intimate connection between the internal order prevailing in communist and liberal democratic nations and their external behavior.

The grand strategies of Presidents Truman and Reagan emanated from a set of assumptions substantially at variance with neorealism's foundational principles: the Soviet Union was not a nation-state with limited aims and objectives, but an evil, repressive, expansionist empire driven by an evil ideology as perverse as Nazism. The Cold War was a geopolitical as well as a moral struggle in which the United States was on the right side of history. At the outset President Truman expressed confidence "in the eventual tri-

umph of universal moral order based on liberal values over Soviet totalitarianism," which he considered "an implacable enemy of human freedom."[21]
This struggle would continue, however, so long as Joseph Stalin remained
in power and the depraved regime that he and Vladimir Lenin had built
remained in place. The source of the Soviet Union's unquenchable animosity toward the United States lay not in specific American conduct, but in
its very existence. Or as the former Soviet foreign minister and ambassador
to Washington Maxim Litvinov put it with regard to Stalin, "The ideological conception prevailing" in the Soviet Union was "that conflict between
Communist and capitalist worlds is inevitable." Western acquiescence to
the "Soviet Union's territorial demands" would not satisfy Stalin but merely
lead "to the West being faced with the next set of demands."[22]

Just as the nature of the Nazi and imperial Japanese regimes constituted the root cause of the aggression they perpetrated in World War II, the
nature of the Soviet regime constituted the root cause of the Cold War. So
President Truman accepted the logic and policy recommendations of NSC
68, outlined by the National Security Council in April 1950. This document
crystallized and dictated the main lines of American foreign and defense
policy for much of the Cold War, which were in the long term "to foster
fundamental change in the nature of the Soviet system" and in the short
term to thwart the Soviet Union's grand geopolitical design to achieve dominance of the Eurasian landmass.[23]

Beginning in the late 1940s, American statesmen accordingly sought
to contain Soviet expansion with a combination of military and economic
power. Though a liberal democracy with a strong tradition of isolationism
and exceptionalism, the United States implemented containment in ways
that largely resembled classic great power politics because external pres-
sures gave the nation little alternative. American statesmen established and
sustained the NATO alliance and the Mutual Defense Treaty of 1952 with
Japan as a shield behind which these allies could restore their economic
power. Simultaneously, the United States promoted Western European
and Japanese economic recovery through the Marshall Plan, the General
Agreement on Tariff and Trade, the International Monetary Fund, the encouragement of Western European integration, and acceptance of an imbalance of trade in Japan's favor.

Contrary to neorealist assertions that the United States could achieve
more by doing less, American statesmen assumed that the burdens of pre-

vention paled in comparison to the cost and risk of cure. Take, for example, American policy toward Western Europe. The goal of containment was not just to deter the Soviet Union but to prevent a recurrence of the rivalries among the states of Europe that culminated in two cataclysmic world wars. The clarity, capability, credibility, and commitment of American power served as indispensable conditions for the success of NATO, European integration, and Germany's reconciliation with its former enemies. Western European states did not counter the Soviet threat or cooperate with one another spontaneously. They cooperated because a credible American commitment protected them from the Soviet Union and freed them from having to fear one another. Without a visible American presence, Western Europe might have reverted to the dangerous balance of power rivalries that had caused war in the past, and France and Great Britain surely would have worried far more after World War II about growing German strength and perhaps tried to prevent German rearmament. The Soviet Union could have played on the fears and divisions of the Western European powers to dilute and delay effective balancing behavior as Nazi Germany had successfully during the interwar years.[24]

It is worth quoting at length Robert Cooper's assessment of the important role the United States played in reinforcing the basic fact that Western European states no longer want to fight one another:

> More important was the existence of a common friend. The presence of U.S. forces enabled Germany to keep forces at a lower level than its strategic position would have warranted: without them, Germany would have needed to maintain forces large enough to deal with wars on two fronts—against France and Russia simultaneously. Such forces would always have been a cause for alarm to both its neighbors and would probably provoke an arms race as well. . . . The same reasoning would have applied to the nuclear sphere too. As it was, the U.S. nuclear guarantee enabled Germany to remain non-nuclear. But even if Germany had pursued a low level of armaments and had chosen to remain non-nuclear, that would not have been enough. . . . France or Britain might still have suspected a secret German troop build-up or a secret nuclear weapons programme. What mattered above all therefore was the openness NATO created. NATO was and is a massive intra-Western

confidence-building measure. This is why the reunification of Germany within NATO was so important. In a curious way, it is part of how NATO won the Cold War: not by beating Russia but by changing the strategic position of Germany.[25]

Neorealism and the Democratic Peace

Yet the Truman Doctrine and the policy of vigilant containment did not reflect geopolitical calculation alone. It also reflected the judgment that our vital interests and our deepest beliefs often coincided. After World War II, American statesmen strove to create stable, liberal democracies in Western Europe in the belief that stable, liberal democracies do not fight one another and make better allies than other types of regimes. They were right.[26]

The Truman administration and its most far-sighted successors prudently recognized what still eludes neorealists and most classical realists: our vital interest lies in promoting a zone of democratic peace, especially in crucial geopolitical areas. The norms of stable, liberal democracies not only render the threat of force among them illegitimate, but encourage a significant—though by no means complete—convergence of interests among such regimes. The institutional constraints of checks and balances, the separation of powers, and the need for public support preclude statesmen in stable, liberal democracies from resorting to massive violence when the prospects of a satisfactory peaceful resolution remain high. The perception that statesmen in other stable, liberal democracies operate under similar restraints exerts a reciprocal pacifying effect among such regimes.[27] Natan Sharansky's general proposition is therefore right: the United States is always better off with stable, liberal democracies, even those that hate it, than despotisms, even those that love it. It is to America's great advantage to spread and sustain stable, liberal democracy when it is prudent to do so.[28]

Granted, this argument requires substantial qualification. First, the adjectives *stable* and *liberal* are crucial for the democratic zone of peace to operate. Liberalism requires freedom from arbitrary authority, freedoms that include freedom of conscience, a free press, equality under the law, religious liberty, the right to hold and exchange property, the right of private contract, and firm constitutional boundaries beyond which the state cannot go. The protection and vindication of these freedoms require a representative government based on democratic elections and the consent of the governed.

Fareed Zakaria warned correctly that illiberal democracies such as the theocracy in Algeria and the militant mullahs of Iran can pose significant threats to freedom and to their neighbors. Likewise, states in the process of democratization also are often quite aggressive.[29] Even with the positive changes in the Middle East that President Bush's invasion of Iraq unleashed, democratic reform in the region will proceed slowly and laboriously, with cyclical ebbs and flows. Recent elections in Egypt and the Palestinian territories did not result in victory for the forces of political reform and moderation.

Second, democratic triumphalists make the opposite mistake of structural realists by treating the democratic peace as a permanent rather than contingent phenomenon.[30] The spread of stable, liberal democracy is not inevitable, irreversible, or necessarily universal. Although stable, liberal democratic allies always are the preferred option, such allies are not always the available option. Desperate times often require desperate measures. During the Second World War, the West had no choice but to make a temporary tactical arrangement with Stalin to thwart the greater evil of a total Nazi victory. The mistake lay in FDR's thinking that the United States could or should perpetuate that arrangement.

Prudence justifies choosing the lesser moral and geopolitical evil to prevent the greater one. During the Cold War few potential stable, liberal democratic allies existed outside Western Europe and Japan. The choice was usually between authoritarian regimes of the right and totalitarian regimes of the left. President Kennedy trenchantly expressed this perennial dilemma for American foreign policy after the 1961 assassination of Rafael Trujillo, dictator of the Dominican Republic: "There are three possibilities in descending order of preference: a decent democratic regime, a continuation of the Trujillo regime, or a Castro regime. We ought to aim at the first, but we really can't renounce the second until we are sure we can avoid the third."[31]

Similarly, in *Dictatorship and Double Standards,* Dr. Jeane Kirkpatrick made a compelling moral and practical case for supporting the former types of regime against the latter. Authoritarian regimes such as Taiwan and South Korea were likely to be less repressive, more amenable to benign evolutionary reform, and more reliably pro-American and anti-Soviet than totalitarian regimes such as Cuba and North Korea. History confirmed her judgment. South Korea and Taiwan became full-fledged, prosperous democracies under the umbrella of American protection, thanks to the considerable leverage over both countries that the United States possessed and eventually exercised. Cuba and North Korea remain poor and brutal tyrannies operated along Stalinist lines.[32]

Premature efforts to choose a stable, liberal democratic option when no viable one exists can lead to worse rather than better results. For much of the Cold War, that was especially true of the Middle East, where only Israel stood out as a stable, liberal democracy amid various forms of authoritarianism and despotism. Consequently, the United States had to collaborate tactically with an autocratic quasi-medieval Saudi regime and the mujahideen in Afghanistan to avert the greater moral and geopolitical evil of direct or indirect Soviet domination of the region. Our mistake lay not in collaborating but in striving to perpetuate these arrangements when fundamental conditions changed. Without the Soviet threat to induce cooperation, the fundamental differences between the United States and many autocracies in the Middle East began to loom much larger than the convergence of interest that existed during the Cold War.

During the 1970s the United States also sensibly collaborated tacitly with communist China for the limited purpose of constraining the greater danger of surging Soviet power. Our mistake lay in thinking this arrangement with Chinese dictators could or should be permanent beyond the collapse of the Soviet Union.[33]

Even in a unipolar world, with conditions more propitious for the United States, spreading democracy or choosing a democratic ally is not always the prudentially available option. Although the United States should welcome the successful national elections in Palestine and Iraq, as well as local elections in Saudi Arabia and the end of Syrian rule in Lebanon, stable, liberal democracy has yet to take hold in the Middle East. It will take time, patience, and the capacity to accept serious reverses along the way for the United States to succeed in spreading democracy durably rather than just contingently. The recent victory of the radical Hamas in the Palestinian territories underscores the critical distinction between stable, liberal democratic regimes, which are benign, and illiberal democracies, which are often menacing. In some cases, moreover, the United States will have to engage with regimes—such as Pakistan under Musharraf—that fall far short of our ultimate preferences.

Stable, liberal democracy is, however, always the preferred option. Alliances with such regimes rest on a far more reliable foundation than tactical arrangements with dictatorships. Convergences of enlightened self-interest among stable, liberal democracies are much more likely to transcend changes in time and circumstance—to become permanent rather than tactical interests. In this regard, our burgeoning relationship with democratic India should have greater priority than our collaboration with authoritarian Pakistan, though the Bush administration wisely sought to retain good relations with Pakistan for the larger goal of winning the war on terror. Fareed Zakaria explains why:

> Most countries have relationships that are almost exclusively between governments. Think of the links between the United States and Saudi Arabia, which exist among a few dozen high officials [have] and never really gone beyond that. But sometimes bonds develop not merely between states and between societies. Twice before the United States had developed a relationship with a country that was strategic, but also with much more—with Britain and later with Israel. In both cases, the resulting ties were broad and deep, going well beyond governmental officials and diplomatic negotiations. The two countries knew each other and understood each other and as a result became natural and almost permanent partners. America has the opportunity to forge such a relationship with India. . . . That does not mean the United States and India will agree on every policy issue. Remember that even during their close wartime alliance, Roosevelt and Churchill disagreed about several issues, most notably India's independence. America broke with Britain over Suez. It condemned Israel for its invasion of Lebanon. Washington and New Delhi have different interests and thus will inevitably have policy disputes. But it is precisely because of the deep bonds between these countries that such disagreements would not alter the fundamental reality of friendship, empathy, and association.[34]

Third, sustaining and spreading stable, liberal democracy often require an imbalance of power heavily favoring the forces of freedom. For instance, the collapse of liberal democracy in Europe during the interwar years occurred because of an insidious interaction between deteriorating internal and external conditions. America's withdrawal into isolation, Great Britain's indifference, and French weakness conspired to undermine the favorable security environment on which the survival of fragile democracies in Germany and Eastern Europe largely hinged. The failure to enforce the defective but potentially effective Versailles Treaty emboldened German opponents of Weimar democracy to overthrow the regime and the treaty. At the same time the progressive erosion of French willingness and capability to back its allies' commitments to Eastern Europe demoralized the democrats there and encouraged already powerful antidemocratic forces in the region.[35] In the early 1920s, for example, almost all of Europe's twenty-eight regimes west of the Soviet Union, including those in Eastern Europe, were democracies. By the end of 1938 that number had dwindled to twelve, and none remained in Eastern Europe. By 1941 only five democracies remained intact.[36]

Conversely, a felicitous interplay between the establishment of stable, liberal democracies and the benign effects of American power accounts largely for the tremendous success of vigilant containment in Western Europe after World War II. Consider the case of Germany, the linchpin of the NATO alliance. On the one hand, the substantial American commitment increased the odds that democracy in West Germany would succeed after the Second World War, despite past failures. On the other hand, cooperation of the Western European states presupposed a stable, democratic Germany, anchored to the West. Before 1945 a united Germany was a militaristic and aggressive Germany, a Germany that willed, as others had not, two catastrophic world wars. Whether postwar Germany became a menace or an asset to Western Europe depended as much on the regime type of the German state as on external causes. As historical experience makes clear, a totalitarian Germany, the Germany of Adolf Hitler, was the most dangerous type of Germany for Germans and for the world. An authoritarian, militaristic Germany, the Germany of Kaiser Wilhelm, was less dangerous—but still very dangerous. The stable, liberal democratic Germany of Konrad Adenauer and his successors is the least dangerous type of Germany: a peaceful Germany more likely to cooperate with the other states in Western Europe, and to reconcile successfully its historic differences with France that led to three major wars. If liberal democracy alone did not suffice to ensure that post–World War II European states would cooperate with each other or with the United States, it contributed greatly to fostering shared values and eliminating the possibility of war or fundamental conflicts of interest among them.[37]

The American success with Japan after World War II also illustrates the interplay among democracy, external security, stability, and peace. Since Japan's emergence as a major power early in the twentieth century, the character of its impact on East Asia hinged significantly on the nature of Japan's internal regime. As was true of Germany, Japan's relentless aggression that culminated in World War II in the Pacific stemmed from the authoritarian, militarist, and fanatical nature of the regime. As was true of Germany, the establishment and maintenance of liberal democracy in Japan facilitated its smoother, more benign transition from vanquished to full-fledged world power. As was true of Germany, the history of the interwar years warns that problems of trade and economic rivalry, which merely irritate Japanese-American relations today, become potentially explosive when the Japanese maintain a militaristic and authoritarian regime. As was true of Germany, a vigorous American presence in Japan not only kept it firmly in the democratic camp, but also reassured China and the weaker states of East Asia that they had less to fear from Japan's reemergence than before.[38]

Samuel Huntington has argued persuasively that even in the developing world, where the American record remains more controversial, a significant correlation exists between the rise and fall of American power and the rise and fall of liberty.[39] He suggests, likewise, that external actors such as the United States, the Vatican, and the European community contributed significantly to a major third wave of democratization in Europe, East Asia, and Latin America during the final phase of the Cold War in the 1980s.[40]

What was true during the Cold War remains true today. The robustness of American power is generally good for the spread of stable, liberal democracy; correspondingly, the spread of stable, liberal democracy is generally good for the United States. Consider the benign effects of NATO expansion, which prominent neorealists unwisely oppose. Unlike the interwar years, when the withdrawal of the United States, the indifference of Britain, and the erosion of the French alliance system created a power vacuum that doomed democracy in Eastern Europe, NATO membership and the prospect of attaining it have expanded the zone of democratic peace, eased the transition from communism to freedom in the region, and provided a hedge against possible resurgence of Russian nationalism under an authoritarian regime. The United States has already benefited consider-ably from its indispensable role in liberating Eastern Europe from Soviet tyranny, encouraging the spread of democracy there, and sustaining it with the expansion of NATO. In the war on terror, grateful Eastern European democracies continue to support President Bush overwhelmingly. They do so, despite some reservations, because this generation of Eastern Europe-ans does not take its freedom for granted, as many of their counterparts in Western Europe tend to do. Indeed, the durability of the Democratic peace in Europe after the Cold War has utterly confounded the prediction of John Mearsheimer that Europe would return to the dangerous pattern of rivalry reminiscent of the years before World War I. Again, his neorealist disdain for the importance of regime type accounts for this whopping error.[41]

Consider Russia as well. What marked the genuine end of the Cold war was the collapse of the Soviet regime—the pivotal variable neorealists dismiss in their flawed conception of American grand strategy. As the great historian of Russia Richard Pipes has argued insightfully, a Russia without a totalitarian regime is a less menacing adversary than the Soviet Union.[42] Nevertheless, an authoritarian Russia would remain a greater geopolitical threat than a liberal democratic Russia, based on czarist experience. A com-parison of Boris Yeltsin's foreign policy with those of his successors again illustrates the important interest the United States has in a democratic Rus-sia. Whereas Yeltsin at the height of his popularity and authority extolled the virtues of free markets, democracy, and a nonimperialistic foreign policy, Vladimir Putin, his more authoritarian successor, attempted more aggressively to reassert Russian authority in constituent parts of the Soviet Union, though not with the zeal or success of czarist or Soviet times.[43] The more authoritarian Russia becomes, the less cooperative it is likely to be.[44] The United States therefore should find it most disturbing that President Putin laments the collapse of the Soviet Union, calling it a "tragedy."

No doubt the United States would face less difficulty in East Asia, the geopolitical pivot of the twenty-first century, were China to become stable, liberal, and democratic. It is therefore a legitimate and prudential goal of American foreign policy to encourage the evolution of the authoritarian and expansionist People's Republic of China (PRC) into a more benign re-gime: through trade that will strengthen the private sector, which will even-tually demand greater political as well as economic freedom, and through credible containment of Chinese ambitions in the meantime, with Japan and India the linchpins of an American-led democratic alliance system in the region.

Neorealism, the Democratic Peace, and the Middle East since 9/11

This study will defer until later chapters an extended analysis of the Bush Doctrine, its application to the Iraq War, and the rationale of and requirements for the United States' remaining vitally engaged in the world's major power centers, especially East Asia. It suffices here to make a few observations highlighting why we should also reject what neorealists advocate for the Middle East.

First, the policy of deterrence toward Iraq that John Mearsheimer and Stephen Walt offered as their preferred alternative to invasion would have no plausibility whatsoever had the United States or other countries previously heeded their advice.[45] Without Israel's preemptive attack of May 1981 on the Osirak nuclear reactor in Iraq, Saddam Hussein almost certainly would have possessed nuclear weapons when he invaded Kuwait in August 1990, which would have made the cost of liberating it prohibitive.[46] Without the Gulf War of 1990–1991, which most neorealists opposed, Saddam might have achieved a nuclear capability within two years, according to the inspectors of Iraqi facilities sent in pursuant to UN resolutions 685–88, which suspended hostilities so long as Saddam abided by their terms. Without driving Saddam out of Kuwait and demolishing his conventional forces, the United States would have had to leave the "footprints" of an even larger force in Saudi Arabia—which bin Laden himself invokes as one of his prime motivations for perpetrating the dastardly attacks of September 11, 2001. William Shawcross hits the mark squarely: "The policy of containment . . . meant that U.S. troops had had to remain in Saudi Arabia since 1991 to deter Saddam from further attacks on the region. Osama Bin Laden cited 'these armed Christian soldiers' in the sacred land of the two mosques as the ultimate sacrilege that his jihad had to end. It is legitimate to speculate that had Saddam been overthrown in 1991, and had U.S. troops then been withdrawn from Saudi Arabia, Osama Bin Laden's greatest proclaimed grievance and rallying cry would have been removed."[47]

Second, Mearsheimer and Walt employ a flawed analogy in assuring us that a nuclear-armed Saddam would behave with the same caution as the Soviet Union did during the Cold War. All regimes, even evil regimes, do not calculate risks the same way. The wisest American statesmen drew an important distinction, for example, between the Soviet and the Nazi regimes, not morally or by the scale of their ambitions, but in their degree of recklessness and their capacity to be deterred. Whereas Hitler was a man in a hurry, bound and determined to wage war sooner rather than later, war with the Soviet Union was not inevitable. Marxist ideology counseled tactical flexibility in the pursuit of limitless objectives, tactical predispositions that the traditional caution of great Russian diplomacy reinforced. Nor was the Soviet Union all that cautious. The world avoided the stark choice between nuclear war and surrender to tyranny not because both sides possessed abundant numbers of nuclear weapons, but because the United States did. If the Soviet Union had possessed the same wide margin of unassailable nuclear superiority as the United States from 1945 until the mid-1960s, it defies probability to think that Soviet leaders would have conducted themselves with the same degree of self-restraint as American statesmen.[48]

Third, following Walt's approach of continuing the UN inspections process rather than fighting would not have resulted in "a resounding diplomatic victory." On the contrary, the United States would have remained paralyzed, the French would have remained obstructionist, Saddam would have remained defiant—all while the danger mounted. Was it truly realistic in the best sense to invest the UN with the responsibility for monitoring Saddam's WDM programs as he exploited the corrupt oil-for-food program to bribe members of the UN Security Council? As later chapters will examine in greater detail, Saddam's propensity for risk taking also fell closer on the spectrum to Nazi Germany's under Hitler than to the Soviet Union's during the Cold War. True, the United States has yet to find the weapons of mass destruction we legitimately feared, on the basis of past experience, that Saddam had developed; nevertheless, the Kay Commission and Duelfer Report also affirm that it was only a matter of time before Saddam obtained such capabilities once the sanctions so painful to the Iraqi people inevitably broke down.[49] WMD exponentially increased the potential danger of waiting too long to eliminate Saddam, prudently viewed through the prism of 9/11 and Saddam's refusal to abide by the inspection regime.

Fourth, Walt's neglect of ideology and regime type leads him to treat American support for Israel as the cause rather than the symptom of the surge in Islamic animosity against us. Efraim Karsh exposes the fallacy of this neglect in his magisterial study of Islamic imperialism:

> Contrary to widespread assumptions, . . . Arab and Muslim anti-Americanism have little to do with U.S. international behavior or its Middle Eastern policy. America's position as the pre-eminent world power blocks Arab and Islamic imperial aspirations. As such, it is the natural target for aggression. Osama bin Laden and other Islamists' war is not against America per se, but is rather the most recent manifestation of the millenarian jihad for universal Islamic empire (or umma). This is a vision by no means confined to the extremist version of Islam, as illustrated by the overwhelming support for the 9/11 attacks throughout the Arab and Islamic world. In the historical imagination of many Muslims and Arabs, bin Laden represents nothing short of the new incarnation of Saladin. The House of Islam's war for world mastery is a traditional, indeed venerable, quest that is far from over. Only when the political elites of the Middle East and Muslim world reconcile themselves to the reality of state nationalism, forswear pan-Arab and pan-Islamic imperial dreams, and make Islam a matter of private faith rather than a tool of political ambition will the inhabitants of these regions at last be able to look forward to a better future free of would-be Saladins.[50]

The road to stability in the Middle East lies through promoting democratic regime change that addresses the real root cause of the danger: the culture of tyranny and oppression that spawns radical, implacably aggressive despotism such as Saddam Hussein's regime, the militant mullahs in Iran, and the PLO under Arafat.[51] In making the ugly accusation that the Israel lobby has masterminded not only the war in Iraq, but the war in Lebanon, Walt and Mearsheimer sound more like gutter anti-Semites such as Charles Lindbergh and Father Coughlin than the disinterested scholars they profess to be.[52]

Nor do conspiracy theories or Walt and Mearsheimer's more euphemistic Israel lobby explain the depth and intensity of America's support for Israel. The dynamics of American religion provide a better explanation, according to Walter Russell Mead, who cites the growing influence of evangelicals as a powerful source of pro-Israeli sentiment, especially in the Republican Party. "Evangelicals . . . find the continued existence of the Jewish people to be a strong argument for the existence of God and his power in history. . . . Evangelicals have been gaining social and political power, while liberal Christians and secular intellectuals have been losing it. This should not be blamed on Jews."[53]

Josef Joffe demolishes the argument of those who mainly blame Israel for American problems in the Middle East. Far from creating tensions, Joffe argues, Israel actually contains more antagonism than it causes, antagonism that would become even worse were Israel to disappear as its enemies hope:

> Can anybody proclaim in good conscience that the . . . dysfunctionalities of the Arab world would vanish along with Israel? Two U.N. Arab Human Development Reports say no. . . . Stagnation and hopelessness have three root causes. The first is lack of freedom. . . . The second root cause is lack of knowledge: Sixty-five million adults are illiterate, and some ten million children have no schooling at all. . . . Third, female participation in political and economic life is the lowest in the world. Economic growth will continue to lag as long as the potential of half the population remains largely untapped. Will all of this right itself when the Judeo-Western insult to Arab pride suddenly vanishes? Will the millions of unemployed and bored young men, cannon fodder for the terrorists, vanish as well—along with one-party rule, corruption, and closed economies? This notion only makes sense if one cherishes single-cause explanations, or worse, harbors a particular animus against the Jewish state and its refusal to behave like Sweden. . . . Finally, the most popular what-if question of them all: Would the Islamic world hate the United States less if Israel vanished? . . . Arab-Islamic hatred of the United States preceded the conquest of the West Bank and Gaza. Recall the loathing left behind by the U.S.–managed coup that restored the shah's rule in Tehran in 1953, or the U.S. intervention in Lebanon in 1958. As soon as the British and the French left the Middle East, the United States became the

dominant power and the No. one target. Another bit of suggestive evidence is that the fiercest (unofficial) anti-Americanism emanates from Washington's self-styled allies in the Arab Middle East, Egypt, and Saudi Arabia. Is this situation because of Israel—or because it is so convenient for these regimes to "busy giddy minds over foreign quarrels" (as Shakespeare's Henry IV put it) to distract their populations from their dependence on the great Satan. . . . The Cairo Declaration against "U.S. Hegemony," endorsed by 400 delegates across the Middle East and West in December 2002 . . . mentions Palestine only peripherally. . . . In short, global America is responsible for all the afflictions in the Arab world, with Israel coming a distant second.[54]

Like Nazi Germany, imperial Japan, and the Soviet Union, Osama bin Laden went to war against the United States not primarily for what it did, but for who its citizens are—a free people committed to sustaining well-ordered liberty. His implacable enemy is the very freedom America personifies. Mary Habeck has reached a similar conclusion in her brilliant analysis of the jihadist ideology that bin Laden epitomizes. Her remedy for the threat largely parallels the logic of the Bush Doctrine:

> Only democratization . . . will attack the jihadist ideology while creating democracies that are most responsive to their citizens. The jihadist argument is that democracy is completely antithetical to Islam and moreover is specifically designed to destroy the religion. If democracies can flourish in Islamic lands without disturbing the practices and beliefs of Islam, the entire jihadist argument will collapse. While there are many reasons to hope and work for democracies in the Middle East—that they might end despotic regimes, create the conditions for economic development, end oppression, corruption, and so on—the real possibility of the complete defeat of the jihadists must also be taken into consideration. At the same time, this is not an argument for democracies that will be exact copies of the American or European model. The very different conditions in Islamic countries, including a higher toleration for the integration of religion and government, will lead to the creation of states that reflect different religious, cultural, and

historical traditions in that area of the world. . . . Yet, the fact that the Germans and Japanese, Indians and Central Americans have all been able to adapt democracy to local conditions leaves us with the vital hope that Muslims of the world can find their own path to greater freedom.[55]

What Habeck writes also applies to our implacable enemies in the Middle East, who use Israel as an excuse for their animosity toward us.[56] No sensible person can plausibly deny any longer that the former PLO chairman Yasser Arafat envisaged the Oslo Peace Accords of 1993 not as a process to generate genuine reconciliation, but as a continuation of war to exterminate Israel by other means. On the basis of his twelve years of experience during the first Bush and two Clinton terms as chief American negotiator in the Israeli-Palestinian "peace process," Dennis Ross concludes authoritatively that "Arafat never prepared his people for the hard compromises" because "he never prepared himself. Our great failing was in not creating the earlier tests that would have either exposed Arafat's inability to ultimately make peace or forced him to prepare his people to compromise."[57]

The tragedy of the Palestinian people is their unrequited suffering, which a more responsible, moderate Palestinian leadership and more enlightened statesmanship among Muslim and European nations could have substantially redressed. The fundamental asymmetry between Israel and the Palestinian Authority has long remained this: although there are extremists in Israel such as the fanatical settlers on the West Bank who reject any compromise, they are a decided minority; the vast majority of Israelis, including former Prime Minister Sharon and his successor, Prime Minister Olmert, accept the idea of a two-state solution to the conflict. Under Arafat the Palestinian leadership did not. In word and deed Israel has demonstrated that it will trade land when offered real peace. Menachem Begin, the Likud prime minister, pulled Israel out of the Sinai when Egyptian President Sadat offered real peace. Israel withdrew from Lebanon in 2000, five years before Syria belatedly and begrudgingly withdrew under the pressure that the American invasion of Iraq catalyzed. Under Ariel Sharon, Israel withdrew from Gaza and built a wall that left 92 percent of the West Bank to the Palestinians.

Confounding Walt's neorealist view that less American effort would achieve better results is the fact that one of the contributing factors to the demise of the Oslo Accords and the surge in anti-American Islamic radicalism was precisely the perceived erosion of American power and the willingness to use it that had crystallized in the minds of radicals in the region by the end of the Clinton administration. American vacillations with Saddam during the 1990s and the irresolution and pinprick responses to his flouting of UN resolutions; President Clinton's eagerness to accommodate Arafat, his most frequent foreign guest at the White House; the precipitous retreat from Mogadishu in 1993; the tepid American reaction to the bombings of the Khobar Towers, the embassy in Kenya, and the USS *Cole*: all interacted insidiously to embolden American enemies in the Middle East. Read bin Laden's own words in the fatwa he issued in the summer of 1996 declaring war against the United States:

Few days ago the news agencies had reported that the Defense Secretary of the Crusading Americans had said that "the explosion at Riyadh and Al-Khobar had taught him one lesson: that is not to withdraw when attacked by cowardly terrorists."

We say to the Secretary of Defense that his talk can induce a grieving mother to laughter and shows the fears that have enshrined you all. Where was this false courage of yours when the explosion in Beirut took place in 1983 A.D. (1403 A.H.). You were turned into scattered pits and pieces at the same time; 241 mainly marine soldiers were killed. And where was this courage of yours when two explosions made you leave Aden in less than twenty four hours!

But your most disgraceful case was in Somalia; where—after vigorous propaganda about the power of the USA and its post cold war leadership of the new world order—you moved tens of thousands of international forces, including 28,000 American soldiers into Somalia. However, when tens of your soldiers were killed in minor battles and one American pilot was dragged into the streets of Mogadishu you left the area carrying disappointment, humiliation, defeat, and your dead with you. Clinton appeared in front of the whole world threatening and promising revenge, but these threats were merely a preparation for withdrawal. You have been disgraced by Allah and you withdrew; the extent of your weakness and impotence became very clear. It was a pleasure for the "heart" of every Muslim and a remedy to the "chests" of believing nations to see you defeated in the three Islamic cities of Beirut, Aden, and Mogadishu.[58]

Contrast this erosion of American credibility during the 1990s to what has happened since 9/11. Although the situation in Iraq remains difficult and the outcome in doubt, Walt and other critics pronouncing the Bush Doctrine a failure have vastly underestimated its achievements. The United States succeeded brilliantly in toppling the Taliban regime in Afghanistan, creating the conditions for the first free elections in the country's history, and facilitating the victory of Hamid Karzai as president. Karzai, unlike his Taliban predecessors, is not only a good man, but moderate, civilized, and pro-American, The military campaign in Iraq also succeeded brilliantly. Despite the difficult insurgency that still continues, Iraq has made substantial political progress, holding free elections in which more than eight million Iraqis turned out in defiance of murderous terror, and forging a constitution that stands a decent chance of transforming the nation into a federal democratic republic based on the rule of law.

The Bush Doctrine also deserves considerable credit for keeping al-Qaeda on the run and thwarting its ambitions to mount another devastating attack on the United States. Removing Saddam also catalyzed a positive domino effect: the Syrian withdrawal from Lebanon; the Libyan suspension of its WMD program; and the emergence of genuine, albeit precarious, reform movements throughout the Middle East.[59] President Bush deserves much credit as well for abandoning the failed policy of propitiating a radical and corrupt PLO at Israel's expense. In his June 2002 address at West Point, the president rightly defined liberal, democratic regime change for Palestine and the removal of the implacable Arafat as the preconditions for achieving his roadmap to peace, which the administration hopes will eventually culminate in an open Palestinian state committed to living in peace with a stable, secure, democratic Israel.[60] The president rightly refuses to negotiate with Hamas until it recognizes Israel's legitimate right to exist within secure boundaries. Tragically, any durable settlement with the Palestinians will emerge only in the aftermath of a power struggle within the Palestinian Authority that breaks the forces of radicalism and rejectionism. This will not happen soon or without bloodshed. In the meantime, Israel should continue the policies of Ariel Sharon, which were aimed at sealing the Jewish State off from the Palestinian territories and unilaterally establishing a final frontier.

Likewise, the president deserves much credit for giving Israel the green light to defeat Hezbollah in Lebanon. In this case Israel's fight is our own: we are at war with an insidious axis of jihadist terrorist organization such as Hezbollah (which murdered 241 U.S. Marines in October 1983) and their sponsors, such as the militant Iranian regime. Israel and the United States therefore must defeat rather than negotiate with such an enemy. The unsatisfactory outcome of the Israelis' 2006 war with Hezbollah—a UN truce that is likely the prelude to the next war—owed mainly to the poor and halting leadership of Israeli Prime Minister Olmert and Israel's underestimation of a tenacious enemy rather than any shortcomings on the American side. The good news is that Hezbollah suffered much more extensive damage than many seem to realize. As Victor Davis Hanson observes, too, "Iran and Syria unleashed Hezbollah because they were facing global scrutiny, one over nuclear acquisition and the other over assassination of Lebanese reformer Rafik Hariri. The problems will not go away for either of them—nor, if we persist, will democratic fervor in Afghanistan and Iraq on their borders."[61] Count, too, on the impotence of the UN and the resilience of an excellent Israeli defense force that will learn from its mistakes in the war of 2006. This will put Israel and the United States in a much more favorable position when the next round of fighting occurs. The defeat of Hezbollah and ultimately their Iranian and Syrian patrons is a vital endeavor in the war against Islamic fascism, a war every bit as vital to win as the wars against German Nazism and Soviet totalitarianism.

Finally, neorealists vastly exaggerate the danger that the Bush Doctrine will provoke states to make common cause against us and vastly underestimates the risks of this minimalist grand strategy of offshore balancing.[62] Stephen Brooks and William Wohlforth have argued powerfully that the current international system is not only unipolar and prone to peace but durable:

> Bounded by oceans to the east and west and weak, friendly powers to the north and south, the United States is both less vulnerable than previous aspiring hegemons and less threatening to others. The main potential challengers to its unipolarity—China, Russia, Japan, and Germany—are in the opposite position. They cannot

augment their military capabilities so as to balance the United States without simultaneously becoming an immediate threat to their neighbors. Politics, even international politics, is local. Although American power attracts a lot of attention globally, states are usually more concerned with their own neighborhoods than with the global equilibrium. Were any of the potential challengers to make a serious run at the United States, regional balancing efforts would almost certainly help contain them, as would the massive latent power capabilities of the United States, which could be mobilized as necessary to head off an emerging threat.[63]

The United States has another huge advantage to forestall effective balancing, which interacts synergistically with its offshore position: the character of the American regime, whose defining principle of separation of powers imposes formidable restraints on the arbitrary use of power at home and abroad.[64] Aristotle says that the mark of intelligence is the ability to make reasonable distinctions. Even for the controversial episodes in American foreign policy, it insults Aristotle's dictum to equate a stable, liberal, democratic United States with other potentially preponderant powers, especially the evil totalitarian regimes of Nazi Germany and the Soviet Union.

Though much of Western Europe—what Donald Rumsfeld calls the Old Europe—may not agree with us on Iraq or the Middle East, that does not mean that our NATO allies—France excepted—are tempted to join a strongly anti-American coalition. Since World War II the luxury of Europe's escape from the burdens of power politics has depended largely on American protection and the credibility of America power. Robert Kagan formulates best the great paradox of Europe's current situation:

> Europe's new Kantian order could flourish only under the umbrella of American power exercised according to the rules of the old Hobbesian order. American power made it possible for Europeans to believe that power is no longer important. Because Europe neither has the will nor the ability to guard its own paradise and keep it from being overrun, spiritually as well as physically, . . . it has become dependent on America's willingness to use its military might to deter or defeat those around the world who still believe in power politics.[65]

In the final analysis, Western Europeans are not so self-destructive—with possibly France excepted—to jettison the fundamental relationship that has generated such unprecedented peace and prosperity for them. Do the new democracies of Eastern Europe really prefer Franco-German hegemony in Europe to the presence of the Americans? Their support for the United States in defiance of France during the Iraq War of 2003 speaks loudly and clearly that the answer is no.

Does democratic Japan or India or the other powers in East Asia fear the robustness of American power more than they fear the United States may not do enough to contain a rising, authoritarian, assertive China? Would East Asian nations really prefer the United States to adopt the more minimalist strategy of deterrence that neorealists and others recommend? Are we really better off in the Middle East without a strong, active American presence, committed to spreading freedom and thwarting menacing threats arising from the insidious linkage between mounting radicalism and the proliferation of WMD technology? Will appeasing Arab radicalism at democratic Israel's expense really bring peace or honor? Or do the dismal results of Western Europe's twenty-five-year propitiation of the PLO under Arafat, Iraq under Saddam, and Iran under the militant mullahs reveal the moral and geopolitical bankruptcy of such a strategy?

The history of American diplomacy since the beginning of the twentieth century underscores the wisdom of Wohlforth's conclusion that the United States' doing too little is a greater danger than its doing too much.[66] The United States entered World War I and World War II almost too late and dangerously unprepared. Even in the Cold War, the United States did not fund the military dimensions of containment adequately until the shock of the Korean War of 1950–1953 spurred the Congress to triple the defense budget. The United States did not respond adequately to the massive Soviet military buildup that began in the 1960s until the election of Ronald Reagan in 1980. During the 1990s the United States largely lived off the borrowed capital of the Reagan military buildup that not only won the Cold War, but also laid the foundation for winning the conventional combat phase of two wars against Iraq at remarkably low cost and risk.

Neorealist policy prescriptions epitomize that greater danger of doing too little—for the past, present, and future. It is, instead, far more prudent to give the benefit of the doubt to the clarity, credibility, and muscularity of American power. As Michael Mandelbaum wisely observes:

The abdication by the United States of some or all of the responsibilities for International Security that is has come to bear, in the first decade of the twenty-first century would deprive the international system of one of its principal safety features, which keeps countries from smashing into each other, as they are historically prone to do. . . . Their awareness, sometimes dim and almost never explicitly spelled out, of the political, military, and economic dangers that would come with the retreat of American power causes other countries to refrain from trying to displace the United States from its place at the center of the international system. Virtually all of them harbor some grievance or another against the twenty-first century international order, but none of them would welcome the absence of any order at all, which is what the collapse of American power might well bring. Grudgingly, tacitly, silently, other countries support the American role in the world's government out of the well-grounded fear that while the conduct of the United States may be clumsy, overbearing, and occasionally even insufferable, the alternative would be even worse, perhaps much worse.[67]

3

The Unrealistic Realism
of Classical Realists

Republican critics of the Bush Doctrine generally come from the classical realist tradition associated with E. H. Carr, Hans Morgenthau, George F. Kennan, President Richard M. Nixon, and Henry Kissinger. The most prominent of these critics, such as former National Security Advisor Brent Scowcroft and former Secretary of State Lawrence Eagleberger, worked directly with Kissinger during the Ford administration, though Kissinger dissented from his former colleagues by supporting the American invasion of Iraq in 2003.[1]

The Precepts of Classical Realism

Classical realism draws from a wider range of variables than just the structure of international relations. It arises from a pessimistic view of human nature, which identifies man's lust for power as his dominant characteristic. For classical realists the absence of a monopoly on the use of violence in international politics not only amplifies the worst aspects of man's flawed nature, but imposes stark limits on the degree of limited cooperation states can achieve.[2] There are of course important distinctions among classical realists, which a spectrum would best convey, on issues ranging from the comparative importance of ideology, regime type, and shared values. Classical realists also differ in their degree of pessimism about human nature; those who are more optimistic about man's capacity for good as well as evil have greater confidence in the possibility of ameliorating, if not eliminating, international conflict and discord. No American realist holds as grim a view of human nature or its baleful effect on international politics as, say, St. Augustine or Machiavelli.[3]

For all their differences, however, classical realists in the Anglo-American tradition largely adhere to several core propositions: (a) because of man's irredeemable imperfection and the anarchic nature of international politics, the national interest must drive American foreign policy; (b) what constitutes the national interest or vital interests is easily discernable by geopolitical criteria that should be the exclusive measure of ranking; (c) morality and the national interest are often not complementary, but basically in tension; (d) therefore, morality should not drive foreign policy; (e) international politics will remain primarily a struggle for power and equilibrium rather than a quest for justice; (f) foreign policy should not aim to transform the domestic structures of other states.

In his seminal exposition of classical realism, *Politics among Nations,* Hans Morgenthau instructs statesmen to embrace the concept of "interest defined as power" as the guiding principle of foreign policy.[4] He warns of the dangers of applying universal moral principles to international politics, where selfishness and self-interest taint all nations' claims to higher values, including our own.

E. H. Carr, another seminal figure in the pantheon of Anglo-American realism, takes Morgenthau one step further by embracing moral relativism in international politics. Or as Carr wrote, "The weapon of relativity of thought must be used to demolish the utopian concept of a fixed and absolute standard by which policies and actions can be judged."[5] Ultimately, he identifies the statesman's prime imperative as accommodating peacefully to the changing correlation of forces measured in terms of power.

Similarly, George F. Kennan repudiates the moralist-legalistic tradition in American foreign relations, which, in his view, led the nation astray from its true interest of pursuing fixed, finite, and limited foreign policy goals devoid of moral arrogance or the pretense of virtue. A pervasive theme of Kennan's writing is that objective morality cannot provide a basis for peace among nations, because morality is a thoroughly relative matter. Instead, foreign policy should reflect our own concrete interests, which represent the limits of our competence to discern: "Let us not assume that our moral values, based as they are on the specifics of our national tradition and various religious outlooks represented in the country necessarily have validity for people everywhere. In particular, let us not assume that the purposes of the state are fit subjects for measurement in moral terms."[6]

Although Morgenthau rejects Carr's and Kennan's moral relativism in theory, he largely divests international politics of its ethical content by treating the lust for power as all-pervasive by dismissing as mere pretense the invocation of moral principles in international politics, and by magnifying the daunting difficulty facing statesmen trying to discern what transcendent morality calls for before or during the fact.[7] Even Greg Russell, Morgenthau's excellent and sympathetic biographer, concedes that "the pervasive evil in human nature and politics rendered his formal ethic so transcendent that it could not easily function as a vital force directing man's creative energies in a more imperfect world." Like George Kennan and other classical realists in the same vein, Morgenthau did not defend a fixed, finite conception of the national interest as the sole reference point for foreign policy out of cynicism. He believed that it was more honest, more moral, and more likely to minimize deadly ideological crusades for nations to confess their real motives, rather than pretend to have noble ones.[8]

The dominant trajectory of classical realist thought is likewise at odds with the logic of the Bush Doctrine and vigilant containment, which view democratic regime change as a precondition for addressing the root cause of rivalries with our most dangerous and aggressive adversaries. Henry Kissinger is the classical realist most ambivalent on this subject. On the one hand, his seminal study of the nineteenth-century balance of power, *A World Restored*, concedes the linkage between domestic political structures and international stability; on the other hand, his policy of détente with the Soviet Union explicitly denied that linkage. He also deplores "ideological crusades" based on abstract principles, and warns of the consequences: "When one or more states claim universal applicability for their particular structure, schism grows deep indeed."[9]

Brent Scowcroft and other critics of the president from the realist wing of the Republican Party largely adhere to these underlying assumptions of classical realism and their policy implications. He also depreciates the importance of ideology or regime type in assessing America's true interest in the Middle East, which he defines as the achievement of stability and equilibrium. He doubts that democratic regime change can succeed in the Middle East, or that it matters very much in the grand scheme of things even if it does. In his view, "The notion that inside every human being is a burning desire for freedom and liberty, much less democracy, is probably not the case."[10] Scowcroft believes that resolution of the Arab-Israeli conflict would contribute significantly more to the region's stability than the removal of Saddam and the establishment of stable, liberal democracy in Iraq. So he favored containing rather than removing Saddam in 2003.

Like the neorealists, Scowcroft assumed Arafat was a suitable partner for genuine peace, without reference to Arafat's ideology or the PLO's despotic internal characteristics.[11] He also considered the intransigence of democratic Israel the culprit for the failure to resolve the Arab-Israeli conflict. Unlike the pro-Israeli administration of George W. Bush, Scowcroft despaired that Israeli Prime Minister Ariel Sharon agreed to pull Israeli troops from Gaza, because in his view Israel then "could control a Palestinian state atomized enough that it can't be a problem."[12] Scowcroft also dismisses regime type as a critical variable in the United States' addressing the emerging Iranian nuclear threat.[13]

Classical realism illuminates some essential truths that statesmen ignore at their peril. It reminds us of the permanence of evil and tragedy in international politics, which a policy grounded in prudence can significantly alleviate but never eliminate. It relentlessly exposes the dangerous fallacies of utopian thinking: faith in the moral force of public opinion; a belief in the automatic harmony of interests among men and states; confidence in the United Nations as the arbiter of international legitimacy; confidence in achieving perpetual peace or peace without power. It inoculates us against the danger of equating good intentions with moral outcomes in international relations.

The Defects of Classical Realism

Yet the defects of unalloyed classical realism outweigh its virtues as a guide for American grand strategy. Man neither lives without power nor lives by power alone. Or as the great theologian Reinhold Niebuhr put it: "Pure idealists underestimate the perennial power of particular and parochial loyalties. . . . But the realists are usually so impressed by the power of these perennial forces that they fail to recognize the novel and unique elements in a revolutionary world situation. . . . A view more sober than that of idealists or realists must persuade us that, if hopes are dupes, fears may be liars."[14]

The deep pessimism and moral relativism pervasive in classical realist thought underestimate man's imperfect but still significant residual capacity for justice and devotion to a larger good. Although security concerns form the irreducible core of the national interest, nations are not totally incapable of adhering to interests and values beyond the national interests. Nor are their statesmen totally incapable of legitimately defining the national interest with some reference to transcendent ideals, or with some regard for the good of other nations. This is especially true for the United States, which has always rejected narrow, coarser conceptions of self-interest in favor of what George Washington calls interest guided by justice, or what Alexis de Tocqueville calls self-interest rightly understood:

> Americans . . . are pleased to explain almost all of the actions of their life with the aid of self-interest well understood; they complacently show how the enlightened love of themselves constantly brings them to aid each other and disposes them willingly to sacrifice a part of their time and their wealth to the good of the state. I think that in this it often happens that they do not do themselves justice; for one sometimes sees citizens in the United States as elsewhere abandoning themselves to the disinterested and unreflective sparks that are natural to man; but Americans scarcely avow that they yield to movements of this kind; they would rather do honor to their philosophy than to themselves.[15]

This more enlightened, enlarged conception of the national interest reflects greater practical insight about the prerequisites for sustaining public support in a democracy than Morgenthau's, Kennan's, Carr's, or other mainstream versions of classical realists. The problem with reflexively invoking the national interest as a self-evident guide to foreign policy is that the idea is a truism. Everyone is for the national interest. Even Woodrow Wilson favored it. For American foreign policy the issue is how to define the national interest among rival conceptions and then choose the most effective means for pursuing it. Historically, the United States has always defined the national interest not just geopolitically, but through the tug and pull of domestic politics, and partly by reference to transcendent ideals.

Those realists who attempt to sever ideals and transcendent morality from conceptions of the national interest are completely unrealistic. President George Herbert Walker Bush discovered this during the First Gulf War when his secretary of state first depicted the rationale for fighting as merely oil and jobs; Richard Nixon and Henry Kissinger discovered this in their attempt to pursue a policy of détente based on a restrictive conception of the national interest when Realpolitik was not sufficient to win the domestic support necessary to sustain an effective foreign policy. The foreign policy troubles of Woodrow Wilson, Jimmy Carter, and Bill Clinton also demonstrate that idealism alone cannot suffice to win such support. Americans must believe that U.S. foreign policy is right, legitimate, and in their self-interest.[16]

Classical realists make the same mistake as neorealists by discounting ideology and treating all regimes as essentially alike. The great French political scientist Raymond Aron offers a devastating rebuttal to the notion that states, despite changes in regimes, pursue the same kind of foreign policy:

> Is it true that states, whatever their regime, pursue the same kind of foreign policy? This statement is admirably ambiguous. Are the foreign policies of Napoleon, Hitler, and Stalin of the same kind as those of Louis XVI, Adenauer, or Nicolas II? If one answers yes, then the proposition is incontestable, but not very instructive. The features which all diplomatic-strategic behavior have in common are formal; they come down to selfishness, to the calculation of forces, to a variable mixture of hypocrisy and cynicism. But the differences in degree are such that a Napoleon or a Hitler suffices with the help of revolutionary circumstances to change the course of history.[17]

Often, ideology is not just a rationalization for a ubiquitous will to power but a partially autonomous force that could either temper the ambitions of regimes or make them more ruthless and dangerous. Frequently the internal characteristics of states do vitally affect how they define and pursue their interests. George Kennan's more modest conception of containment did not take these variables or the notion of enlightened self-interest sufficiently into account. The United States, Kennan believed wrongly, merely needed to keep West Germany and Japan, centers of industrial capability, out of Soviet hands. He opposed the NATO alliance as unnecessary and the idea of incorporating a liberal West Germany into it unduly provocative. Assuming that ideology did not determine alignment decisions in international politics, he also believed wrongly that the United States could even tolerate a communist Germany or Japan so long as they were not satellites of the Soviet Union.[18]

The United States, our allies in Western Europe, and Japan owe much to President Truman for having a more enlarged, enlightened, and realistic conception of our true national interest than Kennan did. A truly neutral Germany was neither desirable nor possible. For one thing, the Soviet Union would have never accepted it. Soviet leaders proposed neutrality as a way of decoupling Germany from NATO, and NATO from the United States, their ultimate goal being domination of Germany and then the rest of Europe. For another thing, German integration into a democratic alliance was by far the more prudential option for Americans and Europeans. It meant that Germany would no longer threaten their neighbors and themselves as they had as the world's loose cannon between 1870 and 1945. It meant that Germans would become part of democratic Europe rather than strive implacably to make Europe German.[19]

There is, moreover, no retreat from moral reasoning in international politics by retreating to the abyss of moral relativism, as Kennan, E. H. Carr, and other classical realists who reify power have done. Granted, we should always be on guard against a moral pretense that conflates particular, self-interested claims with universal, moral ones. No nation has a monopoly on moral virtue, not even our own. Every nation has contributed at least some share of inhumanity, injustice, and arrogance. Also, ethics in foreign policy is a moral discipline related, though not identical, to personal ethics. The danger arises not from objective morality per se, but from moralism, which naively conceives of political morality as directly applying the injunctions of the Sermon on the Mount, which measures ethics in terms of just intentions, and which harbors a suspicion of power and interest as legitimate guides for action. Man has an ineradicable capacity for evil as well as good, and the relative anarchy of international politics often significantly constrains statesmen's range of moral choices.

Nevertheless, the sagest statesmen in the Anglo-American tradition have always recognized the absolute standards of Judeo-Christian morality as the basis for evaluating moral and geopolitical evil. The cardinal moral virtue of these statesmen was prudence: the art of applying general principles to particular circumstances informed by a realistic assessment of the desirable, the possible, and the probable consequences of alternative courses of action. Without fixed moral standards, statesmen lack the valid criteria to make critical distinctions: between legitimate and illegitimate challenges to the existing order; between flawed but decent democratic regimes and their more odious alternatives; between the lesser evil of authoritarianism and the greater evil of totalitarianism; between the decent opinions of mankind that deserve some respect, if not always our deference, and the indecent opinions, such as the UN Conference on Racism of 2002, that we should greet with indignation and contempt.[20]

All the worst features of unrealistic classical realism converge in the thought and policy prescriptions of E. H. Carr, whose book *The Twenty Years' Crisis, 1919–1939*, published in 1940, remains one of the seminal statements of classical realism. His moral relativism and tendency to treat all states equally made him obtuse to the malignity and gravity of the Nazi and Soviet threats. His Hobbesian view of the international environment made him insensitive to the significant if imperfect amity that stable, liberal democracies could achieve among themselves even in anarchy. Revealingly, Carr considers the infamous Munich Agreement of September 1938 "a successful model of combining realism with utopianism," the nearest approach to the settlement of a major international issue by the procedure of peaceful change: "If the power relations of 1938 made it inevitable that Czecho-Slovakia should lose part of her territory, and eventually her independence, it was preferable (quite apart from any question of justice or injustice) that this should come about as the result of discussions round the table in Munich rather than as a result of war between the Great Powers or a local war between Germany and Czecho-Slovakia."[21]

This appalling statement casts all the deficiencies of Carr's classical realism in bold relief. Nazi Germany was not just another revisionist power that appeasement by status quo powers could satisfy. The obvious shortcomings of the Treaty of Versailles did not render Nazi Germany's position morally equivalent to those of the democracies, nor did they justify Hitler's demolition of the treaty by force any more than did the sins real or imagined of American policy toward the Middle East justify 9/11. Democratic Czechoslovakia's loss of independence in 1938 was neither inevitable nor desirable. A sober evaluation of the nature of the Nazi regime and its ideology was not irrelevant in calculating the efficacy of a policy of conciliation or firmness.

The same flawed assumptions led Carr to treat the United States and the

Soviet Union as morally equivalent superpowers having limited freedom of action. He advocated a policy of appeasing Stalin after the Second World War. He not only accepted the Soviet regime as legitimate and permanent, but predicted it was the wave of the future: "The missionary role which had been filled in the First World War by American democracy and Woodrow Wilson passed in the Second World War to Soviet democracy and Marshall Stalin."[22] Most classical realists are not nearly as fatuous as Carr, though George Kennan also defended the Munich Agreement, a position he had the sense and decency to repudiate later.[23]

Contrast the moral and practical consequences of Carr's moral relativism with the salutary results of Winston Churchill's statecraft, grounded in absolute, transcendent, Judeo-Christian principles as well as in geopolitics. Unlike E. H. Carr, Churchill rejected the idea of cooperation with Hitler for ethical as well as practical reasons: "There can never be friendship between the British democracy and the Nazi power, that power which spurns Christian ethics, which cheers its onward course by a barbarous paganism, which vaunts the spirit of aggression and conquest, which derives strength and perverted pleasure from persecution, and uses, as we have seen, with pitiless brutality, the threat of murderous force. That power can never be the trusted friend of the British democracy."[24]

Although Churchill accepted the necessity of a tactical arrangement with Stalin during World War II to prevent the greater evil of a total Nazi victory, he likewise rejected the possibility of genuine friendship between the democracies and the Soviet Union:

> Personally, I am in favor of the utmost freedom of thought and discussion. In the open clash of conflicting opinions in the Parliamentary arena, the right of public meeting, and the unfettered and independent press, I see the surest guarantee of ordered progress. But the Communist, like the Nazi, seeks to abolish these things. The idea of both is the totalitarian state, in which opposition is treason and criticism a crime. . . . The Communist will denounce all things—as they exist in Nazi Germany. But a totalitarian state does not change its nature because the Swastika has been replaced by the Hammer and the Sickle. These evils are inherent in Communism as in every system which deifies the state and debases its citizens.[25]

Churchill recognized, conversely, that Anglo-American cooperation reflected shared ideals that informed self-interest, well understood: "The unity of policy that exists throughout the English-speaking world does not arise because of any bargaining or treaties, but from the fact that there is a natural agreement between Great Britain and the United States on almost all questions that arise. This is because we pursue the same ideals and have a common inheritance in literature and laws."[26]

Thus, Churchill's statecraft largely succeeded in striking a prudential balance between the classical realists who unmoor power from principle and the idealists who view principles or multilateral institutions as an adequate substitute for national power: "It is not against any state or nation that we range ourselves. It is not against tyranny in all its forms, ancient or modern, new or old, that we take our stand. Tyranny presents itself in various forms. . . . Hence we also find ourselves in great harmony with the Great Republic of the United States, whose services to mankind . . . demand our full cooperation. Any alliance that the British nation makes with another free government is not directed against any particular country or people, but the power of evil, wherever that may be and whoever that may be."[27]

The Unrealism of Scowcroft's Realism

The version of classical realism that Brent Scowcroft and other Republican internationalists espouse is more robust than Kennan's and less prone to dire consequences than Carr's. Like Henry Kissinger, Scowcroft at least regarded the Soviet Union during the Cold War as an imperial threat that required American power to contain. He supported the use of force in the First Gulf War to liberate Kuwait, an imperfect outcome but still superior to accepting Saddam's faits accomplis, as a vast majority of Democratic senators urged at the time.[28] Scowcroft assisted President George H. W. Bush in his masterly management of the final stages of German reunification in 1990, which ended the Cold War on Western terms with Germany as part of the NATO alliance. In this instance, George H. W. Bush deftly persuaded a reluctant France, a skeptical Great Britain, and a displeased Soviet Union to accept this vital and hugely beneficial outcome.[29]

Yet Scowcroft's unalloyed realism more often than not yielded serious policy errors. In defiance of overwhelming contrary historical evidence, including the testimony of the great Soviet dissidents, Scowcroft does not believe that Ronald Reagan's calling the Soviet Union "the evil empire" got anybody anywhere.[30]

As national security advisor for President George H. W. Bush, Scowcroft was too eager to resume negotiations with Beijing without reproach six months after the massacre of young Chinese who protested for freedom in Tiananmen Square.[31] He badly advised President Bush to bolster Gorbachev rather than encourage the breakup of the Soviet Union. He inspired one of the president's most egregious foreign policy blunders, the infamous Chicken Kiev speech of 1991 warning Ukrainians on the verge of achieving their well-deserved independence to beware of suicidal nationalism. Although President George H. W. Bush has insisted recently this statement merely "meant not so fast," Scowcroft has never conceded his error or qualified the interpretation of his ill-advised strategy to keep the Soviet Union from disintegrating.[32]

Even now Scowcroft defends the error of advocating a halt to the use of force in the First Gulf War, which left Saddam in power and those we encouraged to rebel to suffer the terrible consequences. He dismisses the counterargument that the very failure to eliminate Saddam and transform the Iraqi regime during the Gulf War of 1990–1991 made the war of 2003 to remove Saddam necessary and inevitable. Scowcroft denies that the democratic stirrings in Lebanon are related to the Iraq War. More fearful of instability than tyranny, he worries about, rather than celebrates, the brutally despotic Syrian regime's withdrawal from Lebanon.[33]

Scowcroft has consistently misread the essence of the war on terror, what the United States needs to do to win it, and the dynamics of the Arab-Israeli conflict because he does not understand the prime importance of ideology and regime type in international relations. After fifteen years of failing to contain Saddam, the United States needed to crush his regime and replace it. After decades of futilely negotiating with Arafat's corrupt, tyrannical PLO bent on Israel's destruction, the United States needed to insist on Arafat's departure and a fundamental reform of the Palestinian Authority. After decades of trying to manage the Middle East in the quest for illusory stability, the homicide bombings of 9/11 underscored the prudence of addressing the real root cause of that deadly aggression: the culture of repression that spawns secular and religious despotisms neurologically hostile to the United States. The proliferation of weapons of mass destruction underscores the prudence of taking decisive action now rather than later.

In *A World Transformed,* which Scowcroft wrote with President George H. W. Bush, he unintentionally but revealingly concedes much of the substance of this critique of his realism. He praises the harshness and determination of the Reagan administration as a corrective to the delusions of détente with the Soviet Union during the 1970s.[34] Yet Scowcroft shared many of these delusions as President Ford's national security advisor. The failed policy of détente will receive extended analysis in subsequent chapters. Consider, for now, this example, emblematic of the deficiencies of Scowcroft's unalloyed realism.

On July 2, 1975, President Ford announced that he would not meet with the great Soviet dissident and Nobel Prize–winning author, Alexander Solzhenitsyn. The administration spurned Solzhenitsyn because of his hostility toward détente. Governor Ronald Reagan and Senator Henry "Scoop" Jackson, Democrat from Washington State, the two most formidable opponents of détente, assailed the decision. It was primarily Scowcroft and Kissinger who had convinced President Ford not to invite Solzhenitsyn. Kissinger considered Solzhenitsyn's three-volume *Gulag Archipelago,* which chronicled the grotesque horrors of the Soviet regime under Stalin, a great moral event. He even showed it to President Ford. When, however, some of Kissinger's aides suggested the administration use *Gulag Archipelago* to generate support for a strong foreign policy among liberals rediscovering their anticommunism, Kissinger refused, dismissing the idea as too provocative. Kissinger had a congenital distrust of ideological movements, even our own. "If I understand the message of Solzhenitsyn, it is that the United States should pursue an aggressive policy to overthrow the Soviet system. . . . I believe the consequences of these views would not be acceptable to the American people." Kissinger especially did not want to risk sabotaging future agreements with a Soviet state he regarded as permanent and legitimate.[35] Scowcroft advised President Ford to accept Kissinger's recommendations and rationale.[36]

President Reagan's policies contributed mightily to winning the Cold War precisely because he then repudiated the policies of classical realists such as Brent Scowcroft. President George W. Bush has demonstrated similar foresight by repudiating the policies of such classical realists now.

4

The Perils of Liberal Multilateralism

The most politically potent critique of President Bush's foreign policy comes from liberal multilateralists dominant in the Democratic Party, among Western European elites, and in large parts of the academy. Charles Krauthammer identifies four of the core premises of multilateral liberalism: (a) an emphasis on legalism, the binding effect of treaties, and international norms; (b) a belief in the efficacy of multilateral institutions as the arbiters of international legitimacy; (c) a "deep suspicion" of power wielded on behalf of traditional, concrete, geopolitical conceptions of national interest; and (d) greater willingness to use force to achieve humanitarian goals that "the international community" deems legitimate.[1]

Like realism, liberal multilateralism has substantial variations that range along a spectrum. Liberal multilateralists disagree among themselves on whether American primacy is ephemeral or durable. Joseph Nye argues sensibly that the world will remain unipolar for years to come.[2] Conversely, Charles Kupchan and John Ikenberry argue implausibly that the United States must increasingly defer to a rising Europe, oblivious to the powerful demographic trends and political constraints that militate against the emergence of such a European superpower. The French electorate's repudiation of the EU constitution in May 2005 should have delivered the crowning blow to the delusion of a united Europe serving as an effective counterweight to and substitute for American power.[3] Liberal multilateralists also disagree among themselves about which forums should have the power to decide when to use force. Francis Fukuyama is more pessimistic than most of them about the efficacy of the United Nations. He argues that deference to NATO's collective judgment should be the strong presumption of American foreign policy.[4]

The goals of the muscular multilateralism of British Prime Minister Tony Blair and his advisor Robert Cooper have much in common with President Bush's. Where Blair and Cooper differ with the president is in their brimming confidence in the capacity of multilateral institutions to generate consensus for undertaking decisive action against a wide range of threats.[5] Like President Bush and unlike classical realists, liberal multilateralists of all varieties stress the importance of liberal democratic institutions for mitigating rivalry and fostering legitimacy.

The Liberal Multilateralist's Critique of the Bush Doctrine

Where the most prevalent and popular versions of liberal internationalism differ with President Bush is on the issue of what needs constraining and how. The views of John Kerry and virtually every Democratic presidential nominee since 1968 have a long pedigree in the "New Politics" wing of the party, which fears the consequences of what J. William Fulbright calls the "arrogance of American power" as much as the external threats ranged against the United States. Unlike Richard Cooper and Tony Blair, these liberal multilateralists envisage international organizations such as the UN as vehicles to harness as well as to facilitate the exercise of American power. Humanitarian interventions fulfill their criteria for employing force precisely because the imprimatur of international institutions removes the taint of an unbridled pursuit of the American national interest, which they distrust.[6]

Contrary to what Charles Krauthammer suggests, the mainstream of liberal multilateralism has not overcome the Vietnam syndrome. It remains profoundly uncomfortable using force abroad, even for humanitarian concerns. Such interventions as those in Haiti, Somalia, and the Balkans in the 1990s occurred belatedly and haphazardly and with a very low threshold for casualties. Witness the hasty withdrawal from Somalia in 1993 after suffering fewer than thirty deaths in a firefight in Mogadishu. Witness the unwillingness to risk losing even a single aircraft in the Kosovo campaign, which impelled NATO warplanes to drop their payloads from fifteen thousand feet. Witness the strategy of gradual escalation that governed these interventions, which the Vietnam War had utterly discredited. Witness, too, the failure to avert genocide during the 1990s in Rwanda, despite the minimal force it would have required to do so successfully.[7]

Although virtually all liberal multilateralists concede in theory that there are occasions in which the United States must use force unilaterally or with a smaller coalition of the willing rather than the broad approval of NATO or the United Nations, they define such cases as few and far between. Joseph Nye argues that the United States has relied too much on hard power, military power, while slighting soft power, that is, the ability to get what it wants through the attraction of American culture and values. He calls on the United States to abandon the policy of "unilateralism, arrogance, and parochialism" in favor of enlightened multilateralism, which cultivates American relations with allies and other countries. He defines soft power as "the universality of a country's culture and its ability to establish a favorable set of rules and institutions that govern areas of international activity."[8]

Likewise, Ikenberry and Kupchan regard "international rules and institutions" as salutary restraints on America's freedom of action that advance our true interests in the long run. They repudiate Secretary of Defense Donald Rumsfeld's view that "the mission determines the coalition." The United States should pursue the preventive use of force, say Ikenberry and Kupchan, "only as a last resort, only when facing clear and present danger, and only after full consultation with other democratic nations." Instead, "the Bush Administration has . . . unwittingly advanced some of the objectives of Islamic extremists by overreacting and pursuing an errant strategy that has polarized global politics. The Atlantic Community has been stretched to the breaking point, with America's traditional democratic allies now some of its staunchest critics." Finally, Ikenberry and Kupchan lament that the Bush administration's disdain for international legitimacy has had "devastating consequences for America's role in the world, especially among Europeans." During the Cold War, they deem it was "unthinkable for the German chancellor to rescue his bid for re-election by insisting that Berlin stand up to Washington"; now, "in a world of degraded American legitimacy, . . . countries are more reluctant to cooperate with the United States."[9]

The Deficiencies of Liberal Multilateralism

The mainstream versions of liberal multilateralism share some of the deficiencies of neorealism and classical realism that this book has already assessed: the assumption that unipolarity is evanescent; the prediction of strong balancing against the United States unless we jettison the Bush Doctrine; an almost categorical presumption against using decisive force sooner rather than later.[10] What follows addresses the deficiencies of liberal internationalism unique to it. Liberal internationalists make the opposite mistake of realists by overestimating the influence of soft power, the effectiveness of international institutions, and the likelihood of even stable, liberal democracies generating a consensus on the need for undertaking strong, effective action against major threats.

The attributes of soft power Nye rates so highly—such as the appeal of American culture—can enhance, but not substitute for, the hard elements of national economic and military power on which American security ultimately depends. Nor, in all cases, is the influence of our soft power as soothing as Nye assumes. America's most implacable enemies—Nazi Germany, the Soviet Union, imperial Japan, Osama bin Laden, Saddam Hussein, the militant mullahs in Iran—hate the United States precisely because they abhor American culture, political institutions, and commitment to freedom. This applies to the most zealous opponents of globalization as well. No amount of gentle persuasion can defend American values against such enemies without the robustness of American power and the willingness to use it, with as broad a coalition possible that fits the mission. As even Nye concedes, a country that suffers economic and military decline is likely to lose the ability to shape the international agenda as well as its attractiveness.[11]

The issue is not whether a broad coalition is desirable, but when and in what circumstances its maintenance should take precedence over the need for decisive action. Nor is the issue whether legitimacy is an important criterion for American foreign policy. Benign is the key word in Josef Joffe's apt description of American hegemony.[12] Niall Ferguson and others have wrongly branded the United States as an imperial power.[13] Richard Cooper knows better. As he observes perceptively, the United States has been consciously anti-imperial for most of American history:

True, it has interfered relentlessly in Central America, acquired territory by force (as well as by purchase), and it was caught up in the imperial frenzy at the end of the nineteenth century; but it was also one of the first to give up its colonies. It then did its best to ensure that the British and French Empires were dismantled. The United States is founded on ideals and its vocation is the spread of those ideals. Although the United States has more troops deployed abroad than Britain at the height of its imperial glory, they are not used for the same purpose. Typically, they are used to defend America's allies. . . . Usually they arrive at a time of conflict, but stay on to ensure security and perhaps to strengthen the forces of good government—the two are sometimes related—thereafter. This often turns out to be a long business.[14]

The success of American containment policy in Western Europe and Japan stemmed as much from the character of American engagement and the common interests of democratic allies as from the preponderance of American power. In contrast to the brutal Soviet empire in Eastern Europe, the United States pursued a policy of enlightened self-interest in Western Europe and Japan, which the constraints, norms, and reciprocity of American democracy encouraged.[15] Yet true legitimacy does not always hinge on obtaining a broad consensus.[16] On the contrary, making consensus a goal in itself can often end up undermining legitimacy.

The United States cannot prudently allow the United Nations or even the NATO alliance to serve as the arbiter of the legitimacy of the use of force. What Samuel Johnson said of a second marriage should caution those who wish to rely on collective security as a basis for any practicable and decent world order: it is a triumph of hope over experience. A UN–type collective security system has not and cannot ever serve as an adequate substitute for an American alliance system that can preserve and expand the democratic peace, deter major aggression in vital geopolitical regions, and, should deterrence fail, defeat such aggressors at the lowest possible cost and risk.

Although stable, liberal democracies will not fight one another, the logic of collective action and faulty perception of external threat will often inhibit effective cooperation among them, including our NATO allies. Liberal democratic states often will not view threats to peace in the same way; nor will they always be willing to run the same risks in overcoming those threats they may or may not recognize. In the absence of a preponderant power such as the United States, willing to lead alone if necessary, it often becomes prohibitively difficult to implement effective collective action against even dire external threats. The United States cannot make its policy hostage to the lowest common denominator of either a UN or even a NATO consensus. Those liberal internationalists who argue otherwise fundamentally misunderstand the dynamics of these institutions as well as their implications for American grand strategy.

The Folly of UN Collective Security

A brief history of American endeavors to create collective security systems, their underlying precepts, and their dismal records will elucidate why sensible American statesmen and friends of freedom everywhere should recoil from investing too much authority in the United Nations, now and in the near future.

Any informed debate over the role of the UN in American diplomacy must begin with a discussion of the League of Nations and President Woodrow Wilson's vision that inspired it. Horrified by the hideous carnage of World War I, Wilson identified as its major causes not only the ambitions of an authoritarian, militarist Germany but armaments, alliances, and the practice of power politics. He envisaged the League of Nations as an entity that would replace the rule of force with the rule of law, with collective security as its underlying concept.

Whereas alliances and other traditional security arrangements are directed against particular opponents often limited to specific geographic areas (such as NATO with regard to the Soviet Union during the Cold War), collective security organizations are directed against any and every country that commits aggression.[17] The theory Wilson sought to embody in the League of Nations defined any aggressor as the national enemy of every country; consequently, it held that every country had a vital interest in protecting each victim of aggression, no matter what. As critics such as Henry Kissinger have observed, however, nothing like what Wilson proposed had ever occurred in the annals of international politics. Not all states view threats in the same way, nor are they all prepared to expend significant effort and run major risks to resist all acts of aggression.[18]

Wilson's League of Nations thus foundered on the unwillingness of the

Senate to ratify the League's covenant, which required an entanglement in the world at variance with traditional notions of American sovereignty. Thereafter, collective security failed to stop either Nazi or imperial Japanese aggression, as the United States retreated fecklessly into isolation.

Determined to succeed where Wilson had failed, President Franklin D. Roosevelt played a leading role in establishing the United Nations. He sought not only to build on the principle of collective security that President Wilson proclaimed after World War I, but to remedy the League's defects.

The UN charter outlawed the threat of force, except for self-defense or when it involved collective security. In an attempt to link power with responsibility more effectively than the League had, the UN founders created a security council (UNSC) composed of five great permanent policemen (the United States, the Soviet Union, France, Great Britain, and China), plus a rotating pool of temporary members. Each of the five great powers possessed a veto, which could thwart any collective UN action it opposed.

During the Cold War, the UN collective security system worked slightly better than the League's did during the interwar years. The Korean War of 1950–1953 proved the exception to the rule of the United Nations' inability to deal effectively with great power conflict. The United States succeeded in enlisting the authority of the UNSC in resisting North Korean aggression only because the Soviet Union was boycotting the Security Council for its refusal to recognize the People's Republic of China as the legitimate representative of China. Neither the Soviet Union nor any other major power repeated the mistake.

Thereafter, Soviet-American rivalry produced a gridlock in the Security Council that marginalized the United Nations in the great power conflicts that dominated the Cold War. The Soviet veto precluded any effective UN action to stanch Soviet aggression in Eastern Europe, Afghanistan, and the Middle East. No consensus existed among the UNSC members, moreover, on who was the main aggressor in the Middle East conflict or what the United Nations should do about it. During the bleak years of the 1970s, the U.S. veto on the Security Council rightly precluded a rogue assortment of communist tyrannies, Third World radicals, and Arab dictatorships from emasculating Israel, a stable, liberal democracy under siege.

Hopes for the United Nations soared once more with the end of the Cold War and the rivalries that had dominated it. What seemed to give such hopes more credence than usual was the apparent success of the UN security system in reversing Iraq's 1990 invasion of Kuwait. A broad coalition participated in and endorsed the UNSC's authorization of the American decision to resist Iraqi aggression.

Even without the Soviet-American impasse, the Gulf War has proved the exception to the rule of the UN's impotence in dealing with great power conflict since the end of the Cold War. Iraq had committed a brazen act of aggression against a sovereign state. The impending disintegration of the Soviet Union and the international fallout from the Chinese Politburo's decision to order the massacre of students at Tiananmen Square in June 1989 gave leaders in both these countries a powerful incentive to retain American goodwill; thus, neither vetoed the UN action. Residual fear over German reunification and its potential consequences also inspired the French to be more cooperative than usual.

Such a felicitous convergence of conditions is hardly typical. Aggression will often be less clear-cut than Iraq's invasion of Kuwait, and so it will diminish the possibility of generating an effective UNSC consensus. Collective security is particularly difficult to apply in civil wars, where boundaries are fluid and causality more complex than in wars involving interstate aggression. Normally, great powers also disagree about the practicalities and equities of major conflicts. Since the first war against Iraq in 1990–1991, UN failures in the realm of security have dwarfed the marginal contributions its peacekeeping missions have made in such places as Haiti, Cambodia, and East Timor. UN intervention in Bosnia during the 1990s was too weak to succeed but large enough to curtail effective action until stronger NATO forces replaced the hapless, ineffective UN contingents. The UN intervention in Somalia ended in debacle in 1993. The UN bungled even worse in Rwanda in 1994, doing nothing to prevent that sad nation's holocaust, in which some 800,000 Rwandans were killed in one hundred days.[19] Martin Meredith gives this lacerating and authoritative account:

> At the United Nations, members of the Security Council ignored mounting evidence of genocide, reluctant in the wake of Somalia to get involved in another African quagmire. France, still acting to protect its Hutu allies, insisted that the violence in Rwanda was not genocide, but the result of civil war. U.S. officials went to extraordinary lengths to avoid using the term "genocide" for fear that, under the UN genocide convention of 1948, it would create a legal obliga-

tion for them to intervene. . . . President Clinton, still smarting from events in Somalia, declared: "Lesson number one is, don't go into one of these things and say, as the U.S. said when we started in Somalia, 'Maybe we'll be done in a month because it's a "humanitarian crisis."' . . . Because there are always political problems and sometimes military conflicts which bring about these crises."[20]

Another terrible display of UN impotence occurred in the Balkans during the summer of 1995 when Dutch peacekeepers merely watched as Serbs murdered seven thousand Muslim men in Srebrenica, an area that the UN had designated as a safe zone. In 1999 the United States and its NATO allies, including France, decided to ignore rather than rely on the United Nations in order to wage war in Kosovo, where Serbian atrocities had precipitated.[21] The UN's record in the Sudan is little better. When war broke out in Sudan's western region of Darfur, the government responded against the insurgency with a ferocity that threatened "a disaster of a magnitude that had not occurred since Rwanda." More than a million refugees had fled their homes by February 2004 in fear of government-sponsored Arab militias known as Janjaweed, which raped and killed at will. Yet the United Nations responded only belatedly, tepidly, and ineffectively because members of the Security Council such as France and China were reluctant to impose even sanctions on a Sudanese government they had assiduously cultivated.[22]

The resurgence of great power rivalries since 1991 has rendered the United Nations a dangerous obstacle to necessary American action. With increasing frequency the Russians, the Chinese, and the French have invoked the veto or threat of it to constrain the exercise of American power. Nothing reveals the deficiencies of the UN more vividly than its incapacity to enforce seventeen resolutions that Saddam defied with impunity before President Bush had the courage to remove him. The rampant corruption of the UN's oil-for-food program, which Saddam exploited to bribe members of the UNSC, is merely the symptom of a deeper, more fundamental problem. From the early 1990s on, France and Russia worked consistently to thwart any serious punishment of Iraq for its flagrant violations of Security Council resolutions. Simultaneously, both nations worked incessantly to weaken the effectiveness of the UN inspection system right up until the American invasion of Iraq in March 2003.[23] Even formidable modern defenders of the UN, such as the historian Paul Kennedy, concede that its glaring failures in the realm of peacekeeping and security have overshadowed its achievements.[24]

President Bush did not rush to war, as critics claimed, but made a genuine effort to forge a consensus at the UN. He and Secretary of State Powell spent months engaged in extensive consultations among Prime Minister Blair of the United Kingdom, President Chirac of France, and President Putin of Russia. These consultations yielded UN Resolution 1441, which the Security Council unanimously approved—ostensibly, Saddam's last chance to comply before the UN would sanction the use of force to oust him. Yet the French confounded Powell's optimism because they never had any intention of countenancing the use of force against Saddam, regardless of whether he complied with UN resolutions. On the contrary, French Foreign Minister Dominique de Villepin systematically subverted Powell's efforts to convince the Security Council to authorize military action, inciting other nations to oppose the Bush administration. "France will do whatever is necessary to prevent war," declared Dominique de Villepin on January 21, 2003. On February 9, 2003, Germany and Russia joined France in opposing the use of force to uphold Resolution 1441, despite Saddam's regime's being in material breach of it and sixteen previous UN resolutions.[25]

What happened in the case of Iraq is, alas, typical for the UN. Those who oppose the assertion of American power—at home and abroad—will use the UN instrumentally as a means to shackle it. The UN collective security system can do little to restrain China, rogue states such as Iran and North Korea, or a host of other major potential aggressors looming on the horizon. In the case of the Iranian mullahs' brazen determination to build nuclear weapons, the UN is unlikely to agree beyond the lowest common denominator of ineffective action.[26] Add to these failures the UN's appalling performance in Lebanon: Hezbollah mocked UN Resolution 1559, which requires the disarming and dismantling of this murderous terrorist organization. UN peacekeepers did not lift a finger to stop Hezbollah and its Syrian and Iranian sponsors from raising and equipping a veritable army with thousands of missiles. If the past is any guide, the role envisaged for the UN in enforcing the conditional cessation of hostilities between Israel and Hezbollah does not inspire great confidence, to say the least. The United States should place a high burden of proof on the United Nations to demonstrate that it can effectively defang and disarm Hezbollah despite the failures of the past. Do not count on the UN peacekeepers having either the will or the courage to hold Hezbollah to account.

Nor should the United States count on the UN to deal effectively with North Korea's nuclear weapons program. Unlike the sharp divisions about security threats that exist in the Middle East, there is a large degree of regional and international consensus on the grave danger posed by North Korea's nuclear tests and ballistic missile programs. Unlike views of the Middle East, there is a consensus that the North Korean regime is among the worst in the world. Neither the United States nor the major powers of East Asia—Japan, China, and Russia—want North Korea to have nuclear weapons. Nevertheless, at least Russia and China are unlikely to countenance the type of UN sanctions on North Korea that could plausibly constrain or deter the North Korean regime from consummating its nuclear weapons program. The United States will have to rely on a strategy of deterrence, containment, or preemption to deal with the gathering North Korean danger. Whatever happens with North Korea in the coming months, the United States will have to rely on coalitions of the willing to fit the mission rather than the United Nations to implement any strategy that has a reasonable prospect for success.

Ultimately, then, the credibility of American power, unconstrained by the UNSC veto, remains a necessary if not sufficient condition for sustaining an international environment conducive to peace, freedom, security, and prosperity. Of course, the United States should strive to cooperate with other states as much as prudence allows. There are many times, however, when making multilateralism an absolute value is imprudent. As the forthcoming discussion on NATO will demonstrate, muscular multilateralism is difficult enough to attain even among stable, liberal democracies with shared values and a largely complementary perception of interests. It becomes prohibitive and dangerous in a forum structurally inclined to paralysis, such as the United Nations. In these circumstances, multilateralism can easily degenerate into a pretext for inaction, thereby emboldening aggressors.

Expanding the Security Council to include other members—particularly democratic India and Japan, as the Bush administration proposes—has considerable merit for other reasons: equity, to reflect the changing distribution of power since World War II, and the compelling interest in having two major democratic allies with complementary strategic outlooks as members. This, however, will only intensify the already powerful gravitational pull of the Security Council to gridlock because of the divergent interests of the council's members. Deferring to the UN means operationally conferring on the French, Russians, and Chinese the right to block any American use of force these nations deem illegitimate. That is indefensible. Eliminating the Security Council's veto power is an even worse idea, because it merely repeats the mistake of the League of Nations, which severed power from responsibility. The veto is essential for the United States to prevent the UN from running amok, as it is often inclined to do because of the large number of tyrannies represented at the UN and their enablers who appease them.

Neither Americans nor friends of freedom elsewhere should delude themselves about the contributions that the UN can make to U.S. security. Peacekeeping in areas where the major powers have no fundamental clashing interest, rendering various forms of technical assistance, and providing a forum for diplomacy represent the outer boundaries of UN competence, beyond which prudent American statesmen should not go.

Human Rights and the Limits of UN Competence

These same admonitions hold true for the United Nations' role in promoting human rights. Its Universal Declaration of Human Rights, adopted in 1948, may have contributed marginally by at least solidifying the principle that there are basic laws and higher rights that ought to restrain governments. This UN declaration, however, reflects the influence of legal doctrines in tension with more individualistic conceptions of human rights, such at those embodied in the Declaration of Independence and the U.S. Bill of Rights. Unduly skeptical of free markets, unduly enamored with collectivism in all its varieties, the framers of the Universal Declaration did not protect property and contract rights, which are the bedrock of well-ordered liberty.[27]

Furthermore, the United Nations has always done a better job declaiming on human rights than protecting them in practice. During the 1960s and 1970s, particularly, it served as a forum to apologize for rather than alleviate tyranny. Totalitarian communist tyrannies and radical Third World leaders used the United Nations to vent their antipathy toward the United States and all things associated with the Western concept of freedom.

These lamentable efforts, which the United States stoutly resisted, culminated in the notorious UN resolution equating Zionism with racism, which the UN General Assembly passed overwhelmingly in 1974. Idi Amin, the dictator of Uganda who murdered hundreds of thousands of his own people, received a standing ovation for delivering a speech in support of the resolution, a speech that Adolf Hitler could have written and cheerfully delivered.[28]

The vast expansion of the Democratic peace that occurred during the 1980s and early 1990s occurred despite rather than because of the United Nations and the sensibilities it represented. Its foremost cause was the resurgence of American power and purpose that defied those sensibilities. Although the United Nations today is less neurologically hostile to the United States than during the Cold War, a serious problem still persists. Two examples do not augur well for the UN's capacity to promote human rights.

First is the UN's decision to oust the United States, human rights' greatest defender, from the UN Human Rights Commission while packing it with regimes that have abysmal human rights records: Sudan, Sierra Leone, Togo, Syria, Algeria, Libya, and Vietnam. Evidently, many of our European allies, complicit in this decision, prefer quiet diplomacy that is silent about rampant violations of human rights, ranging from slavery in Sudan and tyranny in the Islamic world to systematic political repression in China and North Korea.

Second, the World Conference against Racism, sponsored by the United Nations in Durban, South Africa, in the late summer of 2001, represented "a repudiation of liberal democracy" in general and the United States in particular. President Bush rightly refused to send Secretary of State Colin Powell to attend these deplorable proceedings; then he courageously withdrew our lower-level delegation as the virulence of its anti-American, anti-Semitic, and antidemocratic sentiments mounted. In his devastating critique of the conference, Arch Puddington rightly excoriated it as the "ideological prologue to September 11."[29]

Finally, multilateral schemes such as the International Court of Justice (ICJ) menace rather than enhance the defense and extension of liberty. The Bush administration has wisely joined India, China, Russia, and Japan in refusing to cooperate with this new court, whose broad jurisdiction and extremely broad definitions of crimes would authorize international bureaucrats bearing us ill will "to second-guess the decisions of the American military." No one has written more trenchantly than Jeremy Rabkin about the danger unfettered multilateralism poses for American foreign policy:

> But in general, the disproportion in resources makes it more dangerous for the United States to invest too much authority and prestige in multilateral institutions. . . . The underlying problem is that there is an inherent asymmetry in every American partnership. The United States has military capacities that no country or combination of countries can now match. That means in turn that the United States figures, at least potentially, in almost any conflict in the world. For that reason, a military setback for the United States has ramifications in every part of the world. No international organization can compensate for this problem, but international organizations can certainly complicate it. . . . No one is likely to be saved by a UN resolution, and no one is likely to be deterred by one. To the contrary, in the debate over the war in Iraq, enthusiasm for the UN's "essential role" was the strongest among those governments most anxious to preserve Saddam's regime—precisely because the UN was understood to be incapable of enforcing its own resolutions. When the United States does not provide a strategic guarantee, it loses credibility in dangerous ways if it appears to back off.[30]

What Theodore Roosevelt said about the League of Nations sagely sums up the proper attitude to hold toward the United Nations: "The League of Nations may do little good, but the more pompous it is and the more it pretends to do, the less it will really accomplish."[31] Peace, prosperity, security, and freedom emanate not from the United Nations, but from the power, principle, and prudence of the United States and a coalition of the willing.

Coalitions of the Willing—The Limits of NATO Multilateralism

Although the United States should pay more attention to the views of NATO members than to those of the United Nations at large, it is not in the American interest to make unanimity among them a categorical imperative for when, where, and how to use force. The twenty-five-member alliance is too large and cumbersome to generate a consensus for decisive action, especially in areas outside Europe. NATO remains vitally important not only as a hedge against a resurgence of Russian authoritarianism, but also to consolidate the democratic peace in Eastern Europe. American participation in NATO and its expansion eastward also enhances American influence in Europe and diminishes the possibility that the European community will become a competitor of rather than collaborator with the United States, as the French apparently intend it. In many areas, however, the alliance cannot serve as an adequate substitute for American power, asserted either unilaterally or in collaboration with a coalition of the willing that usually will include many though not all of our democratic allies in Europe.

Those who criticize the Bush administration for its lack of deference to the unanimous council of NATO err in five ways.[32] They fundamentally misunderstand the actual history of the alliance, exaggerate the current level of discontent with the United States, misdiagnose the source of the problem, prescribe the wrong remedy, and derive the wrong implications for American grand strategy.

During the Cold War, NATO operated at its highest level of consensus dealing with the Soviet threat to Western Europe. Frequently, sharp disagreement arose even on this issue, the one least likely to divide the alliance. Charles de Gaulle's return to power in 1958 may have saved France from chaos, but it guaranteed serious discord in the NATO alliance, which he distrusted from the beginning because of American and British participation.[33] Jean-François Revel may have exaggerated, but not by much, in saying that by the end of the 1960s de Gaulle's hatred of the United States became stronger than his fear of the Soviet Union. De Gaulle started off by treating the superpowers as equivalent threats: "We are happy to have you [Khrushchev] to help us resist pressure from the United States . . . just as we are very glad to have the United States help us resist pressure from the Soviet Union." From 1964 on, de Gaulle's foreign policy aimed more at weakening the United States than deterring the Soviet Union, the threat that gave rise to NATO in the first place. Ultimately, he blamed the American alliance for "smothering Europe" and "blocking understanding" with a Soviet Union he no longer thought of as an evil or particularly dangerous empire.[34] In early 1966 he withdrew French forces from the NATO command structure. Franco-American tension abated during the 1980s, during the presidency of François Mitterand, though serious disagreements persisted even then.

So France's inordinate fear of American power is hardly new to this Bush administration.[35] In *The American Enemy*, Philippe Roger exposes the deep roots and long pedigree of French anti-Americanism. He concludes:

> French anti-Americanism is a deep historical construct with deep roots in French culture. If you try to understand it by reading anything into its seasonal varieties, it is bound to slip through your fingers. Developed over and shaped by the long haul, it forces the investigator to plunge into the long haul. It did not start with the Vietnam War or with the Cold War—or even the 1930s when it was at its peak. Nearly all the ingredients were there more than a century ago: its narrative structure had largely been formed, its augmentation polished up, and its rhetoric broken in as early as the 1890s. And even more surprisingly it was already consensual.[36]

Contrary to what Kupchan, Ikenberry, Fukuyama, and other critics of the Bush Doctrine claim, America's disagreements with the Social Democratic government of Gerhard Schroeder in Germany over the war in Iraq also have ample precedent in the annals of the NATO alliance. The decade of the 1970s witnessed a fierce debate on both sides of the Atlantic on whether and how far to pursue détente with the Soviet Union.[37] Unabashed American cold warriors worried, with good reason, that the West German version of détente (Ostpolitik) flirted dangerously with neutralism toward and appeasement of the Soviet Union.[38]

During the 1980s elites in West Germany, much of Western Europe, and the United States ridiculed Ronald Reagan's rhetoric about the evils of communism and the policies he implemented to combat it. Hundreds of thousands of protesters took to the streets across Western Europe and in the United States in support of a nuclear freeze that the Soviet Union supported and in protest of the Reagan administration's determination to deploy Pershing and cruise missiles to offset the Soviet Union's SS-20 intermediate-range missiles in Europe. The size and intensity of these protests in Germany make the protests in Europe over the Iraq War of 2003 look tepid by comparison. The German Social Democrats displayed no more inclination to acquiesce to the Reagan administration in 1983 than the Schroeder government in Germany had in 2002–2003 to support the American invasion of Iraq.

If the Social Democrats rather than the Christian Democrats had won the pivotal election of March 6, 1983, West Germany would have likely reneged on its commitment to deploy Euromissiles so vital for preserving the NATO alliance, thereby blunting Soviet pressure on Western Europe and catalyzing the emergence of efforts at reform in the Soviet Union.[39] If the Christian Democrats rather than the Social Democrats had won the elections in Germany in the fall of 2002, which the Christian Democratic Party (CDU) narrowly lost, West Germany would never have pushed its disagreements with the United States over Iraq as hard or as far as the Schroeder government did.[40]

The fragile but promising coalition government led by the Christian Democrat Angela Merkel has already eased cooperation between the Bush administration and Germany. Schroeder's defeat deprived Chirac's French government of its most ardent collaborator among major European statesmen in the constraint of American power. According to the strongly pro-American Polish president, Alexander Kwasniewski, "Chancellor Merkel understands the driving force of our times, the move to democracy, because she has lived it."[41] She and her Christian Democratic Party have a much more favorable disposition toward the United States than Schroeder and his Social Democratic Party (SPD).

During the Cold War the United States and its NATO allies often disagreed even more sharply and frequently on security issues beyond the Soviet threat to Europe. Much of Western Europe opposed the escalation of the war in Vietnam; France under de Gaulle took the lead in criticizing the United States. No area generated more controversy between the United States and its European allies than the Middle East. The Truman administration and the Bevin Labour government of Great Britain had conflicting views after World War II on whether to establish a Jewish state in Palestine. The Suez Crisis of 1956 precipitated a serious disagreement within the NATO alliance as well.[42] When Egyptian President Nasser seized control of the Suez Canal in July, the French, fearful of the repercussions of his actions on their control of Algeria, the Israelis, harassed by terrorist raids that Nasser sponsored from his territory, and the British, formerly the power of authority in the canal zone, together launched a joint invasion of the Sinai region and Egypt and seized the Suez Canal. President Eisenhower then surprised and humiliated his allies, who did not consult with him before acting, by forcing them to return to Egypt what they had captured.[43]

Since the Six Day War of June 1967, the United States and its European allies also have found themselves increasingly at odds over the Arab-Israeli dispute and its broader implications. American presidents from Nixon through Reagan saw Arab and Palestine Liberation Organization (PLO) rejectionism as a major source of the problem, whereas our Western European allies inclined to accommodate rather than confront the PLO and radical Arab regimes. What our Western European allies called evenhanded, Americans tended to view as appeasement at Israel's expense. What the United States viewed as salutary commitment to the safety of a decent and democratic Israel, other NATO allies viewed as one-sided support that hurt the Western position in the Middle East.

Actually, the United States has enjoyed vastly more support from its European and Asian allies in the Iraq War than it did in the Middle East for the final two decades of the Cold War. Despite widespread domestic opposition, most of our NATO allies formally supported us in the Iraq War. They and a total of more than forty nations provided at least some assistance, and some of those nations provided considerable assistance. Relations between the United States and our democratic allies in Eastern Europe and Asia—particularly Japan—have improved considerably during the Bush administration. Far from being a dogmatic unilateralist, the president has also succeeded in cultivating an important new ally considerably more important than France: democratic India, whose outlook on the dangers of Islamic terror and a rising, undemocratic China largely coincides with our own.

Contrast the state of America's alliances under President George W. Bush with what occurred in the Yom Kippur War of October 1973. Not one of America's Western European allies would give the United States overflight rights to resupply Israel in its time of grave peril until the U.S. Congress managed to buy off Portugal at the eleventh hour to allow American aircraft to use the Azores.[44] Or contrast President Bush's much-derided but comparatively broad coalition of the willing to what occurred in April 1986: several European governments harshly criticized President Reagan's decision to attack military targets in Libya, including the reputed hideouts of the dictator Muammar Qaddafi in retaliation for a terrorist bombing at a West Berlin discotheque, which killed and injured several Americans. Typically, British Prime Minister Margaret Thatcher supported the American effort unstintingly. Typically, the French even refused the United States overflight rights, which made the mission longer and more dangerous.[45]

After the collapse of the Soviet Union in 1991, differences between the United States and its NATO allies inevitably became more pronounced without the Soviet threat, which had muted dissent during the Cold War. What magnified the frequency and intensity of these differences is the shift in focus of American foreign policy since 9/11 to the very area where the perspectives of the United States and Western Europe always diverged the most: the Middle East. The firm, united American and Western European reaction to Russia's vain attempt in 2004 to subvert democracy in Ukraine by aiding and abetting election fraud illustrates the large repository of good-will and common interest that still binds the United States with NATO.

Because of the dynamics of the democratic peace, war remains un-thinkable between the United States and Western Europe. Resolution of our disputes always will fall well short of the threat or actual use of force so long as stable, liberal democracy endures among Western European states. American prestige and legitimacy in Europe and the rest of the world still remain high, much higher than during the dismal decade of the 1970s, when America's post–World War II standing descended to its lowest point.

American statesmen, however, cannot dismiss the considerable wis-dom of Robert Kagan's pathbreaking book, *Of Paradise and Power:* "When it comes to setting national priorities, determining threats, defining chal-lenges, and fashioning and implementing foreign and defense policies, the United States and Europe have parted ways." Kagan attributes this grow-ing divergence to Europe's "turning away from power . . . and moving into a self-contained world of laws. It is entering a post-historical paradise of peace and relative prosperity." Conversely, the United States must still rely heavily on physical power in the dangerous world that still exists outside Europe's self-contained zone of democratic peace. Compared with Europe-ans, Americans are more likely to resort to force and coercion more quickly, more frequently, and more decisively. Compared with Americans, Euro-peans place a higher value on multilateralism, the potentialities of inter-national law, and the efficacy of acting through international institutions. What European critics of American foreign policy really mean by unilater-alism is not that the United States acted alone, but that no European power could constrain it. Legitimacy depends, in their eyes, on the United States acting within the institutionalized alliances such as NATO or through the UN rather than with "coalitions of the willing."[46]

Kagan's insightful and original argument has profound implications for American foreign policy, but it does require qualification to put our problems with Europe into proper perspective and proportion. Although the recent Iraq war was widely unpopular even in the eighteen European nations whose governments supported the Bush administration, Kagan's stark dichotomy between American and European views exaggerates the divergence. American statesmen can grasp the actual situation in Europe with greater clarity by distinguishing among three categories of states.

Britain and the newly independent states of Western Europe are likely to acquiesce to or be more comfortable with the assertions of the hard aspects of American power most if not all of the time. Since the beginning of the twentieth century, America's complementary outlook with Great Britain has largely transcended time, place, or party in power. The administrations of Prime Minister Neville Chamberlain in the late 1930s and Edward Heath in the early 1970s are the exceptions that prove this rule. Similarly, Eastern European members of NATO likely will retain their enthusiastically pro-American orientation well beyond this generation, which remembers Soviet tyranny and America's indispensable role in liberating them from it. Geopolitically, American support for these states will remain essential as insurance against the resurgence of Russian imperialism under an authoritarian government. Their compelling interest in blunting Franco-German domination of the EU at their expense also provides Eastern European states with another strong and enduring incentive to solicit American protection and goodwill. The new democracies of Eastern Europe do not want merely to trade Soviet domination for imperious French attempts to silence them, as French President Chirac tried to do when they supported the Bush administration on Iraq in 2003. Great Britain and what Donald Rumsfeld aptly calls the "New Europe" will often find themselves a part of an American coalition of the willing rather than an impediment to it. Even when all or some of these states disagree with the United States, they will not try to use international institutions or the NATO alliance to obstruct American power.

Whether America's other NATO partners oppose or support assertions of American power will depend on which party is in office: conservative governments will tend either to support or at least to acquiesce to decisive American action, whereas social democratic or more left-leaning governments will strive harder to thwart it on a broader range of issues. This was certainly true for the war in Iraq. Italy and Spain supported it when conservatives were in power; Germany opposed it when the Social Democrats were in power, but it has taken a less hostile position since the Christian Democrat Angela Merkel has replaced the Social Democrat Gerhard Shroeder as chancellor. Spain switched from pro- to antiwar when the Social Democrats came to power after a terrorist attack there in the summer of 2004. A Christian Democratic government in Germany never would have brazenly joined with France to defy the Bush administration on Iraq, as the Social Democratic government of Gerhard Schroeder did.

Kagan thus has exaggerated the seriousness of the rift between the United States and much of Europe. The United States will obtain more cooperation and less widespread resistance than Kagan suggests in many of these states most of the time. Even if the United States cannot count on their active support for many security issues outside Europe, most European states realize that their security and the luxury of their "democratic peace," based on the rule of law, depends on the credibility and capability of American power. The United States has less to fear from acting without the consensus of its Western European allies than critics of the Bush administration suggest. Generally, shared values and common interest will continue to alleviate the frequency, severity, and consequences of disagreements between the United States and its democratic allies in Europe.

Europe has an equal or perhaps greater stake in American success in the Middle East than even the United States does. Geographic proximity and military weakness make Europe more vulnerable than America to the threat of rogue regimes and terrorists in the Middle East. Radical Islamism is a much greater threat to the social cohesion of European states than to our own, particularly in France: witness the chilling spectacle of more than two weeks of riots there, which largely alienated and radicalized Muslim Frenchmen perpetrated. Faced with declining birthrates and a burgeoning unassimilated Muslim population, many Western European democracies would greatly profit from shining examples of the compatibility between Islam and freedom. The Bush Doctrine has already spurred a rise in democratic sentiment in the Middle East that may just have a positive spillover to the Islamic citizens of Western Europe as well.

France is the state in Western Europe where the anti-Americanism Kagan writes about runs most strongly, most deeply, and most dangerously. French hostility to American foreign policy emanates from an unsavory combination of envy and delusions of grandeur that undermines France's true national interest. Jean-François Revel best explains the root cause of this anti-Americanism and its pernicious consequences. He views much anti-Americanism as a surrogate for an attack on capitalism by those in Europe and elsewhere still committed at heart to illiberal doctrines. He also sees European weakness and the desire to find a scapegoat for it as another powerful source of this anti-Americanism, obsessions that are most pronounced in France.[47]

France aspires to nothing less than great power status commensurate with that of the United States, but it lacks the geopolitical heft to achieve this alone. The French envisage the EU as the way to realize their ambition of "balancing" America. They desire the EU to become a global political power to match its economic power, for it to speak in one voice on foreign and defense policy: that is, a pro-French and anti-American voice. French statesmen assume themselves to be the brains and the Germans the brawn of an EU dedicated to restoring Europe to its former, more lofty status. Meanwhile, the French intend to use NATO, multilateral institutions such as the UN, and bilateral arrangements with nations such as Russia and Germany to constrain what they call American hyperpower.

The French effort to subvert the Bush administration on Iraq is not the exception but the norm of French diplomacy. Kagan's dichotomy does not fully explain it. There was much that was genuinely idealistic about the Bush administration's commitment to ending tyranny in Iraq and spreading stable, liberal democracy to the Middle East. There was much that was cynical and Machiavellian in French opposition to the war. For decades France appeased Saddam's murderous regime for oil and money and to placate French Muslims. The French helped Saddam with his nuclear program, supplied him with weapons, turned a blind eye to the slaughter of Kurds and Marsh Arabs, blocked any effective UN action against him after 1991, and stood to gain billions of dollars in secret oil deals negotiated with him.[48]

The danger is not that France will realize its largely delusional ambitions. Even if the EU succeeds, a dim prospect especially now that the French electorate itself has rejected the EU constitution, it cannot likely match a United States that continues to grow while Europe continues to decline demographically, economically, and militarily. History also does not inspire confidence in France's capacity to manage Germany without an active American presence in Europe. On the remote chance that French aspirations for the EU ever become reality, the results would confound their expectations: Germany would inevitably dominate it by dint of its enormous power, not a middle-ranking country such as France.

Nevertheless, France has crossed the line between legitimate dissent and active subversion of American interests. Consequently, the United States cannot make the approval of NATO or the EU the sine qua non for military action. As Max Boot recommends instead, the United States must strengthen its links with more pro-American democratic allies in Europe, such as Spain, Italy, Great Britain, and Poland, and other Eastern European members of NATO. The United States should encourage these states to thwart Franco-German domination of NATO or the EU for anti-American ends. The United States also should remain an active member of NATO to enhance its leverage; to deter Russia from attempting to restore its empire in Eastern Europe; to extend and consolidate the democratic peace in Eastern Europe; and to frustrate French ambitions to transform Europe into a counterweight rather than a complement to American power.[49]

Finally, the United States should strive to create and sustain in Europe as broad a coalition as possible that is consistent with America's mission. That means respecting legitimate dissent and the reasonable opinions of allies, but not slavishly deferring to it. Contrary to what Kupchan, Ikenberry, Fukuyama, and other critics of American foreign policy claim, the United States is more right than wrong in the policy disputes we have had with our European allies since 9/11. For decades European appeasement of Middle Eastern dictators produced only futility. It failed miserably not only with Saddam Hussein in Iraq but with the militant mullahs in Iran. Neither the diplomatic process in which the Europeans have taken the lead nor the United Nations will stop the Iranians from acquiring nuclear weapons.[50] Only American power could possibly do that.

Events have also discredited the European alternative to the American approach to the Arab-Israeli conflict. Imagine if only European states had put pressure on the PLO to reform and jettison Arafat rather than bolster his repressive regime and rejectionism for all these years. Chances for an equitable, durable solution to the Israeli-Palestinian conflict would have increased significantly.

Those who wish to subordinate American foreign policy to multilateral institutions should recall George Washington's warnings against the danger of entangling commitments at variance with America's interests. The record of the twentieth century has demonstrated that the vitality of democratic alliance systems is a more permanent interest than the Founders contemplated. Yet "it is unwise to implicate ourselves by artificial ties" when our enemies or misguided friends make multilateralism a categorical imperative rather than a calculation of prudence.[51] For the sake of America's and Europe's genuine rather than imagined interest, no nation, no alliance, no international organization can have a veto on American action. That is especially true when the French and others regard international institutions as being in pursuit of their misguided balancing strategy against the United States by other means.

5

Moral Democratic Realism

Moral democratic realism offers a more compelling framework for American grand strategy than the alternatives because it takes due measure of the centrality of power and the constraints the dynamics of international politics impose, without depreciating the significance of ideals, ideology, and regime type. It grounds American foreign policy in Judeo-Christian conceptions of man, morality, and prudence that inoculate us against two dangerous fallacies: a utopianism that exaggerates the potential for cooperation without power; and an unrealistic realism that underestimates the potentialities for achieving decency and provisional justice even in international relations. It rests on a conception of self-interest, well understood, and respect for the decent opinions of mankind, without making international institutions or the fickle mistress of often-indecent international public opinion the polestar for American action. The precepts of moral democratic realism emerge from the lessons of American diplomatic history.

First, conflict, evil, and the possibility of war always loom large as the consequences of irredeemable human imperfection. The anarchical system of international politics—with no monopoly on the legitimate use of violence—compounds these dangers arising from flawed human nature itself. The potential for war will always exist in a world of sovereign states, each of which claims the right to take justice into its own hands and to be the sole arbiter in the decision to fight or not to fight. History has not ended, nor will it ever end by man's contrivance alone. Kant's notion of perpetual peace is a dangerous illusion. So is the notion of Woodrow Wilson and his modern admirers that international organizations such as the United Nations can effectively maintain even a provisionally just peace based on the principles of collective security. No generation of Americans should ever take freedom for granted. We will always have to defend it from the devil that always lurks around the corner in international relations. Power is thus the pivotal, inescapable dimension of international politics. Or as Reinhold Niebuhr put it: "There has never been a scheme of justice in history which did not have . . . power at its foundation. If the democratic nations fail, their failure must be partly attributed to the faulty strategy of idealists who have too many illusions when they face realists who have too little conscience."[1] The preservation of American self-interest will continue to depend mainly on the clarity, credibility, and capability of American power. Coalitions of the willing can supplement but not substitute for that power. Multilateral institutions in general and the UN in particular can inhibit the necessary exercise of it if we are unwise enough to defer to them as a matter of course and without regard for the consequences.

Typically, the greatest dangers to the United States arise not from vigilance or the arrogance of American power, but from unpreparedness and an excessive reluctance to fight. So American statesmen must strive to maintain what Churchill called "overwhelming power," with plenty to spare for unforeseen contingencies. This posture will deter most aggressors most of the time and defeat them with less cost when deterrence occasionally fails: "If you are going to do things on a narrow margin, one way or another you are going to have war. But if you get to five or ten to one on one side, then you will have an opportunity to make a settlement that will heal the wounds of the world. Let us be the blessed union of power and justice."[2]

Second, regime analysis is an integral aspect of moral democratic realism. All regimes do not behave alike. Some are more aggressive or more peaceful than others. There is a vital moral and practical distinction between stable, liberal democracies, on the one hand, and totalitarian regimes animated by a messianic ideology, on the other. The United States is right to encourage the spread of stable, liberal democracy that is based not just on ideals but also on what Robert Kagan calls the higher realism: such regimes are more likely to cooperate and less likely to fight one another when they do disagree. Again, Reinhold Niebuhr best expressed this higher realism: "Man's capacity for justice makes democracy possible; but man's capacity for injustice makes democracy necessary. . . . The democratic techniques of a free society place checks upon the power of rulers and administrators and thus prevents it from becoming vexatious. . . . The perils of uncontrolled power are a perennial reminder of the virtues of the Democratic society."[3] The issue is not whether but how to promote democracy prudentially, which depends on the interplay between principles and circumstances.

Granted, the United States should not court enormous risks to establish democracies anywhere, on any pretext. Neoconservatives such as William Kristol and Robert Kagan tend to underrate the obstacles to promoting democracy, just as realists and liberal multilateralists overrate them.[4] In a cautionary tale illustrating the limits of America's capacity to remake other societies, Rich Lowry, the author of friendly critiques of neoconservative thought, notes the dismal record of American interventionism in Latin America early in the twentieth century, failure in Haiti and Somalia, and chaos in the Balkans.[5] He should add South Vietnam to his list, though he also does not fully appreciate the magnitude of American success elsewhere: American power greatly facilitated the emergence of stable, liberal democracy, not just in Germany and Japan, but in all Eastern and Western Europe, Korea, the Philippines, and Taiwan.[6]

Yet sometimes the prospects for democratic forces succeeding are too remote and America's stake in a favorable outcome too limited to justify active U.S. involvement. We should always prefer a stable, liberal democratic outcome; we cannot always get one. A prudent statesman knows when the desirable is possible or not. The diplomacy of John Paul II is a splendid example of prudence worthy of emulation in cases where the democratic option is not directly available. The pope abhorred Soviet totalitarianism, but he understood he could not challenge the Soviet system openly, given the correlation of forces. So, writes Charles Krauthammer, "he nurtured and justified every oppositional trend" in Eastern Europe, thus becoming "one of the great liberators of the twentieth century."[7]

Regime type and ideology account not only positively for the democratic peace so beneficial for American security, but negatively for the most menacing aggression against the United States. American statesmen rightly identified the militaristic regime of Kaiser Wilhelm as the root cause of World War I, Nazi totalitarianism and imperial Japanese militarism as the root cause of World War II, Soviet totalitarianism as the root cause of the Cold War, Saddam Hussein's Ba'ath regime as the root cause of both Iraq Wars, and the culture of tyranny and oppression in the Middle East as the root cause of the war on terror.

Third, moral democratic realism dictates that American foreign policy adhere closely to the imperatives of geopolitics. Realists and many liberal multilateralists have failed to grasp that the unipolar era is enduring and not evanescent. The United States will remain the world's dominant power for a long time to come. Strong balancing against American power is highly unlikely for a combination of practical, moral, and geopolitical reasons. For all nations, however, even a nation as powerful as the United States, resources are finite.

Neoconservatism is vastly more right than wrong in its conception of America's national interest, its diagnosis of the threats the United States faces, and its policy prescriptions for dealing with it. Yet, as Charles Krauthammer warns, the unbridled democratic globalism that some neoconservatives and Tony Blair advocate could squander American resources and morale imprudently on peripheral interests that may be difficult to achieve in any event, such as humanitarian interventions.[8] American foreign policy must give priority to extending the democratic zone of peace to East Asia, Europe, and the Middle East. These are the major power centers of the world, the regions where the absence of liberty could prove most perilous. An unfettered worldwide crusade for democracy risks imperiling our unique capacity to perform the most vital task for American self-interest: preventing hegemonic or other dangerous threats from emerging in the most vital geopolitical regions.

Elsewhere the United States should vigorously support the extension of freedom and the democratic zone of peace, but not by threat, employment, or commitment of American military power, except in rare instances where minimal force with minimal risk, with a prompt and certain exit strategy, can avert mass murder or genocide.[9] Supporters of humanitarian interventions must satisfy a high burden of proof that the United States can satisfy these conditions without detracting from the U.S. military's core missions. The genocide in Rwanda during the 1990s qualifies under this exception: the United States could have easily and safely prevented the horrendous murder of many of the 800,000 victims of the genocide at very little cost or risk. Generally, other countries should take the lead in humanitarian endeavors, which are often well within their more limited military capabilities to undertake.[10]

Fourth, the cardinal virtue of prudence—choosing right ends and right means—must guide when, how, and for what purpose the United States resorts to military force. Prudence requires that the United States keep its powder ready, dry, and ample to defeat actual, imminent, or gathering dangers to vital interests of the United States and its pivotal allies.

Just-war theory rightly requires a moral as well as a geopolitical rationale for using military force, which American statesmen ignore at their peril. The American people will not support long and costly wars unless they meet the dual requirements of being right and in our self-interest. Modern just-war theory and secular guidelines such as the Weinberger-Powell doctrine make the mistake, however, of requiring that force be used only as a last resort.[11] This is imprudent. Whether the United States resorts to force sooner rather than later is a prudential judgment, not a categorical one. It depends upon the gravity of the danger, the probability of its realization, the availability of alternative means, and the prospects for success.[12]

We know from history that sometimes using force sooner can save much blood, toil, tears, and sweat later. No statesman speaks more authoritatively on this subject than Winston Churchill: "If you will not fight for the right when you can easily win without bloodshed; if you will not fight when your victory will be sure and not too costly; you may come to the moment when you will have to fight with all the odds against you and only a precarious chance for survival. There may even be a worse case. You may have to fight when there is no hope of victory, because it is better to perish than to live as slaves."[13] We know that had the democracies heeded Winston Churchill's advice and stopped Hitler at various watersheds during the 1930s, particularly when Nazi Germany invaded the Rhineland on March 7, 1936, in violation of two international agreements, we could have averted the worst war in history. Hitler admitted as much, calling the first forty-eight hours of the Rhineland Crisis the most nervous of his life, because French resistance would have caused his regime to collapse.[14] We know, given the nature of academics, that had the democracies heeded Churchill's advice, generations of ungrateful professors would still be writing tomes complaining about preventive war and exonerating Hitler as a legitimate folk nationalist.

Consider three more compelling examples of when the actual or pre-emptive use of force averted vastly greater moral and geopolitical evil. In July 1940, with Nazi Germany triumphant in Europe, the Soviet Union neutrally pro-Nazi, the United States still isolationist, and Great Britain clinging precariously to freedom, Winston Churchill ordered a preventive strike against the Vichy French fleet harbored in Oran, killing nearly thirteen hundred Frenchmen, despite Vichy's nominal independence, and despite possessing no hard evidence that Vichy's minister of war, Admiral Jean-François Darlan, intended to turn the French fleet over to Hitler. Darlan insisted until his dying day he had no such intention. Yet Churchill was right.[15]

In May 1981 Israel launched a preventive strike against Iraq's nuclear reactor at Osirak, which the United Nations unanimously condemned. Yet Israel was right. Otherwise, Saddam Hussein would have possessed a nuclear capability when he invaded Kuwait in the summer of 1990, which may have deterred the United States from responding decisively or raised exponentially the cost and risk of such a response.[16]

During the Cuban missile crisis of October 1962, the Kennedy administration may have launched a preventive attack against Soviet nuclear missiles deployed in Cuba had the Soviet Union not conceded under pressure to remove them. President Kennedy was right.[17]

Contrary to modern versions of just-war theory such as Jimmy Carter's, which categorically assails war as unjust unless the United States first "exhaust all non-violent options," St. Thomas Aquinas's traditional and superior formulation was silent on the question of whether force should be used as a last resort or sooner.[18] There is also no presumption against war in Aquinas that one often finds in modern versions of just-war theory. Nor, as James Turner Johnson points out in a splendid analysis of the subject, does one find in the arguments of Aquinas the requirement of proportionality that modern just-war theory elevates to a categorical imperative.[19]

Aquinas is wiser than his successors for these deliberate omissions. "In order for war to be just," according to Aquinas, "three things are necessary." First, war must be waged by the duly recognized sovereign, which means, in the case of the United States, the supreme authorities that the Constitution invests with such responsibility: the president with the sanction of the Congress. Second, war must be waged only for just cause; that is, "those who are attacked should be attacked because they deserve it on account of some fault." Third, war must be waged with right intention; that is, statesmen must "intend the advancement of good or the avoidance of evil." We do not "not seek peace to be at war," but go "to war that we may have peace."[20]

Aquinas's casuistry should always have a prominent place in any prudential calculation of when, how, and for what purpose the United States should wage war. A prudential statesman ought to pay special attention to the implications of his third requirement: that war be waged with right intention for a rightly ordered peace. Our greatest military historians, such as Victor Davis Hanson, have demonstrated that the most just and durable peace settlements usually occur when wars have decisive outcomes, which eradicate the root cause of aggression.[21] This insight runs counter to the trend in modern thinking that treats restraint and discrimination in the employment of force as a virtue for its own sake. Especially against implacable foes, it is better to err on the side of decisiveness than to settle for an ambiguous outcome.[22]

One of the major causes of World War II was the failure of the Treaty of Versailles to address the root causes of World War I. By October 1918 German generals knew they were beaten and forced the kaiser to abdicate, expecting that a democratic German government would obtain more lenient peace terms. It did not appear to the German people that defeat was inevitable or imminent as the German army retreated in good order and German territory remained unscathed. When the German people reacted with outrage to the terms of the Treaty of Versailles, German generals did not admit Germany's defeat or the responsibility of the kaiser's regime for the war. Instead, they mendaciously blamed the Weimar democratic regime for "stabbing Germany in the back." The Allies' unwillingness to enforce the Treaty of Versailles compounded the mistake of "letting the Kaiser's regime off the hook" in the first place. Hitler's diabolical exploitation of the "stab in the back" myth facilitated his rise to power, with all its horrendous consequences.[23]

Franklin Roosevelt and Winston Churchill did not make the same mistake during World War II. They would settle for nothing less than unconditional surrender and total defeat of the Nazi regime, in a manner so devastating that the German people could not deny it. They insisted on democratic regime change in Germany and were determined to enforce it in order to create the conditions of Aquinas's rightly ordered peace.[24]

One of the major causes of the Iraq War of 2003 was the ambiguous outcome of the Gulf War of 1990–1991, which left Saddam in power. For a combination of understandable reasons, President Bush halted the use of force too soon: fear of a power vacuum; the limits of the UN mandate that called for the liberation of Kuwait but not Iraq; and the visual images of the so-called highway of death, which conveyed the false impression that

Saddam's Republican Guard was devastated beyond repair. The Iraqi and American people paid a terrible price for this well-meaning but imprudent restraint. President George W. Bush did not repeat the mistake. He understands that a just and durable peace requires Saddam's total defeat and democratic regime change, which the United States must have the perseverance to enforce. Likewise, the Cold War could not end until the collapse of the Soviet Union's malevolent regime that caused it.

The requirements of prudence and Aquinas's three conditions for just war are thus largely complementary. A decisive outcome and democratic regime change are usually prerequisites for a rightly ordered peace that addresses the real root cause of aggression.

Yet sometimes the United States must settle for less than total or immediate victory. In a bipolar era nuclear weapons precluded the United States from defeating the Soviet Union directly by traditional military means. The Korean War of 1950–1953 is a prime example of an occasion when fighting for less-than-total victory was a more prudential alternative than either capitulation or all-out war. The failure to save South Korea from North Korean aggression would have delivered a devastating blow to American credibility with its new NATO allies and perhaps a fatal one to the prospects of securing an alliance with Japan, which deemed a noncommunist South Korea vital to its security. After the Chinese army intervened in Korea in November 1950, the Truman administration abandoned the goal of unifying the Korean peninsula in favor of restoring South Korean independence south of the thirty-eighth parallel. The president managed to convince the nation over the stout objection of General Douglas MacArthur—who demanded total victory and was willing to use nuclear weapons and fight a land war with China if necessary—that such escalation would imperil American ability to deter the Soviet Union, which was by far the greater danger. Truman was right, though Mao's China—particularly in its early phase—was indeed as malevolent and revolutionary as the pro-Nationalist lobby in the United States portrayed it.[25] Stalin would have relished the United States' getting bogged down in a protracted fight with China, leaving the Soviet Union, then the greater danger, free to intimidate Western Europe.[26]

Even in a unipolar world, where the United States faces less daunting constraints than it did during the Cold War, prudence sometimes counsels against attempting to achieve victory by direct military means. Take the case of Iran, which President Bush rightly designated as part of the Axis of

Evil that the United States must defeat. The Iranian regime poses a serious and imminent threat to the United States, American allies, and the entire Middle East. The militant mullahs are bent on developing a nuclear and ballistic missile capability, supporting terrorism, and fueling insurgency, with the ultimate goal of destroying American civilization.[27] The pledge of Iranian President Mahmoud Ahmadinejad to see Israel "wiped off the map" and Arabs who recognize Israel "burn in the fire of Islamic national fury" reveals in bold relief the politics of hate and confrontation that animates the current Iranian regime.[28]

Until recently, however, the Iranian mullahs have been more deterrable and less prone to taking precipitous risk than Saddam Hussein. Moreover, the cost and risk of direct American military action is greater. Iran is much larger than Iraq, its geography more forbidding, and its nuclear program more ripe and difficult to preempt: Iran has widely dispersed its several nuclear facilities, making them a vastly more difficult target for preemption than Iraq's nuclear facility at Osirak. An attack on Iran would cause enormous economic hardship: oil prices likely would skyrocket to more than a hundred dollars a barrel. Iran could blockade the Strait of Hormuz, where 40 percent of the world's oil flows daily. Eventually, the United States would succeed in breaking such a blockade, but it would take much time, treasure, men, and material to do it.[29] Iranians also have a long history of ferocious hostility to foreign intervention, particularly American intervention, in their domestic affairs that would make the difficulties of pacifying Iraq seem minimal by comparison. Unlike Saddam's Iraq, there also are in Iran plausible scenarios for democratic regime change that do not entail the direct use of force. The militant mullahs face a formidable domestic opposition that the United States can embolden by creating a successful democracy in neighboring Shiite Iraq and defeating Iran's chief surrogates, such as Syria, that are more vulnerable to direct military force.[30]

Ultimately, the United States cannot prudently tolerate a nuclear-armed Iran. Neither deterrence nor containment will suffice against a regime bent on returning the world to the twelfth century and destroying Anglo-American civilization and Israel along with it. Edward Luttwak explains why: "Even with no nuclear weapons, with its conventional forces in disarray, and with American power flanking both sides of Iran in Afghanistan and Iraq, the Iranian regime arms, aids, and abets terror defiantly. It is reasonable to expect Iran's extremist rulers will become even more aggressive if they obtain nuclear weapons. Time is running out for alternative solutions to the mounting and unacceptable peril of a radical, nuclear Iran. An air campaign against Iranian nuclear installations would stand a good chance of disrupting the Iranian program in significant and lasting ways."[31]

North Korea's acquisition of nuclear weapons poses yet another formidable challenge to reconcile the desirable with the possible on the basis of the precepts of moral democratic realism. By any fair standard of measure, the regime of Kim Sung and his son, Kim Jong Il, qualifies as a rogue regime responsible for the death of millions of Koreans and bent on obtaining weapons of mass destruction. The story of North Korea illustrates the inadequacy of diplomacy or international organizations to deal with the mounting danger. Repeated failures in Iraq, Somalia, Bosnia, Kosovo, Sudan, and North Korea discredit the United Nations as an effective alternative. North Korea's rampant and clandestine violation of the Agreed Framework of 1994—in which the North Korean regime agreed to free its plutonium rods and not to remove spent fuel rods from supervision—discredits President Clinton's strategy of accommodation and engagement as an alternative. When the Bush administration produced incontrovertible evidence of North Korea's secret program to develop a nuclear bomb by enriching uranium, the North Korean regime simply disavowed the agreement, which it had subverted from the outset. North Korea has a large conventional army, which could inflict massive destruction on South Korea, and a growing nuclear arsenal. It is developing an intermediate and intercontinental ballistic missile menacing to American allies in Asia and eventually to the west coast of the United States.[32]

Having inherited this mounting danger from a Clinton administration that chose to appease rather than confront a rogue North Korean regime, the Bush administration has relied on a strategy of robust deterrence as the least unpalatable alternative. The United States would find it daunting to preempt a North Korean nuclear threat that is already operational. Preemption would run the risk of a North Korean conventional or nuclear response that could devastate much of South Korea, particularly the capital, Seoul, the financial, political, and industrial center of the South Korean regime, which lies just thirty miles from the thirty-eighth parallel dividing North and South Korea. There is, moreover, a greater potential for robust deterrence succeeding with North Korea than with Iraq. For all the malevolence and moral depravity of the North Korean regime, it has not yet displayed the reckless disregard for risks characteristic of Saddam Hussein's Iraq. The American presence in Korea has succeeded in deterring North Korean aggression for more than fifty years. Unlike the Middle East, where Saddam was a symbol of defiance of American power in a region of seething defiance, North Korea is a dying regime, with no appeal regionally or globally as a model to emulate. The formidable task of American strategy is to prevent the North Korean regime from lashing out dangerously as it faces its inevitable demise.[33]

Like the fanatical president of Iran, however, Kim Jong Il, North Korea's tyrannical dictator, has recently embarked on a more reckless and provocative course that could challenge the presumptions in favor of deterrence and against preemption: the North Koreans launched on July 4 and 5, 2006, several intermediate-range ballistic missiles, which were capable of reaching our South Korean, Japanese, and Taiwanese allies. North Korea also launched one long-range missile, a Taepodong-2, with a range of 3,750 miles, far enough to reach Seattle—had not the missile plunged into the Sea of Japan after a mere forty-two seconds in flight. This brazen behavior raises the question whether deterrence will continue to suffice in light of North Korea's escalation of its nuclear program. North Korea's nuclear weapons tests in October 2006 have underscored and magnified the gathering danger.

What we do know is that appeasing Kim Jong II will not work. The *Wall Street Journal* has trenchantly catalogued the dismal failure of diplomacy and accommodation to deal with the North Korean threat. Normalizing relations with North Korea, ending its economic isolation, and offering the regime security guarantees would repeat mistakes of the past.[34] The worst thing the United States could do is what Democrats advocate: a return to bilateral negotiations with North Korea. This would not only reward North Korea for nuclear blackmail, but fecklessly repeat the failed strategy of President Clinton and his envoy, former President Carter. During the 1990s the Clinton administration fatuously subsidized Kim Jong Il in the naive hope that North Korea would abide by its promise to discontinue its nuclear weapons program. Instead, Michael G. Franc argues compellingly, a Korean ballistic missile launch should impel Congress to accelerate the testing and deployment of ballistic missile defense.[35]

Again the president has displayed greater foresight than his liberal critics by abrogating the Anti-Ballistic Missile Treaty of 1972, which probably did not serve the national interest even during the Cold War and certainly does not now. Since Ronald Reagan unveiled his Strategic Defense Initiative in March 1983, liberals in Congress have opposed ballistic missile defense with what Franc calls "near theological intensity." We are now reaping the fruits that opposition has sown. "Had President Clinton and the Congress not abandoned" the missile defense program that the administration of George Herbert Walker Bush laid out in 1991, the United States would have already achieved a significantly greater capacity to intercept missiles such as North Korea's Taepodong or Iran's Shahab-3.[36]

The upshot is this: American statesmen should always heed the adage of the great Chinese strategist Sun Tzu: "To fight and conquer in all your battles is not the supreme mark of excellence; supreme excellence consists in breaking the enemy's will without fighting."[37] When the United States does have to fight, it should be with the presumption of total victory for the purpose of achieving a rightly ordered peace, unless the weight of prudence dictates otherwise.

Fifth, moral democratic realism rejects moral relativism and moral nihilism. Although the relative anarchy of international politics and man's intrinsically flawed nature constrain the range of moral choices in international politics, Judeo-Christian morality refracted through the lens of the cardinal virtue of prudence ought to serve as the guide for evaluating the relative degrees of moral and geopolitical evil. The standards for evaluating public and private morality, or for evaluating morality between states and within states, do not differ as starkly as the realist tradition claims. The differences lie in the circumstances in which states and statesmen act. In a world of sovereign states, where many seek actively to destroy imperfect but decent, stable, liberal democracies, there are times when even good states and good statesmen must choose the lesser evil to prevent the greater one. Also, because democratic statesmen act on behalf not just of themselves but of their citizens, they have a greater burden of proof to discharge before risking major interests than if they acted in self-abnegation solely on their own behalf.

Not even the United States is immune to the temptations of defining its own national interest too selfishly, in terms of wealth and power, and of seeking it by any means. Slavery and the internment of Japanese citizens during World War II are just two sobering reminders that Americans sometimes fall far short of their ideals. Yet the historian David Hackett

Fischer is right to observe that our founders and the leaders of the American Revolution never believed winning was enough. "One of their greatest achievements," writes Fischer, "was to manage the war in a manner that was true to the expanding humanitarian ideals of the American Revolution. It happened in a way that was different from the ordinary course of war in general. In Congress and the army, the American leaders resolved that the War of Independence would be conducted with a respect for human rights, even of the enemy."[38] What Fischer observes about the American Revolution is no less true of our major wars since then, including the current war on terror: great American leaders have always believed that the United States must win in a way that is consistent with the values of American society and the principles of its cause.[39]

Finally, the mark of prudence is the capacity to discern when changing times require different measures to achieve the same goals. Strategies appropriate for one set of circumstances are often inappropriate for others. Isolationism suited the United States in the age of sail, when America was weak in the world of the strong and could take the effective operation of the European balance of power for granted. The conditions the United States faced in the twentieth century required an entirely new grand strategy. Vigilant containment was a prudential response to the Soviet Union during the Cold War. The current war on terror requires a more proactive grand strategy because of the spread of WMD and the lack of inhibition terrorists or rogue regimes may have about using such weapons.

6

Moral Democratic Realism and the Endgame of the Cold War

The grand strategy of President Ronald Reagan for winning the Cold War exemplifies the precepts of moral democratic realism in action. It has become fashionable in many quarters to take for granted the collapse of the Soviet Union, the vast expansion of freedom, and the increase in American prosperity since the 1980s.[1] That was not the conventional wisdom when Ronald Reagan took office in January 1981.

The decade of the 1970s was a dismal one for the United States. Freedom was in retreat. Collectivism was on the rise. The huge expansion of the federal government in all aspects of American life, especially the economy, had stifled incentives for innovation and growth that had propelled the post–World War II economic boom in the United States. The Arab oil boycott following the Yom Kippur War of October 1973 and the oil shocks of 1978–1979 had broadened and deepened the phenomenon of stagflation—low growth and high interest rates—grinding American economic growth to a halt. By the final year of the Carter administration, the economy had reached new post–World War II lows: inflation reached 12 percent and interest rates ran at 21 percent.[2]

During the 1970s American military power declined precipitously. The trauma of the Vietnam War convinced the establishments of both political parties that substantial American retrenchment was a virtue as well as a necessity. By the end of the decade American power had reached its comparative low point since World War II. Defense spending dropped to 4.8

percent of the GDP, half of what the liberal Democrat John Kennedy spent on defense as a percentage of GDP. The Iranian takeover of the American embassy in Tehran in November 1979, in which fifty-two Americans were held hostage for 444 days, epitomized the mounting self-doubt of the Carter administration, the American people at home, and friends and foes abroad about the purposes of American power.[3]

What made America's predicament seem even more ominous was that it coincided with the rising power, self-confidence, and assertiveness of the Soviet regime. The 1970s witnessed the continuation of the Soviet military buildup, the most massive peacetime buildup in history, which consumed more than one-quarter of the Soviet Union's GDP. The decade saw an extraordinary surge in Soviet expansionism, as the Soviet leadership was confident that the correlation of forces had changed in its favor. The decade also witnessed the peak in influence at the UN of a virulently anti-American Third World bloc, egged on by the Soviet Union. The end of the decade observed the Soviet Union escalating the Cold War by invading Afghanistan in December 1979.[4]

Ronald Reagan repudiated the policy of détente that the Republican administrations of President Richard Nixon and Gerald Ford had pursued, as well as the Carter administration's version of it. A deeper understanding of Reagan's pivotal role in winning the Cold War is essential not only to set the record straight, but to clarify contemporary perspectives on American grand strategy.

First, an analysis of Reagan's policies dispels the myth popular among President George W. Bush's critics that the Bush Doctrine is highly partisan and controversial by the standards of American politics. Although genuine bipartisan consensus on foreign policy existed for the first two decades of the Cold War, the Vietnam War catalyzed a lacerating debate over the purpose of American power that spanned the final two decades of the Cold War. After 1968 the Democratic Party largely abandoned President Truman's policy of vigilant containment.[5] The liberal wing that dominated it fiercely contested most of President Reagan's major initiatives that contributed mightily to the Soviet Union's demise.[6] What Joshua Muravchik writes of John Kerry also applies to the vast majority of post-1968 Democratic liberals:

> Kerry opposed every one of . . . Ronald Reagan's . . . pivotal contributions. . . . Reagan's defense buildup disabused Soviet leaders of

any hope that they could ultimately come out ahead of the United States. Kerry derided these military expenditures as "bloated" and "without any relevancy to the threat." In particular, Reagan's plan to seek a new missile defense system against the Soviet Union's ICBMs and NATO's decision to station new missiles in Europe to counteract the new Soviet deployments there rendered futile the Kremlin's vast investment in nuclear supremacy. Instead of these measures, Kerry advocated that we adopt the "one-sided" nuclear freeze. Reagan also showed the Soviets that history was not necessarily on their side by ousting the erratic communist regime in Grenada and arming anti-communist guerrillas to challenge the leftist oligarchs in Nicaragua. Kerry condemned the U.S. action in Grenada as "a bully's show of force," and he opposed our support for guerrillas in Nicaragua. Reagan also put the U.S. on the ideological offensive when he branded the Soviet Union an "evil empire." But Kerry's harshest words were reserved for his own country, which he accused—during his years as an antiwar leader—of "crimes against humanity committed on a day-to-day basis with the full awareness of officers at all levels of command."[7]

Second, the contending approaches from the final two decades of the Cold War continue to dominate current debates over the future of American foreign policy. The assumptions of President George W. Bush's realist critics, such as Brent Scowcroft and Senator Chuck Hagel of Nebraska, largely reflect those informing the Nixon-Ford-Kissinger policy of realpolitik.[8] Similarly, the core assumptions of the liberal multilateralist critique of the Bush Doctrine mirror those of the Carter administration: its depreciation of the importance of American military power; its reluctance to use force; its conception of the role of human rights in American foreign policy. Conversely, the content of and rationale for President George W. Bush's foreign policy bear a striking resemblance to those of Ronald Reagan's.

The Unrealistic Realism of Nixon, Ford, and Kissinger

Richard Nixon, Gerald Ford, and Henry Kissinger (who served as national security advisor and secretary of state for both presidents) sought vainly to constrain Soviet power by defining American interests more narrowly and depicting the Soviet threat less menacingly. Nixon and Kissinger devised and implemented a version of détente that sought to divest American foreign policy of its legalism, idealism, and crusading moralism. The nineteenth-century balance-of-power tradition inspired their statecraft. Nixon and Kissinger distrusted and deemphasized the ideological dominion of American foreign policy to a degree unprecedented during the Cold War. By their reckonings, the diminished salience of ideology and the emergence of multipolarity, a world of five great power centers instead of just two power centers, made substantial global retrenchment prudent.

Nixon and Kissinger also believed that domestic constraints made such a retrenchment a necessity as well as a virtue. Having won the election of 1968 narrowly, Nixon faced a nation convulsed by the Vietnam War. Even after his landslide reelection in November 1972, Nixon faced a Democratic Congress increasingly hostile to defense spending and the maintenance of U.S. global commitments. From 1969 through 1977 American defense spending declined 38 percent, while the massive Soviet military buildup proceeded relentlessly. Nixon and Kissinger assessed the Congress and the American people as hostile to any substantial American combat involvement anywhere abroad.[9]

The policy of détente toward the Soviet Union and China represented a major shift in the perception of American interests and the best framework for preserving and promoting those interests.[10] Ideology and the threat associated with it had become, in the view of Nixon and Kissinger, relatively less important as sources of international conduct when compared with traditional, narrower conceptions of the national interest. Whereas previous administrations had defined the Soviet Union as a relentless and implacable ideological adversary with unlimited ambitions, Nixon and Kissinger conceived of the Soviet Union as a traditional type of empire, dangerous and expansionist but with limited aims, which offered the possibility of achieving a durable equilibrium. Nixon and Kissinger also conceived of China as less communist and more traditionally Chinese in its foreign policy. Both believed the split between the Chinese and the Soviet Union (the "Sino-Soviet split") offered promising opportunities to normalize relations with China and to minimize the adverse geopolitical consequences of withdrawing from Vietnam.[11]

Nixon and Kissinger spoke publicly about removing ideology or regime type as a reference point for measuring threats. "We have no permanent enemies," Kissinger announced in 1969; "we will judge other countries . . . on the basis of their actions and not on the basis of their domestic ideology." Security in the Nixon-Kissinger framework required equilibrium, not ideological parallels. Thus, to counter threats to the global balance, the United States could cooperate with states with different political systems so long as they shared American interests. This de-emphasis on ideology improved the prospect of relations with our erstwhile communist adversaries. As Kissinger, in typical realist fashion, put it with regard to China: "The leaders . . . were beyond ideology in their dealings with us. Their peril had established the absolute primacy of geopolitics."[12]

Nixon and Kissinger also rested their foreign policy framework on the assumption that the era of bipolarity, with Soviet and American power preeminent in international politics, had begun to draw to a close. Anticipating a new era of global and regional multipolarity, they believed there were surrogates that could substitute for American power to meet more traditional threats to American geopolitical interests. "The Nixon Doctrine," as the strategy came to be known, reflected the administration's determination to address what Nixon and Kissinger perceived to be the limited resources and will to meet U.S. commitments. To lighten U.S. foreign policy burdens and thus make them more acceptable to the American people, Nixon and Kissinger sought to transform the American role in resisting Soviet aggression from primary to supporting.[13]

Rapprochement with the PRC was a prime example of the Nixon Doctrine in action. By forging a relationship with China, Nixon and Kissinger hoped to enlist its aid in containing Soviet expansionism, pressuring North Vietnam to accept a peace compatible with U.S. honor, and maintaining geopolitical equilibrium in Asia. In the Middle East Nixon and Kissinger designated the shah of Iran as the primary U.S. surrogate. The United States would supply the arms, while the shah would provide the ground troops and actual military presence to preserve regional equilibrium. The changing distribution of world power, the apparent waning of ideology and regime type as determinants of foreign policy, Nixon and Kissinger's downgrading of the Soviet threat from Leninist to "traditionally imperial," and the probable availability of regional surrogates for American power seemed to make possible what domestic politics made necessary.[14]

Through arms control, Nixon and Kissinger hoped to constrain the Soviet Union's prodigious military buildup. More broadly, the implementation of détente required the engagement of the Soviet Union in building a stable, international equilibrium, one in which the Soviets had a stake in maintaining order and tranquillity rather than undermining them. Through negotiations and agreements, Nixon and Kissinger hoped to change Moscow's approach to international relations by convincing Soviet leaders that it was in their interest to emphasize cooperation rather than competition with the West.

Nixon and Kissinger advocated linking progress on all these issues to induce compromise. They intended "linkage" to impose a conceptual order on American policy and to function as a source of leverage with the Soviet Union and third parties, which would enmesh the Soviets in a web of economic interdependence and thus moderate their external conduct and ambitions. The Strategic Arms Limitation Talks and Treaties (SALT) became the major instrument for implementing this conception of détente. By May 1972 Nixon and Kissinger succeeded in negotiating two agreements: the SALT I interim agreement limiting offensive delivery systems, and the ABM Treaty, which they hailed as the modern equivalent of the Congress of Vienna of 1815.

It was not just optimism about Soviet intentions but also pessimism about America's prospects that affected their judgment about how to deal with the Soviet threat. Nixon and Kissinger both believed that détente was imperative because the Soviet Union was on the rise while the United States was in decline.[15]

Not all of détente was conciliation. When the Soviet Union encouraged Arab countries to attack Israel in October 1973, the United States responded vigorously. Kissinger's skillful shuttle diplomacy succeeded in its aim of isolating the Soviet Union in the Middle East. In Latin America, which both Nixon and Kissinger considered part of America's sphere of influence, they endorsed the Chilean military's overthrow of Salvador Allende's Marxist regime. Nixon and Kissinger recoiled from the logical consequences of their depreciation of ideology and regime type by their unremitting hostility to the phenomenon of "Eurocommunism" in Western Europe. Nixon and Kissinger failed to save South Vietnam, but their strategy of gradual withdrawal helped prevent America's containment policy from unraveling into a precipitous retreat.[16]

Even so, Kissinger himself admits that détente failed to stem the dangerous geopolitical erosion of American power during the 1970s. He attributes this to the effects of Watergate and the obstructionism of détente's hawkish critics rather than to his own flawed conception. This is untenable. Granted, any administration would have found it monumentally difficult to conduct a vigorous foreign policy under the circumstances that Nixon and Kissinger inherited in 1969. Yet Nixon and Kissinger's grand design must bear a greater share of the blame than either is willing to accept. Nixon and Kissinger took much of their extravagant rhetoric about détente more seriously than their later writings imply. They did believe that the Soviet Union had become a traditional imperial power rather than a totalitarian and revolutionary one. They did believe, wrongly, that the world had become multipolar and that there were adequate substitutes for American power as a consequence. Even before the Watergate crisis, the Soviet Union had already perceived détente as a shift in the correlation of forces in its favor and as a sign of American weakness, which the implosion of the Nixon presidency exacerbated.[17]

Although Kissinger professes that theoretically the task of American foreign policy is to reconcile ideals with self-interest rather than choose one side exclusively, his policy of détente honored that principle only in the breach. Many of the actions of Nixon, Ford, and Kissinger had an enervating effect on the prodefense constituencies in Congress and the country at large. During 1973–1974, for example, Kissinger courted William Fulbright and other Senate doves propitiatingly while spurning those in the Senate who opposed his policy of détente. Even a secretary of state less shrewd than Kissinger should have known that embracing Fulbright, the paladin of New Left sensibilities on foreign policy and national defense, would undermine any attempt to rally the American people to support a policy of boldness that the revisionist Kissinger professes to prefer.[18]

What Nixon, Kissinger, and Ford's unrealistic realism failed to grasp was that international agreements could not constrain Soviet ambitions or generate pressure to liberalize so long as the Soviet Union remained a totalitarian state. The historian Martin Malia sums it up best: "For the West détente was a gradual way to transcend the Cold War; for the East, it was a gradual way to win it."[19] Steeped in their historical pessimism, Nixon and Kissinger also badly underestimated the capacity of the United States to recover from the trauma of Vietnam and the willingness of the American people to sustain a vigorous foreign policy when forthrightly alerted to danger. The remarkable success of Ronald

Reagan's grand strategy refutes the notion that détente was the best the United States could do.

Carter's Naive Idealism

No administration before President Clinton's embraced the policy preferences and underlying assumptions of the Vietnam War's liberal critics with such fervor and conviction as President Carter's.[20] Especially during his first three years in office, Carter, like President Clinton, spurned power politics in favor of a foreign policy based on human rights. He and most of his major advisors rejected unilateralism and coalitions of the willing in favor of multilateralism and an enhanced role for the United Nations.[21]

There are of course revisionists who argue that President Carter took a tougher line toward the Soviet Union than his critics recognize. Zbigniew Brzezinski, Carter's more hawkish national security advisor, makes this case by stressing a series of measures the administration implemented late in the president's term of office: his decision to proceed with the MX missile; his approval in 1979 of military aid for mujahedeen Afghanistan; his imposition in 1980 of a grain embargo on the Soviet Union; his establishment in March 1980 of a Rapid Deployment Force; the issuance of Presidential Directive (PD) 59 in May 1980, which gave greater emphasis to targeting our nuclear forces at Soviet military installations, industry, and intelligence facilities rather than population centers; and his support for a 5.4 percent increase in defense spending for FY 1981.[22]

Brzezinski's line of argument is even less tenable than Kissinger's defense of détente. True, Brzezinski himself advocated a more robust policy than his administration usually followed. As Soviet Ambassador Dobrynin attests, Carter's support for prominent Soviet dissidents such as Andrei Sakharov and Natan Sharansky deeply disturbed the Soviet leadership. After the Soviet Union invaded Afghanistan in December 1979, Carter did indeed display greater firmness toward the Soviet Union than he had during his previous three years.[23] His speech on June 7, 1978, at the U.S. Naval academy contained some stern rhetoric presaging what Carter did during his final year in office.

Nevertheless, Jimmy Carter's dovish inclinations largely guided his foreign policy up until 1980 and after he left office. Carter's actions speak louder than Brzezinski's words. Almost all his political appointees to the

Departments of State and Defense came from the New Politics wing of the Democratic Party, largely associated with Senator George McGovern. So did Andrew Young, Carter's first ambassador to the UN, and Ted Sorensen, his nominee (subsequently withdrawn under pressure) to head the CIA.[24] The renowned liberal civil rights lawyer Morris Abram described Cyrus Vance, Carter's secretary of state, as "the closest thing to a pacifist the U.S. ever had as Secretary of State," with the exception of William Jennings Bryan, who resigned over Woodrow Wilson's policies toward Germany.[25] For his chief advisor on Soviet affairs, Vance chose Columbia's Professor Marshall Shulman, one of the most conciliatory and optimistic of Sovietologists.[26]

For his chief arms control negotiator, President Carter chose Paul Warnke, who epitomized the sensibilities of the New Politics wing of the Democratic Party. Warnke believed that the Soviet Union armed prodigiously not to subjugate the West, but because the "giddy heights of American defense expenditure" gave the Soviet Union no choice but to reciprocate. He regarded the arms race as the primary source, not symptom, of a Soviet-American rivalry, which arms control and American unilateral restraint could alleviate.[27] Thus, Warnke wrote in his landmark "Apes on a Treadmill," which encapsulated the outlook of a generation of like-minded arms controllers and liberal multilateralists: "We should . . . try a policy of restraint, while calling for matching restraint from the Soviet Union. . . . The chances are good . . . that highly advertised restraint on our part will be reciprocated. The Soviet Union, it may be said again, has only one superpower model to follow. To date, the superpower aping has meant the antithesis of restraint. . . . It is time for us to present a worthier model. . . . We can be the first off the treadmill."[28]

President Carter sought, moreover, to transcend what he called in his May 1977 speech at Notre Dame University "our inordinate fear of communism" by conciliating our communist adversaries to a degree even Nixon and Kissinger in their euphoric moments over détente never thought prudent. In that speech, writes his admiring biographer Peter Bourne, Carter renounced "the fundamental pillars on which American foreign policy had been based since World War II."[29]

The early policies of the Carter administration reflected the outlook of William Fulbright and the anti–Vietnam War critics that the arrogance of American power posed a greater danger than communist expansion. Carter favored, though he did not achieve, the withdrawal of American combat troops from South Korea. For a long while the Carter administration took a relaxed view as the Soviet Union intensified its aggression in the underdeveloped world, which culminated in the invasion of Afghanistan—an event that deeply shook President Carter, who proclaimed in a moment of painful candor that he learned more about Soviet motives from that event than he had ever known previously. Although Brzezinski mitigated this tendency to some degree, Carter's human rights policy largely inclined in the direction of Patricia Derian, the assistant secretary of state for human rights who focused mainly on the human rights shortcomings of America's authoritarian allies rather than on those of our communist adversaries. Thus, UN Ambassador Andrew Young initially commended the role of Cuban troops acting as Soviet proxies on the African continent as providing a certain stability.[30]

Nor did Secretary of State Vance or Marshall Shulman favor strong human rights action against the Soviet Union. Vance once told *Time* magazine that Carter and Soviet Premier Leonid Brezhnev held "similar dreams and aspirations about fundamental issues."[31] Shulman classified the Soviet Union merely as an authoritarian regime rather than totalitarian. He considered "counterproductive" efforts "to compel changes in Soviet institutions and practices by frontal demands."[32] Both Vance and Shulman preferred quiet diplomacy as an alternative and believed that the imperative of both sides to reduce the danger of nuclear war through arms control transcended Soviet-American disputes on other issues. Both counseled a usually receptive President Carter to avoid vigorous action that Soviet leaders might regard as provocative or destabilizing.

Depreciating the use of military power in the nuclear age, President Carter strove to achieve large reductions in Soviet and American arsenals, not only by formal arms control treaties, but by exercising unilateral restraint in weapons building in the hope that the Soviet Union would reciprocate. Thus, the Carter administration delayed the development and deployment of the Trident submarine, cruise missiles, and the MX missile; shut down Minuteman ICBM production sites; canceled enhanced radiation weapons, sometimes called neutron bombs; and scrapped the B1 bomber—all programs that Nixon, Ford, and Kissinger had initiated and considered vital to maintaining the Soviet-American strategic balance.[33]

The Soviet Union confounded the Carter administration's optimistic expectations by continuing their military buildup. As the historian Patrick

Glynn ruefully observes, the greatest surge in the Soviet Union's strategic nuclear buildup took place after the SALT I agreement in 1972, which purportedly ushered in a new era of détente. Furthermore, the Carter administration responded only belatedly to Moscow's deployment of a new generation of intermediate-range missiles, the SS-20, which had ignited neutralist sentiment in Western Europe by undermining the credibility of the U.S. nuclear guarantee to its NATO allies. At the urging of Chancellor Helmut Schmidt of West Germany, the Carter administration finally committed the United States in 1979 to the two-track approach, whereby the alliance would deploy land-based cruise missiles and Pershing intermediate-range ballistic missiles (IRBMs) to offset this dangerous Soviet advantage.[34]

Defense spending during the first three years of the Carter presidency reflected the administration's optimistic assessment of the Soviet Union, which was in keeping with Secretary of State Vance's outlook. It was President Ford, not Carter, who first proposed to reverse the 38 percent decline in U.S. military spending that had occurred between 1968 and 1976. By raising defense spending by only a modest 3 percent during the first three years of his administration, Carter actually slashed $57 billion from the six-year program the Ford administration had proposed and projected.[35]

Unlike Presidents Nixon and Ford, who wanted to spend more on defense than Congress was willing to appropriate, President Carter wanted to spend substantially less. He fought hard to thwart congressional efforts to raise defense spending annually by at least 5 percent, a figure that Henry "Scoop" Jackson, Sam Nunn, Ernest Hollings, and other Democratic hawks in the Senate recommended. Almost all the measures that Brzezinski and others invoke as evidence of Carter's greater firmness toward the Soviet Union—the grain embargo, the boycott of the Olympics, approval of a 5.4 percent increase in the FY 1981 defense budget—occurred after the invasion of Afghanistan, in the middle of a difficult fight for reelection in 1980.[36]

Carter's born-again hawkishness during the early stages of the presidential campaign of 1980 contrasts sharply not only with the trajectory of his administration's foreign policy during the first three years, but also with his dovish foreign policy inclinations since leaving office. Throughout the fall presidential campaign, he tried to depict Ronald Reagan as a warmonger whose belligerent policies would provoke a dangerous arms race and possibly war. Like most of his fellow liberal Democrats, Carter vigorously opposed the Reagan administration's defense buildup and his approach toward the Soviet Union. During the Gulf War of 1990–1991, Carter so strongly opposed the use of American force that he unsuccessfully lobbied other members of the Security Council to block a resolution sanctioning it.[37] He has opposed with equal vehemence the Bush Doctrine and the American invasion of Iraq in 2003.[38]

Consider this searing indictment of the decade of détente, issued by Senator Henry M. Jackson, its most formidable congressional foe:

> The theory that has animated American foreign policy toward the Soviet Union over the last decade and under three administrations—that the Soviets, lured by cooperative restraints, would match our concessions and reward restraint—is dangerously and demonstrably false. The Soviet invasion of Afghanistan has shown that détente for us was an illusion, and Soviet "restraint" merely the absence of opportunity. And the political, economic, and military policies developed to fit the theory that we have moved from confrontation with the Soviets to cooperation now lies in ruins. For a decade, the Soviets have watched our businessmen stream to Moscow with technology in hand. . . . The Soviets have seen our diplomats naively put forth proposal after proposal—on the Indian Ocean, on weapons in space, on conventional arms sales, on forces in Europe, on strategic arms control—based on the assumption that the Soviet Union shares our desire for accommodation and a stable world order. They have heard our leaders tell the American people that manifestly unequal and unverifiable treaties are equal and verifiable to us. They have seen us stand by idly as their Cuban surrogates have marched over Africa bearing Russian arms and exploiting the instability of fledgling Third World governments. . . . They have listened as we called their combat brigade in Cuba unacceptable one week and acceptable the next. They have heard very little from us as their Vietnamese surrogates have pressed into Laos, into Cambodia, and threatened the border of Thailand. What must the Kremlin think of us?[39]

By 1980 the prestige of American power had declined to its lowest point since before World War II. The Carter administration's botched Iran rescue mission of April 24 symbolized that decline. It was the height of folly to undertake a mission to rescue the hostages in Iran with just eight helicopters when such a mission required at least six to be operational (a mission such as this would need at least twelve—eighteen would be better— to get six). The plan called for flying the helicopters to a remote desert site where cargo planes would refuel them and transfer assault teams before they moved several hundred more miles closer to a secret base in Tehran. The administration arrived at the arbitrary number eight as a compromise between Brzezinski's staunch advocacy of the mission and Vance's categorical opposition. When three of the helicopters experienced mechanical difficulties, the president aborted the mission on the commander's recommendation. Eight men died during the evacuation when an American transport plane and helicopter collided. The president announced the failure of the rescue mission to a stunned nation. Vance resigned in protest because he opposed on principle any use of force to resolve a hostage crisis.[40]

Carter also shared, in large measure, Nixon and Kissinger's pessimism about America's prospects. In his speech during the summer of 1979 after a retreat at Camp David, he admonished the American people to overcome their malaise and learn to accept the declining capacity of America to influence events abroad.[41]

The Reagan Legacy

Ronald Reagan repudiated the policy of détente in any form. Indeed, he proved indispensable to achieving one of the most significant victories ever for the cause of freedom: the defeat of Soviet totalitarianism. He understood more clearly than almost anyone in American politics the evil essence of Soviet communism and how to defeat it. He understood even more clearly than his supporters the vulnerability of the Soviet system to sustained economic, military, moral, and political pressure. His unabashed defense of democratic capitalism and his economic program also succeeded in restoring the nation's prosperity, self-confidence, and capacity for world leadership, badly damaged during the dismal decade of the 1970s.

The personal attributes and world outlook that accounted for Reagan's success as a political leader had their genesis in his early years. The moral clarity he brought to politics arose from his religious upbringing under the guiding hand of his mother and her church, the Disciples of Christ, an optimistic but nonutopian denomination of Protestant Christianity congenial to his sunny disposition. Reagan always operated with a firm and fixed notion of good and evil that was grounded in Judeo-Christian morality. He possessed great faith in the inherent decency of the collective wisdom of the American people, and in the potential for extending freedom, personal liberty, and prosperity.[42] At the same time, he believed that the search for the perfect was the enemy of the good, that, as he put it, "no government schemes are going to perfect man, because living in this world means living with the doctrine of sin." He also did not take freedom for granted. Although optimistic about spreading democracy, he frequently remarked that it was fragile and contingent. Or as he frequently put it: "Freedom is never more than one generation from extinction. We did not pass it to our children in the bloodstream. It must be fought for, protected, and handed on for them to do the same, or one day we will spend our sunset years telling our children and our children's children what it was once like in the United States when men were free."[43]

Reagan also had firm convictions about foreign policy from the start, convictions to which he remained faithful for his entire political career. Even before World War II, he was an outspoken internationalist. He frequently denounced appeasement of Hitler as "suicidal dogma."[44] In the late 1940s he was an unwavering champion of Israel. "No conviction I have ever held," he wrote, "has been stronger than that the United States must ensure the survival of Israel."[45] Reagan said of World War II that "never in the history of man had the issue of right and wrong been so clearly defined, so much so that it makes one question how anyone could have been neutral."[46] Unlike the old Republican right of Senator Robert Taft then and the isolationist Pat Buchanan now, Reagan revered Winston Churchill—the archenemy of appeasement—for doing more than any man "to preserve civilization during its hour of greatest trial."[47]

Reagan thus identified Nazi totalitarianism as one of the two greatest threats to the well-ordered liberty that he dedicated his political career to defending and expanding. After World War II Reagan concluded from his experience as president of the Screen Actors Guild that Soviet totalitarianism posed a threat to freedom as odious and menacing as Nazi Germany had under Hitler. He dedicated much of his political life to defeating rather than accommodating it: "The real fight with this new totalitarianism belongs properly to the forces of liberal democracy, just as did the battle with

Hitler's totalitarianism. There is really no difference except in the cast of characters. On the one hand is our belief that the people can and will decide what is best for themselves and on the other (Communist, Nazi, or Fascist) side is the belief that a few can decide best what is good for the rest."[48]

Ronald Reagan believed that it was the pessimistic proponents of détente, not the American people, who suffered from malaise. In a series of radio addresses and speeches between 1975 and 1979, drafted in his own hand, he formulated and articulated the critical ideas that would dictate his comprehensive strategy for winning the Cold War during his presidency.[49]

First, Reagan considered the Soviet regime a totalitarian state, a malevolent Leninist-driven entity with unlimited aims and ambitions, not a traditional great power, as Nixon and Kissinger considered it, or a defensive one driven to aggression by the arrogance of American power, as the dominant wing of the Democratic Party after 1968 considered it. Like the great Soviet dissidents, Reagan believed that the root cause of Soviet aggression lay in its internal structure, in the nature of its regime and ideology. The Soviet Union would constitute an existential danger to freedom, Reagan emphasized, so long as it was a totalitarian state, so long as a handful of people made the decisions, and so long as there was no public opinion to limit the ambitions and actions of a small totalitarian leadership.[50]

Second, Reagan believed that there were no substitutes for American power to protect vital U.S. interests in geopolitically critical regions. Third, he radiated tremendous confidence in the moral and economic superiority of democratic capitalism. He believed that America's best days lay ahead, that the American economy could compete successfully with any type of regime, so long as the United States curtailed big government, and he unleashed the dynamism of private enterprise by reducing taxes and curtailing regulation. He believed that the United States was potentially much stronger and the Soviet Union much weaker than they appeared—that time was on our side, not theirs. Unlike Nixon, Kissinger, Carter, and a legion of academics impressed by the permanence and stability of the Soviet regime, Reagan believed that the Soviet Union had begun to encounter long-term, fundamental economic trouble that made it highly vulnerable to economic pressure and a sustained military buildup with which Moscow could not ultimately compete.

Fourth, Reagan's outlook on foreign affairs, his conception of the national interest, and his understanding of the means necessary to achieve it derived not from either unalloyed realism or idealism, but from fixed, transcendent principles refracted through the prism of prudence. His staunch support for promoting democracy and unabashed public condemnations of the moral evils of communism put him at odds with realists such as Nixon and Kissinger, who slighted the importance of ideology and conceded the Soviet Union a sphere of influence in Eastern Europe. Reagan's emphasis on the importance of military might, his willingness to employ it, and his belief that conflict was eternally grounded in the ineradicable imperfection of human beings put him at odds with idealists such as President Carter, who neglected these permanent conditions and exaggerated the natural harmony of interests among men and states.

For Ronald Reagan, the duty of the American government to safeguard human rights in the Soviet Union arose from both moral and practical considerations. Nations, especially geopolitically powerful ones, that invoke an expansionist, universalist, militant, and uncompromising ideology to repress their citizens systematically at home are likely to commit or threaten implacable aggression abroad. Yet Reagan also assailed the Carter administration for selectively and counterproductively applying human rights sanctions more vigorously to America's less dangerous, less repressive authoritarian allies than to its more dangerous, more repressive communist adversaries.

These assumptions inspired Reagan's grand strategy during his presidency, a strategy that aimed at defeating rather than just containing or accommodating the Soviet regime. Granted, there are many heroes of the Cold War besides Reagan entitled to acclaim.[51]

There is, to begin with, the Truman administration, which laid out the strategy of vigilant containment during the 1940s. There are Truman's successors and much of the Congress, which implemented it. There are the American people, who willingly sacrificed to support it. There are the heroic dissidents behind the Iron Curtain such as Sakharov, Solzhenitsyn, and Sharansky, who defied Soviet tyranny at great peril to themselves. There is the conservative and neoconservative opposition to détente that had crystallized around Senator Henry "Scoop" Jackson of Washington State, which conferred great legitimacy on Reagan's repudiation of détente and ensured politically that the United States did not lose the Cold War during the 1970s so Ronald Reagan could win it during the 1980s. There is the burgeoning conservative movement, the intellectual godfather of which was William

F. Buckley and his flagship journal, the *National Review*, which shifted the center of gravity of the Republican Party to the South and West, to "Reagan Country," which contributed enormously to his becoming president in the first place.[52] There is the example of British Prime Minister Margaret Thatcher's successful assault on the welfare state in Great Britain during the 1970s, which encouraged Reagan and provided him with an essential collaborator abroad.[53] There is the papacy of the great John Paul II, which vastly magnified Reagan's impact by spreading the complementary message of the dignity of the human person, especially in Eastern Europe in general and in his native Poland.[54]

Yet Ronald Reagan was indispensable. He possessed the unique combination of courage, vision, ability to inspire, and political skills to generate overwhelming pressure on the Soviet Union that gave it no plausible option but to capitulate. President Reagan laid down the gauntlet to the Soviet Union at his first press conference, when he said that Leninist ideology impels the Soviet Union to lie, cheat, and steal to achieve its objective of global domination. In a commencement address in May 1981, he predicted that "the years ahead will be great ones for the country, for the cause of freedom, and for the spread of civilization. The West will not contain communism, it will transcend communism. We will not bother to denounce it, we'll dismiss it as a sad, bizarre chapter in human history whose final pages are now being written."[55]

From start to finish, Ronald Reagan resolutely pursued a policy of vigilant containment and ideological warfare against communism, despite intense opposition at home and abroad. Reagan secured a massive modernization of the American military, doubling the size of the defense budget, badly straining the Soviet economy, and wiping out the military advantage the Soviets had so painstakingly achieved during the 1970s. Facing down skeptics even within his own administration, ignoring potent nuclear freeze movements that had taken to the streets and intimidated many democratic statesmen on both sides of the Atlantic, Reagan succeeded in persuading the NATO alliance to deploy ground-launched cruise missiles and Pershing intermediate-range ballistic missiles to counter the Soviet SS-20 missiles in Europe.[56]

Despite intense diplomatic pressure culminating in the Soviet walkout from arms control talks, President Reagan ultimately succeeded in compelling the Soviet Union to accept his Zero Option as the basis for the

Intermediate-Range Nuclear Force Treaty of 1987, which eliminated an entire category of nuclear weapons. Reversing two decades of arms control theology that derided the practicality and desirability of ballistic missile defense, Reagan launched the Strategic Defense Initiative (SDI). SDI may have failed to convince U.S. skeptics that it could work; nevertheless, Soviet Prime Minister Gorbachev and the Soviet military certainly feared SDI enough to propose unprecedented concessions to eliminate it. Facing down the opposition of his own national security advisor and secretary of state at the Iceland Summit of 1985 and the Reykjavik Summit of 1986, Reagan refused to sacrifice SDI even for Gorbachev's promise of sharp reductions in Soviet arsenals as the quid pro quo. The result of Reagan's perseverance on SDI and his military buildup resulted in a vastly more compliant Soviet Union, which ultimately agreed to accept reductions in their force levels that it had theretofore cavalierly rejected when previous, more conciliatory U.S. administrations proposed them.[57]

Correspondingly, Reagan intensified economic pressure on the Soviet system by cutting American trade and credit to the USSR and collaborating with Saudi Arabia to reduce the price of oil, which deprived the oil-exporting Soviets of desperately needed hard currency; at the same time he supported opposition groups resisting Soviet clients in Asia, Africa, and Latin America (the Reagan Doctrine). President Reagan's National Security Directive 75, which he signed in the summer of 1983 and is no longer secret, defined the object of his grand strategy. He intended to change the Soviet regime, which he identified as the root cause of Soviet aggression.[58] This he sought to achieve by applying unrelenting comprehensive political, economic, ideological, and military pressure on the Soviet regime.

Reagan also envisioned public diplomacy as the key component of his grand strategy. Addressing the British Parliament in June 1982, he forecast the demise of the Soviet Union. "In an ironic sense," Reagan proclaimed, "Karl Marx was right. We are witnessing today a great revolutionary crisis—a crisis where the demands of economic order are colliding directly with the demands of political order. But the crisis is happening not in the free, non-Marxist West, but in the home of Marxism-Leninism, the Soviet Union. What we see here is a political structure that no longer corresponds to its economic base, a society where productive forces are hampered by political ones."[59]

Today these remarks seem prophetic. At the time, however, intellectual elites derided Reagan's remarks as ignorant, belligerent, and morally arrogant. Writing in 1981, the Nobel laureate Paul Samuelson called it "a vulgar mistake to think that most people in Eastern Europe were miserable." In response to Reagan's predictions of the Soviet demise, Columbia University Professor Seweryn Bialer, one of the most eminent Sovietologists of his day, pronounced that "the Soviet Union is not now nor will it be for the next decades in the throes of a true systemic crisis, for it boasts enormous unused reserves of political and social stability that suffice to endure its deepest difficulties." Writing in 1989, Lester Thurow, professor of economics at MIT, assured us that the Soviet Union "was a country whose economic achievements bear comparison with those of the United States."[60]

Ronald Reagan remained undaunted by such criticism. Speaking before the Council of Evangelicals on March 8, 1983, he shocked the foreign policy establishment once more by calling the Soviet Union an evil empire, to the great joy of imprisoned Soviet dissidents such as Natan Sharansky.[61] "Finally," Sharansky wrote, "the leader of the free world has spoken the truth—a truth that burned in each and every one of us."[62]

Those who still deny Reagan his due tend to see Soviet Premier Mikhail Gorbachev as the main hero for ending the Cold War.[63] According to a popular variant of this argument, which Beth Fischer puts forth, Gorbachev induced Reagan largely to abandon the hard-line policies of his first term; this diffused the spiraling cycle of tensions between the United States and the Soviet Union, for which the belligerence of the early Reagan was primarily to blame.[64]

These arguments give Gorbachev too much credit and Reagan not nearly enough. The restoration of American power to which Ronald Reagan contributed so vitally gave the Soviet Union no choice but to take the risk of choosing a reformer such as Gorbachev, who recognized that the Soviet Union could not compete against a rejuvenated, self-confident United States unless it liberalized at home and pursued a more conciliatory policy abroad.

Nor was Gorbachev a true democrat. He aimed only to reform communism, not to abolish it. His regime began to implode under the cumulative effect of decades of U.S. containment of Soviet ambitions, Reagan's confrontational policies, which intensified this external American pressure at a critical moment, and the inherent contradictions of the Soviet regime. Whereas Gorbachev did not intend the breathtaking collapse of communism that his domestic reforms unwittingly unleashed, Ronald Reagan dedicated his political life to achieving this outcome. True, Gorbachev deserves credit for decency, for not resorting to the use of force to reverse the demise of the Soviet empire, as his predecessors likely would have tried to do. Gorbachev's contribution is important, but secondary to that of Ronald Reagan.

When circumstances changed during Reagan's second term, Reagan adjusted his policies, but not the premises underlying them. He responded positively to the changes in the Soviet regime during Gorbachev's tenure. Keep in mind, however, that Gorbachev and the Soviet Union agreed to end the Cold War not on their terms, but on Ronald Reagan's. American pressure on the Soviet regime did not abate at any point during Reagan's presidency, despite his view that Gorbachev was a different type of Soviet leader. Reagan refused to abandon SDI; American defense spending continued to rise, peaking at $302 billion in FY 1988; the United States continued to aid freedom fighters draining Soviet resources—in East Asia, the Middle East, and Latin America. Reagan also kept up the intensity of his moral challenge to the Soviet Union.[65] In June 1987 President Reagan called on Gorbachev to tear down the Berlin Wall, which he derided as the symbol of Soviet totalitarianism.[66] Gorbachev heeded Reagan's call two years later, ending the Cold War, with America triumphant, freedom on the rise, communism in defeat, and the Soviet Union on the brink of dissolution.

By the end of his administration, Ronald Reagan had shifted away from his initial inclinations to back America's right-wing allies unconditionally, as it became apparent in El Salvador, the Philippines, Korea, and Chile that liberal democracy was a plausible alternative to either authoritarianism or communism.[67] Ronald Reagan thus remained faithful to his lifelong vision of not only resisting dangerous tyranny, but extending liberty, prosperity, and the zone of democratic peace.

The Soviet archives have affirmed that Reagan was right: the Soviet Union was an evil, repressive, insatiably expansionist empire driven by an illegitimate regime's implacably hostile, messianic ideology. The Cold War was a moral as well as geopolitical struggle in which the United States was on the right side of history.[68] As Russian President Boris Yeltsin told the U.S. Congress in 1992: "The world can breathe a sigh of relief. The idol of communism, which spread everywhere social strife, animosity, and unparalleled brutality, which instills fear in humanity, has collapsed."[69]

The more conciliatory policies critics proffered as an alternative to Reagan's prolonged rather than hastened the Soviet Union's collapse. The Soviet Union responded to such conciliatory policies, which the Nixon, Ford, and Carter administrations pursued, by intensifying their massive military buildup and brazen interventionism in the underdeveloped world, which culminated in the Soviet invasion of Afghanistan.

Conversely, Reagan's policies of relentlessly exploiting Soviet vulnerabilities helped enormously to convince reluctant Soviet leaders that the Soviet Union could no longer outbuild or outbully the United States. Alexander Bessmertnykh, a former foreign minister of the USSR, and other major ex-Soviet officials cited President Reagan's military buildup and SDI in particular as vital factors hastening the Soviet Union's collapse.[70]

Nor was such a benign or expeditious result inevitable. Reagan promulgated many of his most controversial policies—the Zero Option, the defense buildup, the evil empire speech—in 1982 and 1983 in a hostile political environment: amid severe recession; amid a nuclear freeze movement of international dimensions at the peak of its popularity; amid the doubts of many of his own advisors and "neuralgic hostility" of the preponderance of elite opinion at home and abroad; amid a public approval rating that plunged below 40 percent at its low point. A less courageous president than Ronald Reagan might have abandoned such a bold and visionary course.[71]

America's triumph over Soviet communism ranks as Reagan's greatest legacy. The American victory in the Cold War also depended on the resurgence of American self-confidence and economic power. Reagan rejected liberal Keynesian macroeconomics and traditional Republican fiscal orthodoxy in favor of what is known as supply-side economics, which focuses on the way individuals invest their labor and capital in the market. He gave primacy to cutting taxes, reducing the rate of domestic spending, and slowing the pace of regulation rather than shrinking the size of government or the welfare state.[72]

The downside was a steady growth in deficits, because the growth in federal spending was even more rapid than the significant increases in revenues that Reagan's progrowth tax cuts generated. The much larger upside of "Reaganomics" was the tremendous dynamism in the American economy that continued through the Clinton presidency. Between 1983 and 1988 the American economy grew by one-third, and manufacturing grew by 12 percent after a 10 percent decline in the 1970s. The United States created

18.5 million new jobs in the 1980s, compared to a net increase of zero for Western Europe.[73] The prosperity of the Clinton years largely hinged on the restructuring of the American economy Reaganomics catalyzed during the 1980s and the peace dividend that the end of the Cold War generated.

Ronald Reagan also transformed the image and the agenda of the Republican Party. Thanks largely to Reagan and his legacy, the Republicans have become the party of growth, innovation, optimism, and enterprise rather than the dour and pessimistic budget balancers who had consigned the party to minority status in Congress in previous decades.

One revealing measure of the dominance of Keynesian economics before Ronald Reagan is that the Republican Richard Nixon embraced it in 1971, proclaiming as he imposed wage and price controls that we are all Keynesians now. A true measure of Reagan's enormous influence is that his once-controversial faith in free markets and his belief in the inextricable linkage among capitalism, prosperity, and political freedom have become the conventional wisdom, not just at home but abroad. When President Clinton signed the Welfare Reform Bill of 1996, dismantling the unconditional entitlement that symbolized Great Society liberalism, he, too, proved that even liberal democrats are to some extent Reaganites now. Moreover, the People's Republic of China is an example of how even self-professed Marxists are, in some ways at least, all capitalists now.

Reagan did make his share of serious mistakes. His propensity to delegate and disengage from day-to-day administration of some issues after setting a clear course—a source of great political strength that allowed him to husband his political capital—served him ill in the Iran-Contra scandal, the worst episode of his administration. Although Reagan's geopolitical priorities in the Middle East were sound—preventing either Iraq or Iran from attaining regional hegemony—the implementation of his policies left something to be desired, particularly in the area of terrorism, where his sentiment often got the better of his good judgment.[74] The credibility of Reagan's staunch stand against terror suffered tremendously because of the ill-fated arms-for-hostage deal that culminated in the Iran-Contra scandal. The American intervention in Lebanon in 1982–1983 ended in a debacle. After an American marine barracks in Beirut was blown up, killing 267 Americans, the Reagan administration withdrew precipitously, which damaged American credibility in the Middle East enormously. The American failure in Lebanon was one potent source of the miscalculation of rogue regimes and terrorists, from Saddam's Iraq to al-Qaeda, that the United States was a "great but decadent Satan" too irresolute to fight.

Reagan's tendency to speak in parables—instilled in him by his religious upbringing and by his Hollywood career—sometimes led him to be cavalier with the facts, to the detriment of his credibility. His antigovernment rhetoric, which did not match his more judicious actions, sometimes obliterated a distinction that conservatives ought to make. Conservatives should not yearn for weak government, but rather should advocate strong government that is limited government: strong because it is limited to essential core functions—national defense, justice, public goods such as infrastructure, and the environment—rather than involved in areas in which it does not belong or perform well.

Even so, Reagan's achievements vastly outweigh his mistakes. Ronald Reagan left the towering legacy that the administration of President George W. Bush has sought to emulate.

7

The Bush Doctrine and Iraq
A Sound Application of
a Sound Doctrine

Some conservative critics, such as Patrick Buchanan, Bruce Bartlett, Jonathan Clarke, and Stefan Halper, have accused the neoconservatives and President George W. Bush of betraying the Reagan legacy in foreign affairs.[1] This is false. The foreign and national security policies of President Bush largely reflect not only Ronald Reagan's legacy, but that of other great presidents who prevailed over perilous threats to freedom. Moreover, thoughtful critics of neoconservatism such as Francis Fukuyama also recognize the fundamental affinity between the neoconservatives and Reagan in the realm of foreign affairs:

> Of the two presidents in question [Reagan and Bush], Ronald Reagan in my view more clearly qualifies as a neoconservative. Much as his critics are loath to admit it, Ronald Reagan was an intellectual of sorts: in the first decade of his career, all he had to offer were ideas and arguments about communism and the free market, American values, and the defects of reigning liberal orthodoxy. He also bore a similarity to the City College crowd insofar as he came to anticommunism from the left: he started out as a Democrat and an admirer of Franklin Roosevelt and was a labor leader as president of the Screen Actors Guild. His insights about the nature of

communism seem to have arisen as a result of his struggles with communists or communist sympathizers in Hollywood. . . . He believed firmly that the internal character of regimes defined their external behavior and was initially unwilling to compromise with the Soviet Union because he saw more clearly than most its internal contradictions and weaknesses.[2]

No one speaks more authoritatively on this subject than George Shultz, President Reagan's secretary of state:

I don't know how you define "neoconservatism," but I think it's associated with trying to spread open systems and democracy. I recall President Reagan's Westminster Speech in 1982—that communism would be consigned to "the ash heap of history" and that freedom was the path ahead. And what happened? Between 1980 and 1990, the number of countries that were classified as "free" or "mostly free" increased by about 50 percent. Open political and economic systems have been gaining ground and there is good reason for it. They work better. I don't know whether that is neoconservative or what it is, but I think it's what has been happening. I'm for it. . . . I'm in favor of the vision. Ronald Reagan had a vision.[3]

As Daniel Heninger observes, likewise, neoconservatives did not originate the Bush Doctrine's most controversial tenet—preemption. Shultz himself was the father of that idea during the Reagan administration.[4] "We must reach a consensus in this country," Shultz said in 1984, "that our responses to terrorism should go beyond passive defense to consider active means of prevention and retaliation."[5]

A fundamental affinity exists, too, between the outlooks of Presidents George W. Bush and Ronald Reagan: as happened to President Reagan, critics have lacerated President Bush for his controversial policies. Likewise, as also happened to President Reagan, President Bush's detractors have called him stupid, uninformed, a unilateralist menacing our traditional allies, morally arrogant, a cowboy, and fiscally irresponsible.

Like Reagan with regard to nuclear weapons and strategic defense, President George W. Bush concluded that the events of September 11, 2001, rendered obsolete defensive strategies that assumed our adversaries always calculated risks rationally, especially with the ominous convergence of the proliferation of WMD and the rise of fanatical movements devoted to destroying American freedom. Like Ronald Reagan and Harry Truman with regard to the Soviet Union, and like Franklin Roosevelt with regard to Nazi Germany and imperial Japan, President Bush sought to inject moral clarity into the struggles with our enemies. Like his great predecessors, he defines regime change and the spread of stable, liberal democracy to address the real root cause of aggression as the ultimate goal in the war on terror.

President Bush even echoes President Reagan's very words in making his case for the imperative to spread democracy. Delivering an address to the British Parliament on June 8, 1982, Ronald Reagan declared:

> The objective I propose is quite simple to state: to foster the infrastructure of democracy, the system of a free press, unions, political parties, universities, which allows a people to choose their own way to develop their own culture, to reconcile their own differences through peaceful means. This is not cultural imperialism; it is providing the means for genuine self-determination and protection for diversity. Democracy already flourishes in countries with different cultures and historical experiences. It would be cultural condescension, or worse, to say that any people prefer dictatorship to democracy. Who would voluntarily choose not to have the right to vote, decide to purchase government propaganda handouts instead of independent newspapers, prefer government to worker-controlled unions, opt for land to be owned by the state instead of by those who till it, want government repression of religious liberty, a single political party instead of a free choice, a rigid cultural orthodoxy instead of democratic tolerance and diversity?[6]

Delivering his Second Inaugural Address, President George W. Bush declared:

> America's vital interests and our deepest beliefs are now one. From the day of our Founding, we have proclaimed that every man and woman on this earth has rights, and dignity, and matchless value, because they bear the image of the Maker of Heaven and earth. Across the generations we have proclaimed the imperative of self-

government, because no one is fit to be master, and no one deserves to be slave. Advancing these ideals is the mission that created our Nation. It is the honorable achievement of our fathers. Now it is the urgent requirement of our nation's security, and the calling of our time. So it is the policy of the United States to seek and support the growth of democratic movements and institutions in every nation and culture, with the ultimate goal of ending tyranny in our world.[7]

Presidents Reagan and Bush thus largely agree on first principles of American foreign policy. The differences in the strategic circumstances each faced account for the minor variation that exists in their approach. The existence of the Soviet Union, armed with thousands of nuclear weapons, deprived President Reagan of the same latitude in an era of bipolarity that his successors have enjoyed in a unipolar age, in which American power is preeminent. Virtually all the major figures serving at the upper echelon of the Reagan administration's defense and foreign policy apparatus endorsed President Bush's conduct of and rationale for the war on terror, including the invasion of Iraq.

The Bush Doctrine is indeed a prudential strategy for the post-9/11 world. To be sure, the president has not embraced the strategy of preemption (really prevention) as the norm. This option is just one aspect of a comprehensive strategy that includes building ballistic missile defense, strengthening nonproliferation endeavors, and mounting effective collective diplomatic action when possible. Nevertheless, the president wisely included prevention and preemption (the latter arises when the threat is more imminent) as potential options in the war on terror.

As the lessons of history attest, critics of the president are wrong to object to prevention or preemption categorically. Whether it is prudent to use force preemptively or preventively depends on the interplay of circumstances: the gravity of the danger, the probability of its consummation but for decisive action, the likelihood of the threat's being dealt with successfully by preemptive means, and the availability of other, more plausible, less risky alternatives. The Bush Doctrine constitutes the same type of innovative response to the dynamics and changing conditions of world politics as the belated but necessary abandonment of isolationism during the twentieth century. Facing rogue regimes or terrorists with a dangerous propensity to take enormous risk, a prudent statesmen may have to use decisive force sooner rather than later.

As the lessons of history attest, critics are wrong to object to the Bush Doctrine because it does not defer categorically to the UN Security Council or to multilateralism in any guise as an end in itself. The inability of the UN to operate effectively against powerful aggressors is intrinsic to the institution. The unquenchable hostility of the French to American leadership also precludes unanimous NATO support for any American enterprise outside Europe entailing the vigorous use of force.[8]

As the lessons of history also attest, critics are wrong to deem as arrogant and imprudent President Bush's commitment to spreading democracy to the Middle East. This aspect of the Bush Doctrine is not new; rather, it is tried and true and based on one of the few robust theories of international politics for which there is abundant empirical confirmation: stable, liberal democracies do not go to war with one another. As is consistent with the grand traditions of American diplomacy that World War II and the Cold War vindicated, President Bush also considers regime change a fundamental part of American grand strategy in the war on terror, a war that we did not initiate but our adversaries thrust upon us. As President Bush put it:

> The war we fight today is more than a military conflict; it is the decisive ideological struggle of the twenty-first century. On one side are those who believe in the values of freedom and moderation— the right of all people to speak, and worship, and live in liberty. And on the other side are those driven by the values of tyranny and extremism—the right of a self-appointed few to impose their fanatical views on all the rest. . . . You have seen this kind of enemy before. They're successors to Fascists, to Nazis, to Communists, and other totalitarians of the twentieth century. And history shows what the outcome will be: This war will be difficult; this war will be long; and this war will end in the defeat of the terrorists and totalitarians, and a victory for the cause of freedom and liberty.[9]

Granted, many thoughtful people believe that regime change will fail in the Middle East: that it is too ambitious; that unlike those in Western Europe and Japan after World War II, the conditions there are not propitious for stable, liberal democracy to succeed.[10] Critics of the Bush Doctrine point to the electoral success of the terrorist organization Hamas and the surging violence in Iraq as evidence for the folly of the Bush administration's policy of encouraging democracy in the Middle East. Their argument runs as follows. The United States cannot impose democracy by force; it must wait for it to emerge organically, only when a mature, civil society is in place. Meanwhile, the United States is better off relying on authoritarian dictators such as Mubarak in Egypt, because the real alternatives are terrorism, fundamentalism, and anarchy.[11]

Although these are serious arguments, under current circumstances the case for the Bush approach is more compelling. For one thing, few at the time were optimistic about establishing stable, liberal democracy in Japan or Germany, or throughout a defeated, demoralized Europe confronting a malevolent, powerful, brutal, and insatiably expansionist Soviet Union. Before American occupation after World War II, the only experiences Germany and Japan had with democracy ended badly: the reviled Weimar democracy in Germany between 1918 and 1933, and the not much more highly regarded Taisho democracy in Japan during the 1920s.

Nor are al-Qaeda adherents or the terrorists in Iraq the first homicide bombers the United States has encountered. Imperial Japan employed this gruesome tactic against us formidably during the Second World War. Who, too, would have predicted in 1944, with a Nazi regime still fanatically implementing the "Final Solution" even on the brink of total defeat, that West Germany would emerge as a stable, liberal democracy just four years later, thanks in no small measure to the enlightened but firm use of American military, economic, and political power.

The Marshall Plan and the NATO alliance so pivotal to Western Europe's democratic resurgence came about as responses to conditions in Europe that had deteriorated a full two to three years after the end of World War II. The dispatches of many American foreign policy experts in 1946 and early 1947 brim with pessimism about Europe's prospects and America's purposes.[12]

Many important developments in the Middle East over recent months have contingently confirmed rather than confounded the president's determination to push for regime change and democratization. Witness, in this regard, the Iraqi elections; the drafting of a decent Iraqi constitution; the dismantling of Libya's WMD program; the breakup of the Pakistani A. Q. Khan's nuclear smuggling ring, the largest in history; the end of Syrian tyranny in Lebanon; demonstrations against homicide bombers in Jordan; and mounting demands for reform throughout the region. Though still facing formidable obstacles, those who believe in democracy and civil society are finally emerging as serious actors, thanks in large measure to the American invasion of Iraq. Saad Ibrahim, a democratic activist in Egypt, originally opposed the war, but he changed his mind: "It has unfrozen the Middle East, just as Napoleon's 1798 expedition did. Elections in Iraq force theocrats and autocrats to put democracy on the agenda, even if only to fight against us. Look, neither Napoleon nor President Bush could impregnate the region with political change. But they were able to be the midwives."[13]

If, as even thoughtful critics of the president such as Fareed Zakaria admit, "Iraq, Afghanistan, and perhaps an independent Palestine and a democratic Lebanon are thriving countries with modern political and economic systems, America will be honored and respected—and the talk of anti-American terror will have dissipated considerably." Zakaria is wrong, however, to suggest that the United States will not be significantly better off in the Middle East if these countries remain "more chaotic and troubled," like those in Central Europe.[14] Even this more modest outcome would be a vast improvement, just as Eastern Europe is significantly better off without the Soviet Union, regardless of the region's current troubles.[15] Contrary to the untenable claims of Francis Fukuyama, the United States cannot achieve such benign results merely by relying on a crude historicism, sociology, economics, or other categories of social science. The defeat of radical Ba'athist or Islamist ideologies, menacing to millions in the Middle East and beyond, depends on the decisive use of American power. Or as Fouad Ajami, a professor of Middle Eastern Studies at the School of Advanced International Studies at Johns Hopkins University, incisively put it:

A battle broader than Iraq itself, then, was playing out in the country. There was no need for the United States to apologize to the other Arabs or Iran's theocrats about its presence in Iraq and its aims for that country. The custodians of Arab power, and the vast majority of the political class in the Arab world, never saw or named the terrible cruelties of Iraq under Saddam Hussein. A political culture that averted its gaze from mass graves and worked itself up into self-righteous hysteria had turned its back on political reason.[16]

Keep this in mind, too: critics wrongly assailed Ronald Reagan's demand for democratic regime change in Eastern Europe in the very same terms as those who now criticize President George W. Bush. Democracy has often succeeded in places such as South Korea, India, South Africa, the Philippines, and El Salvador, where many of the purported prerequisites for democracy were wholly or partially lacking.[17] In the Middle East, with the dangerous intersection of radicalism, tyranny, and the spread of WMD, the United States does not have the luxury of waiting for the organic growth of democracy any more than it did with Nazi Germany and imperial Japan. Those who would rely on authoritarian regimes as the bulwark of American foreign policy in the region confuse rigidity for stability: many autocratic regimes such as Saudi Arabia's are neither durable in the long term nor all that reliably moderate. Even in places such as the Palestinian territories, where elections yielded results we justifiably deplore, a brutal and corrupt PLO under Arafat offered no better alternative for peace, provisional justice, or stability. A more decent and responsible leadership will never emerge in Palestine without the necessary if insufficient conditions of elections and transparency. The United States must remain firm and patient until Palestinians renounce at the ballot box the radicalism of either Hamas or Arafat's PLO.[18]

Even if democracy will not succeed swiftly or in all places in the Middle East, promoting it is a more prudential strategy than the alternative of neglecting the real root cause of 9/11 and similarly inspired aggression: the insidious interaction of poverty, brutality, and oppression that spawns secular and religious radicals and rogue regimes implacably hostile to the United States mainly for what it is rather than what it does.

The invasion of Iraq to remove Saddam in March 2003 was necessary and long overdue. Saddam was a symbol of defiance to American power in a region emboldened to defy it, especially after 9/11. Saddam not only had once possessed WMD, but had used them at home and abroad: against Kurds, Shiites, and Iranians. He launched Scud missiles into Israel during the First Gulf War. To the end, Saddam continued to act as if he possessed weapons of mass destruction; every reputable intelligence service shared our assumption that he still possessed them, an error for which Saddam rather than President Bush was to blame. According to the Kay Commission and the Duelfer Report, Saddam never wavered in his determination to reacquire WMD once the UN sanctions (already so porous) inevitably broke down completely. Nor could the United States have prudently relied on the UN inspectors to verify Saddam's compliance with the disarmament resolutions, which the UN lacked the will to enforce. Saddam also exploited the rampantly corrupt UN oil-for-food program to buy off the French, Russians, and Chinese to abet his diabolical plans for developing WMD capability.[19]

For decades Saddam demonstrated a propensity to take enormous risks that rendered inadequate the options of containing or deterring him. He mounted an assassination attempt against an American president, maintained a regime hideous even by the low standards of the Middle East, and routinely assisted homicide bombers on the West Bank of Palestine (if not al-Qaeda directly) by paying the families of such murderers $25,000 per family for blowing up elderly Jews worshiping at a Passover Seder. Saddam also had ample opportunity to save himself and his regime by complying with the UN sanctions, which would have deprived President Bush of the political support necessary to wage a war to remove him.[20] Contrary to the claims of the president's critics, the strategy of containing Iraq had reached the point of diminishing moral and strategic returns. Sanctions imposed monumental suffering on millions of innocent Iraqis without addressing the real root cause of their misery and the source of the danger to Iraq's neighbors: Saddam's odious regime.[21]

In the war on terror, there is simply no substitute for American power and the willingness to use it in collaboration with as many allies as possible and as is compatible with the integrity of the mission. Ponder the lessons of our current predicaments with North Korea and Iran, where negotiations alone have yielded nothing but dissimulation and defiance. This is not to say the United States should use preemptive force against these rogue regimes. Nor should the United States rule out the use of military force against them. The cost of destroying the Iranian WMD program would be greater than in the case of Iraq, the chances of success more remote, the alternatives more plausible, and Iranians perhaps more deterrable. North Korea is not a symbol of defiance to the United States. It is a hideous but dying regime whose extinction we should hasten as much as possible within the bounds of prudence. Nevertheless, the United States is right to aim for regime change in Iran and North Korea as well as Iraq.[22] In the case of Iran, the argument for preemption has become stronger as the Iranian nuclear program has become riper and the Iranian leadership more militant and reckless. Indeed, prudence dictates that the United States ought to pursue regime change in Iran—by vigilant containment if possible but by force if containment fails. The Iranian author Amir Taheri compellingly explains why:

> The Islamic Republic is unlike any of the regimes in its environment, or indeed, anywhere in the world. It is genetically programmed to clash not only with those of its neighbors who do not wish to emulate its political system but also with those powers that all too reasonably regard Khomeinism as a threat to regional stability and world peace. . . . For as long as the Islamic Republic continues to behave as a revolutionary cause, it will be impossible for others, including the United States, to consider it a partner, let alone a friend or an ally. This does not exclude talks, or even periods of relative détente, as happened with the USSR during the Cold War. But just as the Soviet Union remained an enemy of the free world right up until the end, so the Islamic Republic will remain an enemy until it once more becomes a nation-state.[23]

Americans should not minimize the serious difficulties that lie ahead in Iraq or in the war on terror. The United States has lost more than 2,900 lives in the war in Iraq, every one of which is precious. The costs continue to mount. The month of October 2006 was one of the deadliest months for U.S. troops in Iraq. The United States has spent more than $200 billion in the noble attempt to create democracy in Iraq; homicide bombers still blow up innocent Iraqis without remorse. As even its informed supporters have conceded, the Bush administration made some indisputable errors in the implementation of the Bush Doctrine in Iraq: the failure to police the Iraq-Syrian border; "the lack of post-invasion planning; the lack of ground troops; the lack of coordination of oversight; and the lack of electricity."[24] Charles Krauthammer rightly criticizes the administration for mishandling the trial of Saddam Hussein. The United States has allowed Saddam to control the proceedings rather than use them to educate the Iraqi people about the horrors of his regime.[25] Just as the Nuremberg trials enormously bolstered the prospects for democracy in West Germany by exposing the monstrosities of the Nazi regimes, the trial of Saddam could have the same beneficial effect for Iraqi democracy if the Iraqis and their American allies restore order and deny Saddam the capacity to disrupt the proceedings.[26]

The president has reiterated that victory will also take time and persistent effort across many fronts.[27] Iraqis must overcome not only decades of brutal tyranny but Saddam's devastation of the nation, which ravaged its economy, infrastructure, and human capital. The United States and Iraqis face a ruthless enemy in a region with tyrannies such as Syria and Iran actively working to undermine fledgling Iraqi democracy. Many Iraqi Sunni Muslims have yet to come to terms with their unaccustomed role as a minority in a new democracy rather than a pillar of Saddam's Ba'ath Party. The intensity of sectarian violence remains distressingly high, despite the success of the American military in smiting the symbol of the insurgency's fanaticism: the homicidal Abu Musab al-Zarqawi. It will require a long-term, integrated military, economic, and political strategy to prevail over Iraqi terrorism and insurgency.[28] The administration should heed, too, the advice of Willam Kristol and Rich Lowry, stalwart supporters of the Bush Doctrine, that more U.S. troops in Iraq would significantly improve American chances of success.[29]

Yet the United States should not exaggerate the difficulties the Bush administration has faced or underestimate the considerable progress it has achieved. We face a far less dangerous situation now with Saddam gone than we did before; we face a far less dangerous world now than in 1941 or 1961, when two vastly more powerful evil empires menaced us. The first phase of the Iraq War of 2003 went much better than expected; even this more difficult phase, which we should have anticipated better, has been less costly by far than past wars of comparable or even lesser magnitude.[30] For instance, the United States lost more than 4,000 dead pacifying the Philippines between 1898 and 1902—considerably more than the more than 2,900 Americans servicemen killed in Iraq as of the end of October 2006.[31] More than 58,000 American soldiers lost their lives in the Vietnam War, which ended in defeat. Likewise, the tragic loss of American combat lives in Iraq pales in comparison to those in the Civil War (660,000); World War II (450,000); World War I (175,000); and Korea (38,000). Although we have a long way to go, the United States has already accomplished an enormous amount in Iraq, including "the removal of Saddam's tyranny, negotiation of an interim constitution, restoration of full sovereignty, holding of free national elections, drafting of a permanent constitution, ratification of that constitution, introduction of a sound currency, gradual restoration of Iraq's neglected infrastructure, and the ongoing training and equipping of Iraq's security forces."[32] For all the misgivings about the way the administration has handled its policy, even Fareed Zakaria does not consider Iraq a hopeless cause that should be abandoned. Zakaria chides antiwar critics that the old order in Iraq rested on fear and terror. He depicts the situation in Iraq as "stumbling toward nation-building by consent, not brutality" and considers Iraq "as a model for the Middle East.[33]

Dwell on these eloquent words of an Arab merchant, which describe contemporary realities in the Middle East with uncommon clarity and candor:

> The biggest problem . . . is that George Bush opened a can of worms and all of a sudden everybody realized there is no such thing as the Arab world or Moslem world for that matter. With one sweep, he cleared the deck and exposed everyone to the false world they have been living in. A fact that they do not want to recognize and do not want to face. They are scared of the future and fighting to preserve the false world they have been living in. Their dream is to make the U.S. fail.[34]

Critics have judged President Bush on the basis of a utopian standard the world's greatest commanders in chief would have failed to meet. Should we rate Abraham Lincoln poorly and treat him with contempt because of the veritable litany of mistakes, disasters, and poor commanders that made the Civil War the most costly war in our history—exponentially more costly than the war on terror? Have the Bush administration's mistakes and miscalculations reached the level of FDR's and the American military's in World War II—Pearl Harbor, the Philippines, the Kasserine Pass, Tarawa, Anzio, Dresden? Yet no sensible, informed person denies Lincoln or FDR his due rank as being among our greatest commanders in chief. Nor does any sensible, informed person deny Churchill's greatness despite his serious and costly mistakes: the Norway Campaign of 1940; the debacle in Greece in 1940; the sinking of the *Prince of Wales* and the *Repulse;* the fall of Singapore; and his illusions about Italy and Greece constituting the soft underbelly of Hitler's Europe. Nor should we reconsider Truman's justifiably lofty ranking as a foreign policy president because of his administration's monumental failure to anticipate Chinese intervention in the Korean War. It is therefore unfair, unwise, and premature to pronounce President Bush an incompetent commander in chief, given the magnitude of the endeavors the administration has undertaken in response to a clear and gathering danger.[35]

The president also has displayed a firmer grasp of the essentials, specifics, and dynamics of the insurgency than his critics. Consider, for example, the deeply flawed analysis of former ambassador Richard Holbrooke, a leading candidate for secretary of state in any future Democratic administration. In a widely read editorial in the *Washington Post* that represents the conventional wisdom among the president's detractors, Holbrooke assails the president's policies as "a muddle-headed version of Wilsonianism," which he claims has resulted "in an unprecedented decline in America's position in the world," provoked "dangerous, new anti-American coalitions," and encouraged "a new generation of terrorists." Holbrooke calls instead for "unwinding America's disastrous policy in Iraq," negotiating with the Iranians and the Syrians, and reviving the Clinton administration's policies of active engagement with the Arab-Israeli peace process.[36]

Yet what Holbrooke recommends is merely a reprise of the failed policies of the past, which grim experience has discredited. It was during the Carter administration and its inept handling of the Soviet threat and the hostage crisis with Iran that American international prestige sank to its lowest level since before World War II. It was the Clinton administration that pursued a feckless multilateralism oblivious to the reasonable distinction between democratic India's nuclear weapons program and the nuclear aspirations of rogue regimes such as North Korea, Iran, and Iraq. It was the Clinton administration that ineffectually negotiated an arms control agreement North Korea, which tranquilized the United States as the North Korean nuclear program proceeded unabated. It was the Clinton administration that contributed mightily to the dangerous erosion of American credibility that preceded 9/11: by its failure to follow through on Vice President Al Gore's demand for regime change in Iraq; by its precipitous withdrawal from Somalia after the firefight in Mogadishu; by its halting and ineffective responses to the Khobar Tower bombings and the attack on the USS *Cole;* by its incremental, halfhearted use of force against Saddam when he threw out the UN weapons inspectors in 1998. It was President Clinton who invited Arafat to the White House more than any other leader, on the premise that Arafat had abandoned his goal of eliminating Israel—a premise that Dennis Ross, President Clinton's chief negotiator for the so-called Israeli-Palestinian peace process, has repudiated.[37] It was the Clinton administration that stumbled badly in dealing with Serbian aggression in Bosnia and Kosovo until it belatedly and momentarily came to its senses and bypassed rather than deferred to the United Nations. It was the Clinton administration, according to former Secretary of State Madeleine Albright, that systemically slighted the salience of religion and regime type in world politics. It was the Clinton administration that insisted that the Balkans crisis, the Israeli-Palestinian conflict, the al-Qaeda bombings of the U.S. embassy had nothing to do with religion.[38]

It is President Bush who recognizes that negotiating with these rogue regimes will yield only illusions on our side and defiance on theirs. It is President Bush who recognizes the futility of negotiating with Hamas until it abandons its goal of eradicating Israel. It is President Bush who recognizes that the United States must prevail in Iraq lest the blow to American prestige that Holbrooke rightly worries about becomes a reality. It is President Bush who recognizes that the real root cause of the war on terror: the culture of tyranny and oppression that has spawned and sustained an unsavory coalition of Islamo-fascists, jihadists, and secular radicals who identify American freedom as their mortal enemy. It is President Bush who recognizes the imperative of democratic regime change in the Middle East to address this root cause of the conflict.

President Bush is also wiser than his conservative critic George F. Will, who has embraced the unrealistic realism of Brent Scowcroft and James Baker III, which Will so insightfully repudiated during the 1970s when stalwartly opposing détente as Richard Nixon, Gerald Ford, Henry Kissinger, and Jimmy Carter conceived it. What Will strives to achieve—stability in the Middle East—is a dangerous illusion when the real root cause of the war on terror, which is our adversaries' regime types and noxious ideologies, is not addressed.[39] It inspires much less confidence in this writer than it does in Will that James Baker III is chairing the Iraq Study Group. Throughout his political career, Baker has proved to be a superior tactician but an unrealistic realist in the realm of foreign policy who has underestimated the significance of regime type and ideology in the realm of foreign affairs. Baker's own account of his tenure as secretary of state starkly reveals that his vaunted realism blinded him to the full dimensions of the Soviet threat during the Cold War, the robustness of the democratic peace, and the primary responsibility that Palestinian intransigence, rooted in a culture of tyranny, bears for the Arab-Israeli conflict.[40] The president and the nation should reject any of the commission's recommendations to repudiate the Bush Doctrine's pivotal goal of bringing more freedom to people of the Middle East.[41]

Nor, contrary to the conventional wisdom, did the administration err in disbanding the Iraqi army and purging it of Ba'athist elements after the initial phase of the war concluded with the liberation of Baghdad. Keeping the army intact would have made a difficult situation much worse. Imagine the insurgency the United States would face if Sunni Ba'athists still controlled the armed forces responsible for murdering hundreds of thousands of Shiites and Kurds, who collectively constitute the vast majority of the Iraqi population.[42]

Also, critics who focus on the cost of the Bush administration's actions have slighted the cost of inaction. How would American allies, adversaries, and those on the fence have reacted had the Bush administration remained paralyzed in the UN with Saddam still in defiance, flouting seventeen UN resolutions? Felicitously, President Bush rendered these hypothetical questions. Nor can the United States prudently afford to set an arbitrary deadline for the withdrawal of coalition forces. Leaving Iraq too soon risks repeating the catastrophic mistakes of the United States' withdrawing from Europe precipitously after World War I and leaving Saddam in power after the First Gulf War. It would signal to terrorists, tyrants, and rejectionists that the United States lacks the will to prevail. British Prime Minister Tony Blair put it best:

> Today's worldwide struggle against terrorists is not a clash between civilizations. It is a clash about civilization. It is the age-old battle between progress and reaction, between those who embrace and see opportunity in the modern world and those who reject its existence. Critics of intervention in Iraq and Afghanistan advocate a view which sees the world as not without challenge, but basically calm, with a few nasty things lurking in deep waters, which is best to avoid. That stance amounts to a doctrine of benign inactivity. . . . The failure to construct a common global policy based on common values would risk chaos threatening our stability—economic and political—through letting extremism, conflict, and injustice go unchecked. Terrorist violence springs from deeply embedded

ideological roots. Today in well over 30 or 40 countries, terrorists are plotting action loosely linked with this ideology. The struggle against terrorism in Madrid or London or Paris is the same as the struggle against terrorist acts of Hezbollah in Lebanon, or the Islamic Jihad in Palestine or rejectionist groups in Iraq. . . . The fundamental battle is not just a fight against Islamic extremism, but a battle about modernity, about helping unite Islam and democracy. It is a battle of values and progress, and therefore, it is one we must win.[43]

Victory in Iraq is a vital national interest for the United States in waging the war on terror. It will make America safer and stronger by removing a dangerous tyranny, keep terrorists on the run by depriving them of the sanctuary of a rogue regime, and embolden the forces of democratic reform in a region that sorely needs freedom to address the real root cause of terror. Conversely, failure in Iraq would undermine the credibility of American power in the eyes of our friends and enemies, destabilize the entire Middle East, vindicate the brutal tactics of our adversaries, and hence invite more dangerous attacks on the United States and its allies. Courageously defying the prevailing sentiment within his party, Senator Joseph Lieberman, Democrat from Connecticut, found much cause for optimism after his trip to Iraq:

It is a war between 27 million and 10,000; 27 million Iraqis who want to live lives of opportunity and prosperity and roughly 10,000 terrorists who are either Saddam's remnant or Iraqi Islamist extremists or al-Qaeda foreign fighters who know their wretched cause will fail if Iraq becomes free and modern. The terrorists are intent on stopping this by instigating civil war that will produce the chaos that will allow Iraq to replace Afghanistan as the base for fanatical war-making. We are fighting on the side of 27 million because the outcome of the war is critically important to the security and freedom of America. If the terrorists win, they will be emboldened to strike us directly again and to further undermine the growing stability and progress of the Lebanese who have risen up in proud self-determination after the Hariri assassination to eject their Syrian occupiers (the Syrian and Iranian-backed Hezbollah militias should be next), and the Kuwaitis, Egyptians, and Saudis who have taken steps to open up their governments more broadly to the people. In my meeting with the thoughtful prime minister of Iraq, Ibrahim al-Jaafari, he declared with justifiable pride that his country now has the most open, democratic political system in the Arab world. He is right.[44]

Critics of the Bush Doctrine exaggerate likewise the damage the war in Iraq has inflicted on American alliances and underestimate the diplomatic and military costs of inaction. Our problem with some of our NATO allies, particularly France, is deep and structural, and it long predated the Iraq War. Actually, the diplomatic controversy with Europe over Iraq may work in the long run to improve America's overall diplomatic and political situation: the United States not only bolstered its credibility by eradicating Saddam's tyranny, but exposed to the new Europe—Eastern Europe and our traditional British allies—the depth of French antipathy to the very existence of American power and France's delusional obsession with undermining it at every turn. Ultimately, most of Europe will recoil from France's agenda of weakening a United States that continues to underwrite Europe's freedom and prosperity.

Even on the Arab-Israeli conflict, historically one of the most serious issues of contention between the United States and Europe, European opinion has begun tentatively to move in President Bush's direction. Finally, Prime Minister Ariel Sharon has begun to receive at least grudging respect from European leaders for the Israeli withdrawal from Gaza and for his contributions to the peace process in a manner that defied their expectations. Great Britain's foreign Secretary Jack Straw lauds Sharon as "a towering figure, not only in Israel but in the whole region." Sharon's efforts to achieve a settlement of the Palestinian-Israeli dispute "has earned him huge respect across the world," according to Straw.[45]

Europe's recent experiences with Islamic terrorism and fanaticism—the train bombings in Madrid in 2004, murdering 191 people; the subway bombings in London in 2005, murdering 52 more; the recent victory of the militant Hamas in the Palestinian territory; ferocious Islamic riots over the publication of a mere cartoon in the Danish press—have perhaps begun to dispel the illusions of even the French about the desirability and possibility of appeasing terrorism. "We are not at the point where we would use measures Israel does, but we understand them better," conceded François Géré, president of the French Institute for Strategic Analysis.[46]

The most plausible objection to the Bush Doctrine is that it establishes a dangerous precedent. There are, however, in the United States already formidable constraints to the abuse of preemption in the form of the separation of powers and public accountability. These constraints also operated with great effect in the debate leading up to the American invasion of Iraq in March 2003. Contrary to the assertions of critics, the United States did not rush to war against Saddam; it resorted to this option only after more than a year of extensive discussion at home and abroad, and only after more than a decade of Saddam's brazen defiance.[47] As a practical matter, no president can resort to the preventive or preemptive use of force cavalierly. Nevertheless, other nations in different circumstances may not calculate so prudently. We cannot evade but must acknowledge this danger, attempt to minimize it by making reasonable distinctions, and strive to create an international environment that discourages the unjust, precipitous resort to prevention or preemption.

Conclusion

Beyond the War on Terror

Elsewhere President Bush's foreign policy has largely conformed to the tenets of moral democratic realism. The Bush administration has enjoyed good relations with Russia, despite serious differences. The president has cooperated with Russian President Vladimir Putin when possible, but he has pursued an independent course when necessary. Contrary to the dire warnings of the administration's critics, Russia acquiesced to President Bush's abrogation of the ABM Treaty, a necessary if not sufficient condition for devising comprehensive and effective missile defense for the United States to deal with a wide array of potential threats. The administration also helped to foil Russia's attempt to subvert the "Orange Revolution" in Ukraine. Putin heavy-handedly backed Viktor Yanukovych, an authoritarian in his own mold, in the Ukrainian presidential elections of 2004. Emboldened by American and Western European diplomatic pressure on Putin, thousands of Ukrainians wearing orange, the trademark color of Viktor Yushchenko, Yanukovych's Western-oriented opponent, refused to accept the results of a flawed and corrupt election that declared Yanukovych the winner. Consequently, Yushchenko became president in December 2004, in defiance of Putin's ineffectual protests.[1]

None of this adversely affected Soviet-American collaboration in intelligence gathering in the war on terror or in devising a scheme that reduces the danger of loose nuclear weapons from the former Soviet Union getting into the wrong hands. Nevertheless, the antidemocratic trend in Russia over the past five years is disturbing. Although Russia today is not a full-blown dictatorship and Putin still wants good, stable relations with the

West, his rule has significantly weakened Russian democratic institutions. The United States will find an autocratic Russia more difficult to deal with on a wide array of issues, including Iran, though it doubtless will remain much less dangerous and malevolent than the Soviet Union.

The current trajectory of Russian energy policy is a case in point. As Daniel Twining warns presciently, President Putin is "methodically consolidating state control over Russia's energy industry and deploying Russia's energy resources as a tool of international statecraft." Russian officials reasserted state control over their economy in general and energy resources in particular as a way of making Russia a great power. The United States and Western Europe must take heed of the danger in making themselves increasingly dependent on an autocratic Russia that Twining chillingly depicts as using "energy as a geopolitical weapon" to make Russia a great power again.[2] As James Goldgeier and Michael McFaul therefore wisely recommend, the United States has a moral and geopolitical interest in encouraging the forces of democracy in Russia to the extent our limited leverage there allows it.[3] Russia is now neither an eternal rival nor automatic foe of the West, but "a major outside player," according to Dmitri Trenin.[4]

The most significant challenges to President Bush and his successors will arise in East Asia. From the standpoint of traditional geopolitical criteria, this region is replacing Europe as the world's paramount center of power.[5] This trend will likely continue well into the twenty-first century. The need for a strong American presence is even more compelling in East Asia than in Europe. Liberal democracy in East Asia is more fragile and less widespread than it is in Europe. East Asia also lacks regional organizations, such as the European Economic Community, capable of promoting economic cooperation or ameliorating serious conflicts of interests. It is the world's fastest growing region not only economically, but also militarily.

If winning the war against terror remains the most immediate priority for American foreign policy, then constructively managing the rise of China looms as the largest priority for the near future. Geopolitically, the United States has a vital interest in preventing any single hostile power from dominating East Asia. A dynamic but still authoritarian China growing at an annual rate of more than 9 percent may develop the capability and perhaps already harbor the ambition to attain such dominance. China's ultimate path will have a critical effect on world politics.

The range of opinion on how to deal with China spans a more narrow spectrum than most fundamental debates over American foreign policy. Consensus exists on the need to retain a strong American presence in East Asia. Unlike Western Europe, where the zone of democratic peace was buttressed by strong regional institutions, East Asia remains a highly competitive, fractious, and ideologically diverse region. Nor are there adequate regional substitutes for American power to forge an effective balancing coalition should China embark on an expansionist course. Even the combination of India and Japan could not suffice, in its own right, to contain Chinese power.

Consensus also exists that trade with China is largely desirable. Even those most wary of Chinese ambitions distinguish between the effects of engagement with China and the failed policy of détente with the Soviet Union, which rested on many of the same premises but operated in less felicitous circumstances. Engagement with the Soviet Union failed because it was a totalitarian state with no private sector. In these circumstances, Western trade and credits subsidized the very Soviet military apparatus so menacing to the United States and ameliorated the pressure for fundamental political reform. Conversely, trade with China could have a more benign result by strengthening and emboldening China's burgeoning private sector. Eventually, China's entrepreneurial middle class may demand commensurate political rights, which could lead to regime change that would tame Chinese ambitions.

Consensus exists, too, that a high level of trade with China is now a necessity as well as a virtue. China's membership in the World Trade Organization (WTO) has deprived the United States of significant leverage to link trade to other aspects of Chinese foreign policy, whether we like it or not. Instead, American statesmen should concentrate their efforts on the more limited but significant goal of constraining the sale of those technologies that could dangerously magnify the threat the Chinese military poses to American vital interests in East Asia. Even here, the United States will encounter resistance from the EU and its own business community.

The most vigorous debate on China revolves around two questions: how much deterring does China prudently require? What configuration should such deterrence prudently take? There are two alternative strategies for addressing these fundamental questions, with hybrids in between. Proponents of engagement believe that China has become a status quo power seeking peace, security, and prosperity, and not hegemony. By fostering trade with China and immersing it in the international system, they further believe that the United States can foster a durable equilibrium in East Asia that is consistent with the national interests of both countries.[6] Liberal proponents of engagement such as President Clinton and realist proponents such as Henry Kissinger disagree about whether the internal characteristics of the Chinese regime affect its external goals and behavior. Unlike the realists, the liberals accept that a more open, democratic China would be a more benign China to its citizens and its neighbors, which they assume is just what engagement will facilitate.[7] President Clinton explained the logic behind his policy of engagement this way: "Will we do more to advance the cause of human rights if China's isolated or if it is engaged in a growing web of political and economic cooperation and contact? I am persuaded that the best path for advancing freedom in China is for the United States to intensify and broaden its engagement with that nation. I believe . . . that there are far more likely to be human-rights advances when it is not under the cloud of annual renewal of Most Favored Nation (MFN)."[8]

What unites liberal and realist proponents of engagement is their fear that excessive belligerence by America could make a needless conflict with China a self-fulfilling prophecy. Consequently, they generally oppose deploying a theater or national missile defense that degrades the Chinese nuclear deterrent, forming a strong democratic alliance system to contain China, or encouraging Taiwanese independence.[9]

Proponents of a more robust policy of containment and deterrence conclude that China strives to displace the United States as the preeminent power in East Asia. Arthur Waldron and Aaron Friedberg nicely sum up the mounting evidence in support of this interpretation: a concerted program of military spying; the large size and broad dimensions of the Chinese military buildup, which includes a push to deploy a blue-water navy (that is, a navy that has deep ocean power-projection capabilities); the impending deployment of a new generation of nuclear missiles capable of striking the continental United States; unrelenting efforts to intimidate Taiwan by words and deeds, including firing ballistic missiles over the island; fomenting anti-Japanese sentiment and opposing Japan's becoming a permanent member of the UN Security Council; seizing the Paracel Islands from Vietnam and the Mischief Reef from the Philippines; extinguishing freedom in Hong Kong; opposing the American alliance with Japan and our military presence in the region; and the PRC's now defining the United States as its paramount strategic enemy.[10]

According to Eric McVaden, a retired U.S. Navy admiral who served as defense attaché in China in the early 1990s, "The Chinese are converting their surface navy into a truly modern anti-ship cruise-missile surface navy. . . . The modernization of their Navy has taken a great leap forward. Their nuclear sub program has taken off like wildfire." China aspires to "become the dominant power in the Western Pacific, to displace the United States back to Hawaii or beyond," according to Richard Fisher Jr., an analyst at the International Assessment and Strategic Center in Washington, D.C.[11] Michael Pillsbury wrote and edited a series of pathbreaking studies warning that the Chinese military harbors ambitions of defeating the American "hegemon" over time and strives to build a military that will eventually serve that end.[12]

China's burgeoning demand for energy is also a serious cause for American concern. The Chinese have employed bilateral trade agreements, aid, and debt relief to win the goodwill of various resource-rich states, even in America's own backyard. According to David Zweig and Bi Jianhai, Beijing's assertive strategy of challenging Washington in the realm of trade and access to energy has made remarkable inroads, venturing into the United States' traditional sphere of influence.[13] China's failed attempt to buy the American oil company Unocal Corporation has justifiably raised the level of apprehension about the ultimate object of this strategy.

John Mearsheimer stands nearly alone among proponents of more robust containment and deterrence in discounting regime type in his somber assessment of the Chinese threat. Like realist proponents of engagement such as Henry Kissinger, he sees no qualitative difference in the realm of foreign policy between a repressive China and a liberal democratic one. Unlike them, he treats China as a menacing adversary bent on hegemony that the United States must thwart.[14]

Most prominent proponents of muscular containment and deterrence consider the nature of the Chinese regime as the root cause of its hegemonic ambitions. Ross Terrill identifies the source of the Chinese imperialism as a "polity" he calls a hybrid of Chinese traditionalism and Western Marxism.[15] Wilhelmine Germany is, according to Arthur Waldron, the best if imperfect parallel for thinking about China: a powerful, aggressive state seeking its place in the sun in a way menacing to the legitimate interests of other great powers, and featuring an authoritarian government pitted against a dynamic society.[16] Terrill, Waldron, Aaron Friedberg, Michael Pillsbury, Constantine Menges, and others who argue along these lines do not discount the possibility of the Chinese regime evolving in a more benign direction. They warn, however, that engagement without robust deterrence will reinforce rather than undermine the current Chinese regime, which seeks to stay in power by substituting for genuine reform a policy of national prestige abroad and repression at home.[17]

A mixed strategy—continuing to engage China economically but containing Chinese military power vigilantly—accords best with the lessons of American diplomacy and with the policy of moral democratic realism. First, regime type matters in East Asia as much as in other areas of the world. As was true in Germany, Japan, and the Soviet Union, regime change in the direction of stable, liberal democracy offers the only permanent solution to the threat China poses. Engagement alone will magnify rather than ameliorate the threat, as was the case with appeasement in Nazi Germany and détente with the Soviet Union. As we saw in Europe after World War II, a democratic alliance system offers the best framework for constraining Chinese ambitions and providing a hedge against a tumultuous transition of the Chinese political system that will occur sooner or later.

The Chinese regime staved off but will inevitably face a fundamental crisis of legitimacy that will arise from the inherent contradiction between sustaining prosperity and maintaining the Communist Party's monopoly on political power. In these circumstances an authoritarian Chinese leadership may find even more enticing the options of provoking dangerous foreign crises and intensifying their bid for hegemony in East Asia, unless the United States and its democratic allies sustain a clear, credible, and capable deterrent to such a dangerous course. Arthur Waldron lays out this chilling but plausible scenario:

> Beijing has carried out none of the difficult reforms Moscow managed more than a dozen years ago, even before the Communist system imploded once and for all. How likely can it be that the People's Republic will expire quietly, with little bloodshed and with a reasonably smooth institutional transition? By contrast, how likely is it that its demise will be accompanied by a violent death-rattle, in the form of massacres and/or flailing-out abroad? That

rival factions will descend into civil war? That the army and se-curity apparatus will attempt to restore order by means of a coup against the party and by installing a regime of repression at home and xenophobia abroad—that is, Chinese fascism?[18]

The analysis of even the most thoughtful advocates of engagement, such as Avery Goldstein, actually makes a better case for the policy conclusions of American hard-liners. Goldstein argues that China's grand strategy aims to sustain a peaceful setting for the country's rise to the ranks of a great power. Even if Goldstein is right for the short term, which is debatable, this approach may reflect China's begrudging accommodation to reality; the Chinese may well pursue a more dangerous agenda once their country's capabilities have expanded to a degree that is commensurate with the grander ambition of supplanting the international order that the United States created and led. The analogy Goldstein provides to suggest China is a status quo power—Bismarck's Germany—offers little reassurance. Even if Goldstein is right that Bismarck envisaged Germany as a permanent, satisfied power, an interpretation that is dubious, his successors could not and would not sustain that policy. The authoritarian, illiberal nature of the German regime inclined it to a revisionism incompatible with the legitimate interests of the other major powers in Europe, and World War I ensued.[19] What Goldstein's analogy really suggests is the inherently contingent and unstable commitment of rising, powerful, authoritarian regimes to the status quo—even in the best of times.[20] Robert Sutter rightly worries that China's "peaceful rise" is merely a tactic rather than a permanent strategy.[21]

Japan and India constitute the foundation of an American-led alliance in East Asia. Events in the region since September 11, 2001, have belied the claims of President Bush's critics that the Bush Doctrine undermined American alliances. On the contrary, the United States strengthened its already strong alliance with Japan, one based on shared democratic values, a well-justified alarm about North Korea's nuclear ambitions, and a complementary perception of the imperative of channeling China's dynamism in a constructive direction through a combination of economic engagement and military containment.[22]

The war on terror has actually accelerated the evolution of the emerging strategic partnership between the United States and democratic India.

With the possible exception of Israel, no other country in the world is as pro-American as India. Correspondingly, Fareed Zakaria observes, Americans also find India understandable: "They are puzzled and disturbed by the impenetrable decision-making elites like the Chinese Politburo or the Iranian Council of Guardians. A quarrelsome democracy that keeps moving backward, forward, and sideways—that they know. Take the current situation on nuclear issues. Americans watch what is going on in New Delhi, with people inside the government who are opposed to the nuclear deal leaking negative stories to the media, political opponents using the issue to score points, true ideological opponents being utterly implacable—and all this seems very familiar. Similar things happen every day in Washington."[23]

Unlike some of our European allies, India shares with the United States a compelling interest in dealing with the two major challenges of the early twenty-first century: preventing China from dominating East Asia and defeating radical Islam, which also menaces the Indian state. No nation has lost more to terrorism over the past fifteen years than India. No nation, besides the United States and Great Britain, has a greater incentive or determination to prevail over Islamic extremism than India. The bombings of Bombay's commuter trains in July 2006, killing at least 183 people and wounding more than 660, underscore the danger Islamic terror poses to India and our common interests with the Indian government in combating it. Few nations are more sympathetic to the Bush administration's belief that the promotion of democracy and freedom in the Islamic world is necessary to address the root cause of aggression than democratic India. Or as Robert D. Blackwill, America's ambassador to India between 2001 and 2003, instructively put it:

> Think first of the vital national interests of the United States: prosecuting the global War on Terror and reducing the staying power and effectiveness of the jihadi killers; preventing the spread of weapons of mass destruction including to terrorist groups; dealing with the rise of Chinese power; ensuring a reliable supply of energy from the Persian Gulf; and keeping the global economy on track. Now consider the key countries of the world. Which shares with us these vital national interests and a willingness to do something about threats to these interests—in an unambiguous way, over the long term—for their own reasons? India may lead the list.[24]

India is a potentially powerful as well as philosophically congenial ally for the United States. India, the world's fourth-largest economy, will soon surpass Japan as the third largest. What also bodes well for Indian-American relations is that free enterprise and the entrepreneur have propelled the rise of Indian power, often despite the state.[25] The Bush administration prudently has committed the United States to helping India become a great power, a goal consistent with the global implications of the Bush Doctrine and with the ethical and geopolitical logic of moral democratic realism.[26] The Bush administration has recently taken a major step in this direction by accepting the reality of India's nuclear weapons program and agreeing to provide India with civilian nuclear technology. As Robert Kagan rightly observes, those who oppose this deal on the grounds that it creates a dangerous double standard damaging to the cause of nonproliferation miss the larger point: a U.S. "double standard for India makes strategic, diplomatic, ideological, and political sense."[27] Another concrete step the United States should take immediately is to support India's and Japan's permanent membership on the UN Security Council, in accordance with their emerging great-power status. "A rising India will be difficult at times," predicts C. Raja Mojan, "but it will act broadly to defend and promote the many interests it shares with Washington."[28]

Militarily, the United States must maintain its ability to project conventional air and naval power anywhere in the western Pacific. This means building national and theater missile defense to ensure that China does not develop the capacity to deter the American deterrent. This means monitoring the Chinese military buildup closely and maintaining unassailable military superiority, lest China develop the capacity to neutralize current American advantages so crucial for the credibility of American deterrence in East Asia. This means preventing China from imposing its will on democratic Taiwan by force, or by indirectly intimidating it into reunification. Whether Taiwan becomes independent or ultimately decides to unite with a decent, open, democratic China remains a question. Nevertheless, appeasement of an authoritarian China at democratic Taiwan's expense would yield nothing but moral and geopolitical disaster, which a preponderance of American power and the will to maintain it can avert.[29]

Finally, American grand strategy should have as its ultimate goal for China "political liberalization leading to true democracy." For, as Constantine Menges has warned us, peace with an authoritarian communist regime will never be secure. The United States should dauntlessly encourage peaceful progress in the observance of human rights, the preservation and deepening of political democracy, and the emergence of political pluralism leading to political democracy in China.[30]

Moral democratic realism offers no panacea for American foreign policy. Neither perfect nor perpetual peace will ever exist. War and strife will still occur. Dangerous threats will still arise. Events in international politics will continue to defy even the best-laid plans and the most reasonable expectations. In international politics, justice even in the best of times remains more imperfect and contingent than in well-ordered domestic regimes. There is always a devil lurking around the corner in international relations, no matter how tranquil things seem to be. Geopolitical criteria will continue to impose wrenching trade-offs between the desirable and possible.

Yet the lessons of history offer grounds for cautious optimism: moral democratic realism offers a more compelling framework for American grand strategy than the alternatives. It incorporates the importance of fixed principles of Judeo-Christian ethics and regime type without slighting the equally important imperatives of power and geopolitics. It transcends the unrealistic realism of realists, who underestimate the possibility for provisional justice, and the dangerous illusions of unalloyed idealists, who underrate the obstacles to achieving it. It can facilitate expanding the democratic zone of peace, minimizing the number and gravity of threats the United States faces. It can facilitate the defeat of such threats at the lowest possible cost and risk when—inevitably—even the most robust deterrent fails. We would be remiss to strive either for more or for less than that.

Epilogue

As the book goes to press, the war in Iraq has entered a pivotal phase. American forces in Iraq experienced a terrible October and November 2006; combat deaths and sectarian violence increased significantly. The situation has deteriorated seriously even in the weeks since I submitted the final revisions for chapter 7 of this book, where I defended President Bush's decision to invade Iraq. I still do. Nevertheless, we cannot continue on our present course, which has no clear measure of victory or means to achieve it. As the noted military analyst and historian Fred Kagan observes, the United States must decide whether the pain of trying to succeed is greater than the catastrophic consequences of defeat. The government of Prime Minister Nouri al-Maliki lacks the will and the vision to forge a cross-sectarian coalition of moderate Shiites, Kurds, and those Sunnis who recognize that the alternative to a parliamentary regime is unbridled Shiite domination at their expense.[1] We will lose in Iraq, and much elsewhere in the Middle East, unless the administration decides to stay and win, which will require at least 50,000 more troops, their first object being the securing of Baghdad and key cities and towns in the Sunni Triangle.[2] None of the alternatives—withdrawal; gradual or complete redeployment of American troops; accelerating the transfer of responsibility to the Iraqi army; engaging Syria and Iran; or any combination thereof—will provide even the semblance of a decent interval for staving off a defeat that will embolden our adversaries and result in the slaughter of perhaps hundreds of thousands of Iraqis who depend on us.

It is not certain that President Bush is now committed to pursuing a strategy of victory along the lines that Kagan recommends. The smashing Democratic victory in the congressional elections of 2006 is, to some degree at least, a negative referendum on his handling of Iraq.[3] Many thoughtful commentators, such as Fareed Zakaria, have moved from qualified to un-qualified criticism of the president's vision and his strategy for implement-ing it. Henry Kissinger, one of the principal architects of the failed policy of détente, has pronounced the war in Iraq unwinnable.[4] Even some neo-conservatives who were prominent advocates of the war—Richard Perle, Kenneth Adelman, and David Frum—have turned against it.[5]

Worse, President Bush gave his blessing to the establishment of the Baker Commission, which has recommended a veiled but phased with-drawal from Iraq that will yield nothing but disaster for Iraqis and a dangerous erosion of American credibility. The commission's recommen-dations to negotiate with Syria and Iran merely reprise the unrealistic real-ism emblematic of James Baker's entire diplomatic career. During the elder Bush's administration, Secretary of State Baker favored engaging Saddam Hussein in the name of stability right up until the Iraqi invasion of Kuwait dispelled that illusion. He has relentlessly and wrongly placed the blame for the Arab-Israeli conflict on a decent and democratic Israel rather than on a thuggish and corrupt PLO bent on Israel's elimination—a position that one of his chief negotiators, Dennis Ross, has demolished in his authoritative account of Israeli–PLO peace negotiations since Oslo. Also during the first Bush administration, Baker and his fellow unrealistic realist, National Se-curity Advisor Brent Scowcroft, repudiated Ronald Reagan's greatest legacy by fatuously opposing the breakup of the Soviet Union in the name of sta-bility. This tandem also favored accommodating rather than standing firm against the dictators of the People's Republic of China.[6] Contrary to the claims of the Baker Commission, attempts to engage rogue regimes such as Iran and Syria will prove no less futile than they have in the past. Likewise, Baker's preferred strategy of propitiating Palestinian radicalism at Israel's expense will not succeed in staving off the dangerous intersection of tyr-anny and radicalism that is the root cause of World War IV.

Nor does the president's choice of Robert Gates to replace Donald Rumsfeld as secretary of Defense bode well for anyone who believes the United States should prevail in Iraq. Like James Baker, Gates, a close con-fidant of President George Herbert Walker Bush, comes from the realist wing of the Republican Party, which has consistently failed to appreciate the critical importance of regime type, democratic regime change, and the ideological dimension of international relations.

Beware of veiled and not-so-veiled calls for an exit strategy. As Mark Steyn wrote:

> For a serious power, the correct answer to "What is an exit strategy" is: There isn't one; and there shouldn't be one, and it's a dumb expression. The more polite response came in the President's second inaugural speech: "The survival of liberty in our land depends increasingly on the survival of liberty in other lands. . . . The British went into India without an exit strategy, stayed for generations, and midwifed the world's most populous democracy and a key U.S. ally in the years ahead." Which looks like the smarter approach now? Those American conservatives—the realpolitik crowd—who scorn "nation-building" ought to reflect on what the Indian subcontinent would look like if the British had been similarly skeptical: today it might well be another Araby—a crazy quilt of authoritarian sultantates [sic], Hindu and Muslim, punctuated by thug dictatorships following Baath-type local variations on Fascism or Marxism.[7]

I have not yet lost hope that the president will remain faithful to the Bush Doctrine. Despite the formidable and sobering difficulties American forces have encountered in their efforts to create a free and democratic Iraq, the United States still has a chance to achieve a decent outcome if it does not snatch defeat from the jaws of an attainable victory by withdrawing too soon. We should celebrate, in particular, the Iraqi court's felicitous decision to hang Saddam Hussein for his war crimes. The elimination of Saddam once and for all is a necessary condition for the emergence of an Iraq that is not a menace to its people or its neighbors.

I have much greater confidence that the general principles of the Bush Doctrine will endure as a guide for American foreign policy no matter what happens in Iraq, just as the lacerating controversies over the Korean War, the Vietnam War, and détente did not invalidate the strategy of vigilant containment that contributed so mightily to winning the Cold War. There are deep practical and historical reasons for this confidence. Eventually, the gathering danger of Iran and North Korea, the global aspirations of the dictators in Beijing, and the neo-authoritarian revival of Putin's Russia will reveal the grave deficiencies of any of the vaunted alternatives to the Bush Doctrine, whether they are the unrealistic realism of neo- and classical realists, isolationism, or liberal multilateralism. What is novel about the Bush Doctrine—explicitly including preemption in the repertoire of possible options—is necessary in light of the dangerous convergence of radicalism, tyranny, and WMD. What is familiar about the Bush Doctrine—a commitment to democratic regime change as a war aim to address the real root cause of aggression against the United States—represents one of the most successful and noble traditions of American grand strategy since Franklin Roosevelt.

For all the problems we face in Iraq, the Bush Doctrine has presciently diagnosed the danger we face and prescribed the remedy for it. Senator John McCain seems to recognize that, even if others do not.[8] May President Bush and his successors have the foresight to persevere with the best practicable grand strategy consistent with American ideals and self-interest, rightly understood. Our security, and the security of much of the free world, depend on it.

The National Security Strategy of the United States of America, September 2002

Overview of America's International Strategy

The United States possesses unprecedented—and unequaled—strength and influence in the world. Sustained by faith in the principles of liberty, and the value of a free society, this position comes with unparalleled responsibilities, obligations, and opportunity. The great strength of this nation must be used to promote a balance of power that favors freedom.

For most of the twentieth century, the world was divided by a great struggle over ideas: destructive totalitarian visions versus freedom and equality.

That great struggle is over. The militant visions of class, nation, and race which promised utopia and delivered misery have been defeated and discredited. America is now threatened less by conquering states than we are by failing ones. We are menaced less by fleets and armies than by catastrophic technologies in the hands of the embittered few. We must defeat these threats to our Nation, allies, and friends.

This is also a time of opportunity for America. We will work to translate this moment of influence into decades of peace, prosperity, and liberty. The U.S. national security strategy will be based on a distinctly American internationalism that reflects the union of our values and our national interests. The aim of this strategy is to help make the world not just safer but better. Our goals on the path to progress are clear: political and economic freedom, peaceful relations with other states, and respect for human dignity.

And this path is not America's alone. It is open to all.

To achieve these goals, the United States will:

- champion aspirations for human dignity;
- strengthen alliances to defeat global terrorism and work to prevent attacks against us and our friends;
- work with others to defuse regional conflicts;
- prevent our enemies from threatening us, our allies, and our friends, with weapons of mass destruction;
- ignite a new era of global economic growth through free markets and free trade;
- expand the circle of development by opening societies and building the infrastructure of democracy;
- develop agendas for cooperative action with other main centers of global power; and
- transform America's national security institutions to meet the challenges and opportunities of the twenty-first century.

Champion Aspirations for Human Dignity

In pursuit of our goals, our first imperative is to clarify what we stand for: the United States must defend liberty and justice because these principles are right and true for all people everywhere. No nation owns these aspirations, and no nation is exempt from them. Fathers and mothers in all societies want their children to be educated and to live free from poverty and violence. No people on earth yearn to be oppressed, aspire to servitude, or eagerly await the midnight knock of the secret police.

America must stand firmly for the nonnegotiable demands of human dignity: the rule of law; limits on the absolute power of the state; free speech; freedom of worship; equal justice; respect for women; religious and ethnic tolerance; and respect for private property.

These demands can be met in many ways. America's constitution has served us well. Many other nations, with different histories and cultures, facing different circumstances, have successfully incorporated these core principles into their own systems of governance. History has not been kind to those nations which ignored or flouted the rights and aspirations of their people.

America's experience as a great multi-ethnic democracy affirms our conviction that people of many heritages and faiths can live and prosper in peace. Our own history is a long struggle to live up to our ideals. But even in our worst moments, the principles enshrined in the Declaration of Independence were there to guide us. As a result, America is not just a stronger, but is a freer and more just society.

Today, these ideals are a lifeline to lonely defenders of liberty. And when openings arrive, we can encourage change—as we did in central and eastern Europe between 1989 and 1991, or in Belgrade in 2000. When we see democratic processes take hold among our friends in Taiwan or in the Republic of Korea, and see elected leaders replace generals in Latin America and Africa, we see examples of how authoritarian systems can evolve, marrying local history and traditions with the principles we all cherish.

Embodying lessons from our past and using the opportunity we have today, the national security strategy of the United States must start from these core beliefs and look outward for possibilities to expand liberty.

Our principles will guide our government's decisions about international cooperation, the character of our foreign assistance, and the allocation of resources. They will guide our actions and our words in international bodies.

We will:

- speak out honestly about violations of the nonnegotiable demands of human dignity using our voice and vote in international institutions to advance freedom;
- use our foreign aid to promote freedom and support those who struggle non-violently for it, ensuring that nations moving toward democracy are rewarded for the steps they take;
- make freedom and the development of democratic institutions key themes in our bilateral relations, seeking solidarity and cooperation from other democracies while we press governments that deny human rights to move toward a better future; and
- take special efforts to promote freedom of religion and conscience and defend it from encroachment by repressive governments.

We will champion the cause of human dignity and oppose those who resist it.

Strengthen Alliances to Defeat Global Terrorism and Work to Prevent Attacks Against Us and Our Friends

The United States of America is fighting a war against terrorists of global reach. The enemy is not a single political regime or person or religion or ideology. The enemy is terrorism—premeditated, politically motivated violence perpetrated against innocents.

In many regions, legitimate grievances prevent the emergence of a lasting peace. Such grievances deserve to be, and must be, addressed within a political process. But no cause justifies terror. The United States will make no concessions to terrorist demands and strike no deals with them. We make no distinction between terrorists and those who knowingly harbor or provide aid to them.

The struggle against global terrorism is different from any other war in our history. It will be fought on many fronts against a particularly elusive enemy over an extended period of time. Progress will come through the persistent accumulation of successes—some seen, some unseen.

Today our enemies have seen the results of what civilized nations can, and will, do against regimes that harbor, support, and use terrorism to achieve their political goals. Afghanistan has been liberated; coalition forces continue to hunt down the Taliban and al-Qaida. But it is not only this battlefield on which we will engage terrorists. Thousands of trained terrorists remain at large with cells in North America, South America, Europe, Africa, the Middle East, and across Asia.

Our priority will be first to disrupt and destroy terrorist organizations of global reach and attack their leadership; command, control, and communications; material support; and finances. This will have a disabling effect upon the terrorists' ability to plan and operate.

We will continue to encourage our regional partners to take up a coordinated effort that isolates the terrorists. Once the regional campaign localizes the threat to a particular state, we will help ensure the state has the military, law enforcement, political, and financial tools necessary to finish the task.

The United States will continue to work with our allies to disrupt the financing of terrorism. We will identify and block the sources of funding for terrorism, freeze the assets of terrorists and those who support them, deny terrorists access to the international financial system, protect legitimate charities from being abused by terrorists, and prevent the movement of terrorists' assets through alternative financial networks.

However, this campaign need not be sequential to be effective, the cumulative effect across all regions will help achieve the results we seek.

We will disrupt and destroy terrorist organizations by:

- direct and continuous action using all the elements of national and international power. Our immediate focus will be those terrorist organizations of global reach and any terrorist or state sponsor of terrorism which attempts to gain or use weapons of mass destruction (WMD) or their precursors;
- defending the United States, the American people, and our interests at home and abroad by identifying and destroying the threat before it reaches our borders. While the United States will constantly strive to enlist the support of the international community, we will not hesitate to act alone, if necessary, to exercise our right of self-defense by acting preemptively against such terrorists, to prevent them from doing harm against our people and our country; and

- denying further sponsorship, support, and sanctuary to terrorists by convincing or compelling states to accept their sovereign responsibilities.

We will also wage a war of ideas to win the battle against international terrorism. This includes:

- using the full influence of the United States, and working closely with allies and friends, to make clear that all acts of terrorism are illegitimate so that terrorism will be viewed in the same light as slavery, piracy, or genocide: behavior that no respectable government can condone or support and all must oppose;
- supporting moderate and modern government, especially in the Muslim world, to ensure that the conditions and ideologies that promote terrorism do not find fertile ground in any nation;
- diminishing the underlying conditions that spawn terrorism by enlisting the international community to focus its efforts and resources on areas most at risk; and
- using effective public diplomacy to promote the free flow of information and ideas to kindle the hopes and aspirations of freedom of those in societies ruled by the sponsors of global terrorism.

While we recognize that our best defense is a good offense, we are also strengthening America's homeland security to protect against and deter attack.

This Administration has proposed the largest government reorganization since the Truman Administration created the National Security Council and the Department of Defense. Centered on a new Department of Homeland Security and including a new unified military command and a fundamental reordering of the FBI, our comprehensive plan to secure the homeland encompasses every level of government and the cooperation of the public and the private sector.

This strategy will turn adversity into opportunity. For example, emergency management systems will be better able to cope not just with terrorism but with all hazards. Our medical system will be strengthened to manage not just bioterror, but all infectious diseases and mass-casualty dangers. Our border controls will not just stop terrorists, but improve the efficient movement of legitimate traffic.

While our focus is protecting America, we know that to defeat terrorism in today's globalized world we need support from our allies and friends. Wherever possible, the United States will rely on regional organizations and state powers to meet their obligations to fight terrorism. Where governments find the fight against terrorism beyond their capacities, we will match their willpower and their resources with whatever help we and our allies can provide.

As we pursue the terrorists in Afghanistan, we will continue to work with international organizations such as the United Nations, as well as non-governmental organizations, and other countries to provide the humanitarian, political, economic, and security assistance necessary to rebuild Afghanistan so that it will never again abuse its people, threaten its neighbors, and provide a haven for terrorists.

In the war against global terrorism, we will never forget that we are ultimately fighting for our democratic values and way of life. Freedom and fear are at war, and there will be no quick or easy end to this conflict. In leading the campaign against terrorism, we are forging new, productive international relationships and redefining existing ones in ways that meet the challenges of the twenty-first century.

Work with Others to Defuse Regional Conflicts

Concerned nations must remain actively engaged in critical regional disputes to avoid explosive escalation and minimize human suffering. In an increasingly interconnected world, regional crisis can strain our alliances, rekindle rivalries among the major powers, and create horrifying affronts to human dignity. When violence erupts and states falter, the United States will work with friends and partners to alleviate suffering and restore stability.

No doctrine can anticipate every circumstance in which U.S. action—direct or indirect—is warranted. We have finite political, economic, and military resources to meet our global priorities. The United States will approach each case with these strategic principles in mind:

- The United States should invest time and resources into building international relationships and institutions that can help manage local crises when they emerge.
- The United States should be realistic about its ability to help those who are unwilling or unready to help themselves. Where and when people are ready to do their part, we will be willing to move decisively.

The Israeli-Palestinian conflict is critical because of the toll of human suffering, because of America's close relationship with the state of Israel and key Arab states, and because of that region's importance to other global priorities of the United States. There can be no peace for either side without freedom for both sides. America stands committed to an independent and democratic Palestine, living beside Israel in peace and security. Like all other people, Palestinians deserve a government that serves their interests and listens to their voices. The United States will continue to encourage all parties to step up to their responsibilities as we seek a just and comprehensive settlement to the conflict.

The United States, the international donor community, and the World Bank stand ready to work with a reformed Palestinian government on economic development, increased humanitarian assistance, and a program to establish, finance, and monitor a truly independent judiciary. If Palestinians embrace democracy, and the rule of law, confront corruption, and firmly reject terror, they can count on American support for the creation of a Palestinian state.

Israel also has a large stake in the success of a democratic Palestine. Permanent occupation threatens Israel's identity and democracy. So the United States continues to challenge Israeli leaders to take concrete steps to support the emergence of a viable, credible Palestinian state. As there is progress towards security, Israel forces need to withdraw fully to positions they held prior to September 28, 2000. And consistent with the recommendations of the Mitchell Committee, Israeli settlement activity in the occupied territories must stop. As violence subsides, freedom of movement should be restored, permitting innocent Palestinians to resume work and normal life. The United States can play a crucial role but, ultimately, lasting peace can only come when Israelis and Palestinians resolve the issues and end the conflict between them.

In South Asia, the United States has also emphasized the need for India and Pakistan to resolve their disputes. This Administration invested time and resources building strong bilateral relations with India and Pakistan. These strong relations then gave us leverage to play a constructive role when tensions in the region became acute. With Pakistan, our bilateral relations have been bolstered by Pakistan's choice to join the war against terror and move toward building a more open and tolerant society. The Administration sees India's potential to become one of the great democratic powers of the twenty-first century and has worked hard to transform our relationship accordingly. Our involvement in this regional dispute, building on earlier investments in bilateral relations, looks first to concrete steps by India and Pakistan that can help defuse military confrontation.

Indonesia took courageous steps to create a working democracy and respect for the rule of law. By tolerating ethnic minorities, respecting the rule of law, and accepting open markets, Indonesia may be able to employ the engine of opportunity that has helped lift some of its neighbors out of poverty and desperation. It is the initiative by Indonesia that allows U.S. assistance to make a difference.

In the Western Hemisphere we have formed flexible coalitions with countries that share our priorities, particularly Mexico, Brazil, Canada, Chile, and Colombia. Together we will promote a truly democratic hemisphere where our integration advances security, prosperity, opportunity, and hope. We will work with regional institutions, such as the Summit of the Americas process, the Organization of American States (OAS), and the Defense Ministerial of the Americas for the benefit of the entire hemisphere.

Parts of Latin America confront regional conflict, especially arising from the violence of drug cartels and their accomplices. This conflict and unrestrained narcotics trafficking could imperil the health and security of the United States. Therefore we have developed an active strategy to help the Andean nations adjust their economies, enforce their laws, defeat terrorist organizations, and cut off the supply of drugs, while—as important—we work to reduce the demand for drugs in our own country.

In Colombia, we recognize the link between terrorist and extremist groups that challenge the security of the state and drug trafficking activities that help finance the operations of such groups. We are working to help Colombia defend its democratic institutions and defeat illegal armed groups of both the left and right by extending effective sovereignty over the entire national territory and provide basic security to the Colombian people.

In Africa, promise and opportunity sit side by side with disease, war, and desperate poverty. This threatens both a core value of the United States—preserving human dignity—and our strategic priority—combating global terror. American interests and American principles, therefore, lead in the same direction: we will work with others for an African continent that lives in liberty, peace, and growing prosperity. Together with our European allies, we must help strengthen Africa's fragile states, help build indigenous capability to secure porous borders, and help build up the law enforcement and intelligence infrastructure to deny havens for terrorists.

An ever more lethal environment exists in Africa as local civil wars spread beyond borders to create regional war zones. Forming coalitions of the willing and cooperative security arrangements are key to confronting these emerging transnational threats.

Africa's great size and diversity requires a security strategy that focuses on bilateral engagement and builds coalitions of the willing. This Administration will focus on three interlocking strategies for the region:

- countries with major impact on their neighborhood such as South Africa, Nigeria, Kenya, and Ethiopia are anchors for regional engagement and require focused attention;
- coordination with European allies and international institutions is essential for constructive conflict mediation and successful peace operations; and
- Africa's capable reforming states and sub-regional organizations must be strengthened as the primary means to address transnational threats on a sustained basis.

Ultimately the path of political and economic freedom presents the surest route to progress in sub-Saharan Africa, where most wars are conflicts over material resources and political access often tragically waged on the basis of ethnic and religious difference. The transition to the African Union with its stated commitment to good governance and a common responsibility for democratic political systems offers opportunities to strengthen democracy on the continent.

Prevent Our Enemies from Threatening Us, Our Allies, and Our Friends with Weapons of Mass Destruction

The nature of the Cold War threat required the United States—with our allies and friends—to emphasize deterrence of the enemy's use of force, producing a grim strategy of mutual assured destruction. With the collapse of the Soviet Union and the end of the Cold War, our security environment has undergone profound transformation.

Having moved from confrontation to cooperation as the hallmark of our relationship with Russia, the dividends are evident: an end to the balance of terror that divided us; an historic reduction in the nuclear arsenals on both sides; and cooperation in areas such as counterterrorism and missile defense that until recently were inconceivable.

But new deadly challenges have emerged from rogue states and terrorists. None of these contemporary threats rival the sheer destructive power that was arrayed against us by the Soviet Union. However, the nature and motivations of these new adversaries, their determination to obtain destructive powers hitherto available only to the world's strongest states, and the greater likelihood that they will use weapons of mass destruction against us, make today's security environment more complex and dangerous.

In the 1990s we witnessed the emergence of a small number of rogue states that, while different in important ways, share a number of attributes. These states:

- brutalize their own people and squander their national resources for the personal gain of the rulers;
- display no regard for international law, threaten their neighbors, and callously violate international treaties to which they are party;
- are determined to acquire weapons of mass destruction, along with other advanced military technology, to be used as threats or offensively to achieve the aggressive designs of these regimes;
- sponsor terrorism around the globe; and
- reject basic human values and hate the United States and everything for which it stands.

At the time of the Gulf War, we acquired irrefutable proof that Iraq's designs were not limited to the chemical weapons it had used against Iran and its own people, but also extended to the acquisition of nuclear weapons and biological agents. In the past decade North Korea has become the world's principal purveyor of ballistic missiles, and has tested increasingly capable missiles while developing its own WMD arsenal. Other rogue regimes seek nuclear, biological, and chemical weapons as well. These states' pursuit of, and global trade in, such weapons has become a looming threat to all nations.

We must be prepared to stop rogue states and their terrorist clients before they are able to threaten or use weapons of mass destruction against the United States and our allies and friends. Our response must take full advantage of strengthened alliances, the establishment of new partnerships with former adversaries, innovation in the use of military forces, modern technologies, including the development of an effective missile defense system, and increased emphasis on intelligence collection and analysis.

Our comprehensive strategy to combat WMD includes:

- *Proactive counterproliferation efforts.* We must deter and defend against the threat before it is unleashed. We must ensure that key capabilities—detection, active and passive defenses, and counterforce capabilities—are integrated into our defense transformation and our homeland security systems. Counterproliferation must also be integrated into the doctrine, training, and equipping of our forces and those of our allies to ensure that we can prevail in any conflict with WMD-armed adversaries.
- *Strengthened nonproliferation efforts to prevent rogue states and terrorists from acquiring the materials, technologies, and expertise necessary for weapons of mass destruction.* We will enhance diplomacy, arms control, multilateral export controls, and threat reduction assistance that impede states and terrorists seeking WMD, and when necessary, interdict enabling technologies and materials. We will continue to build coalitions to support these efforts, encouraging their increased political and financial support for nonproliferation and threat reduction programs. The recent G-8 agreement to commit up to $20 billion to a global partnership against proliferation marks a major step forward.
- *Effective consequence management to respond to the effects of WMD use, whether by terrorists or hostile states.* Minimizing the effects of WMD use against our people will help deter those who possess such weapons and dissuade those who seek to acquire them by persuading enemies that they cannot attain their desired ends. The United States must also be prepared to respond to the effects of WMD use against our forces abroad, and to help friends and allies if they are attacked.

It has taken almost a decade for us to comprehend the true nature of this new threat. Given the goals of rogue states and terrorists, the United States can no longer solely rely on a reactive posture as we have in the past. The inability to deter a potential attacker, the immediacy of today's threats, and the magnitude of potential harm that could be caused by our adversaries' choice of weapons, do not permit that option. We cannot let our enemies strike first.

- In the Cold War, especially following the Cuban missile crisis, we faced a generally status quo, risk-averse adversary. Deterrence was an effective defense. But deterrence based only upon the threat of retaliation is less likely to work against leaders of rogue states more willing to take risks, gambling with the lives of their people, and the wealth of their nations.
- In the Cold War, weapons of mass destruction were considered weapons of last resort whose use risked the destruction of those who used them. Today, our enemies see weapons of mass destruction as weapons of choice. For rogue states these weapons are tools of intimidation and military aggression against their neighbors. These weapons may also allow these states to attempt to blackmail the United States and our allies to prevent us from deterring or repelling the aggressive behavior of rogue states. Such states also see these weapons as their best means of overcoming the conventional superiority of the United States.
- Traditional concepts of deterrence will not work against a terrorist enemy whose avowed tactics are wanton destruction and the targeting of innocents; whose so-called soldiers seek martyrdom in death and whose most potent protection is statelessness. The overlap between states that sponsor terror and those that pursue WMD compels us to action.

For centuries, international law recognized that nations need not suffer an attack before they can lawfully take action to defend themselves against forces that present an imminent danger of attack. Legal scholars and international jurists often conditioned the legitimacy of preemption on the existence of an imminent threat—most often a visible mobilization of armies, navies, and air forces preparing to attack.

We must adapt the concept of imminent threat to the capabilities and objectives of today's adversaries. Rogue states and terrorists do not seek to attack us using conventional means. They know such attacks would fail. Instead, they rely on acts of terror and, potentially, the use of weapons of mass destruction—weapons that can be easily concealed, delivered covertly, and used without warning.

The targets of these attacks are our military forces and our civilian population, in direct violation of one of the principal norms of the law of warfare. As was demonstrated by the losses on September 11, 2001, mass civilian casualties is the specific objective of terrorists and these losses would be exponentially more severe if terrorists acquired and used weapons of mass destruction.

The United States has long maintained the option of preemptive actions to counter a sufficient threat to our national security. The greater the threat, the greater is the risk of inaction—and the more compelling the case for taking anticipatory action to defend ourselves, even if uncertainty remains as to the time and place of the enemy's attack. To forestall or prevent such hostile acts by our adversaries, the United States will, if necessary, act preemptively.

The United States will not use force in all cases to preempt emerging threats, nor should nations use preemption as a pretext for aggression. Yet in an age where the enemies of civilization openly and actively seek the world's most destructive technologies, the United States cannot remain idle while dangers gather.

We will always proceed deliberately, weighing the consequences of our actions. To support preemptive options, we will:

- build better, more integrated intelligence capabilities to provide timely, accurate information on threats, wherever they may emerge;
- coordinate closely with allies to form a common assessment of the most dangerous threats; and
- continue to transform our military forces to ensure our ability to conduct rapid and precise operations to achieve decisive results.

The purpose of our actions will always be to eliminate a specific threat to the United States or our allies and friends. The reasons for our actions will be clear, the force measured, and the cause just.

Ignite a New Era of Global Economic Growth through Free Markets and Free Trade

A strong world economy enhances our national security by advancing prosperity and freedom in the rest of the world. Economic growth supported by free trade and free markets creates new jobs and higher incomes. It allows people to lift their lives out of poverty, spurs economic and legal reform, and the fight against corruption, and it reinforces the habits of liberty.

We will promote economic growth and economic freedom beyond America's shores. All governments are responsible for creating their own economic policies and responding to their own economic challenges. We will use our economic engagement with other countries to underscore the benefits of policies that generate higher productivity and sustained economic growth, including:

- pro-growth legal and regulatory policies to encourage business investment, innovation, and entrepreneurial activity;
- tax policies—particularly lower marginal tax rates—that improve incentives for work and investment;
- rule of law and intolerance of corruption so that people are confident that they will be able to enjoy the fruits of their economic endeavors;
- strong financial systems that allow capital to be put to its most efficient use;
- sound fiscal policies to support business activity;
- investments in health and education that improve the well-being and skills of the labor force and population as a whole; and
- free trade that provides new avenues for growth and fosters the diffusion of technologies and ideas that increase productivity and opportunity.

The lessons of history are clear: market economies, not command-and-control economies with the heavy hand of government, are the best way to promote prosperity and reduce poverty. Policies that further strengthen market incentives and market institutions are relevant for all economies—industrialized countries, emerging markets, and the developing world.

A return to strong economic growth in Europe and Japan is vital to U.S. national security interests. We want our allies to have strong economies for their own sake, for the sake of the global economy, and for the sake of global security. European efforts to remove structural barriers in their economies are particularly important in this regard, as are Japan's efforts to end deflation and address the problems of non-performing loans in the Japanese banking system. We will continue to use our regular consultations with Japan and our European partners—including through the Group of Seven (G-7)—to discuss policies they are adopting to promote growth in their economies and support higher global economic growth.

Improving stability in emerging markets is also key to global economic growth. International flows of investment capital are needed to expand the productive potential of these economies. These flows allow emerging markets and developing countries to make the investments that raise living standards and reduce poverty. Our long-term objective should be a world in which all countries have investment-grade credit ratings that allow them access to international capital markets and to invest in their future.

We are committed to policies that will help emerging markets achieve access to larger capital flows at lower cost. To this end, we will continue to pursue reforms aimed at reducing uncertainty in financial markets. We will work actively with other countries, the International Monetary Fund (IMF), and the private sector to implement the G-7 Action Plan negotiated earlier this year for preventing financial crises and more effectively resolving them when they occur.

The best way to deal with financial crises is to prevent them from occurring, and we have encouraged the IMF to improve its efforts doing so. We will continue to work with the IMF to streamline the policy conditions for its lending and to focus its lending strategy on achieving economic growth through sound fiscal and monetary policy, exchange rate policy, and financial sector policy.

The concept of "free trade" arose as a moral principle even before it became a pillar of economics. If you can make something that others value, you should be able to sell it to them. If others make something that you value, you should be able to buy it. This is real freedom, the freedom for a person—or a nation—to make a living. To promote free trade, the Unites States has developed a comprehensive strategy:

- *Seize the global initiative.* The new global trade negotiations we helped launch at Doha in November 2001 will have an ambitious agenda, especially in agriculture, manufacturing, and services, targeted for completion in 2005. The United States has led the way in completing the accession of China and a democratic Taiwan to the World Trade Organization. We will assist Russia's preparations to join the WTO.
- *Press regional initiatives.* The United States and other democracies in the Western Hemisphere have agreed to create the Free Trade Area of the Americas, targeted for completion in 2005. This year the United States will advocate market-access negotiations with its partners, targeted on agriculture, industrial goods, services, investment, and government procurement. We will also offer more opportunity to the poorest continent, Africa, starting with full use of the preferences allowed in the African Growth and Opportunity Act, and leading to free trade.
- *Move ahead with bilateral free trade agreements.* Building on the free trade agreement with Jordan enacted in 2001, the Administration will work this year to complete free trade agreements with Chile and Singapore. Our aim is to achieve free trade agreements with a mix of developed and developing countries in all regions of the world. Initially, Central America, Southern Africa, Morocco, and Australia will be our principal focal points.
- *Renew the executive-congressional partnership.* Every administration's trade strategy depends on a productive partnership with Congress. After a gap of 8 years, the Administration reestablished majority support in the Congress for trade liberalization by passing Trade Promotion Authority and the other market opening measures for developing countries in the Trade Act of 2002. This Administration will work with Congress to enact new bilateral, regional, and global trade agreements that will be concluded under the recently passed Trade Promotion Authority.

- *Promote the connection between trade and development.* Trade policies can help developing countries strengthen property rights, competition, the rule of law, investment, the spread of knowledge, open societies, the efficient allocation of resources, and regional integration—all leading to growth, opportunity, and confidence in developing countries. The United States is implementing The Africa Growth and Opportunity Act to provide market-access for nearly all goods produced in the 35 countries of sub-Saharan Africa. We will make more use of this act and its equivalent for the Caribbean Basin and continue to work with multilateral and regional institutions to help poorer countries take advantage of these opportunities. Beyond market access, the most important area where trade intersects with poverty is in public health. We will ensure that the WTO intellectual property rules are flexible enough to allow developing nations to gain access to critical medicines for extraordinary dangers like HIV/AIDS, tuberculosis, and malaria.
- *Enforce trade agreements and laws against unfair practices.* Commerce depends on the rule of law; international trade depends on enforceable agreements. Our top priorities are to resolve ongoing disputes with the European Union, Canada, and Mexico and to make a global effort to address new technology, science, and health regulations that needlessly impede farm exports and improved agriculture. Laws against unfair trade practices are often abused, but the international community must be able to address genuine concerns about government subsidies and dumping. International industrial espionage which undermines fair competition must be detected and deterred.
- *Help domestic industries and workers adjust.* There is a sound statutory framework for these transitional safeguards which we have used in the agricultural sector and which we are using this year to help the American steel industry. The benefits of free trade depend upon the enforcement of fair trading practices. These safeguards help ensure that the benefits of free trade do not come at the expense of American workers. Trade adjustment assistance will help workers adapt to the change and dynamism of open markets.
- *Protect the environment and workers.* The United States must foster economic growth in ways that will provide a better life along with widening prosperity. We will incorporate labor and environmental concerns into U.S. trade negotiations, creating a healthy "network" between multilateral environmental agreements with the WTO, and use the International Labor Organization, trade preference programs, and trade talks to improve working conditions in conjunction with freer trade.
- *Enhance energy security.* We will strengthen our own energy security and the shared prosperity of the global economy by working with our allies, trading

partners, and energy producers to expand the sources and types of global energy supplied, especially in the Western Hemisphere, Africa, Central Asia, and the Caspian region. We will also continue to work with our partners to develop cleaner and more energy efficient technologies.

Economic growth should be accompanied by global efforts to stabilize greenhouse gas concentrations associated with this growth, containing them at a level that prevents dangerous human interference with the global climate. Our overall objective is to reduce America's greenhouse gas emissions relative to the size of our economy, cutting such emissions per unit of economic activity by 18 percent over the next 10 years, by the year 2012. Our strategies for attaining this goal will be to:

- remain committed to the basic U.N. Framework Convention for international cooperation;
- obtain agreements with key industries to cut emissions of some of the most potent greenhouse gases and give transferable credits to companies that can show real cuts;
- develop improved standards for measuring and registering emission reductions;
- promote renewable energy production and clean coal technology, as well as nuclear power—which produces no greenhouse gas emissions, while also improving fuel economy for U.S. cars and trucks;
- increase spending on research and new conservation technologies, to a total of $4.5 billion—the largest sum being spent on climate change by any country in the world and a $700 million increase over last year's budget; and
- assist developing countries, especially the major greenhouse gas emitters such as China and India, so that they will have the tools and resources to join this effort and be able to grow along a cleaner and better path.

Expand the Circle of Development by Opening Societies and Building the Infrastructure of Democracy

A world where some live in comfort and plenty, while half of the human race lives on less than $2 a day, is neither just nor stable. Including all of the world's poor in an expanding circle of development—and opportunity—is a moral imperative and one of the top priorities of U.S. international policy.

Decades of massive development assistance have failed to spur economic growth in the poorest countries. Worse, development aid has often served to prop up failed policies, relieving the pressure for reform and perpetuating misery. Results of aid are typically measured in dollars spent by donors, not in the rates of growth and poverty reduction achieved by recipients. These are the indicators of a failed strategy.

Working with other nations, the United States is confronting this failure. We forged a new consensus at the U.N. Conference on Financing for Development in Monterrey that the objectives of assistance—and the strategies to achieve those objectives—must change.

This Administration's goal is to help unleash the productive potential of individuals in all nations. Sustained growth and poverty reduction is impossible without the right national policies. Where governments have implemented real policy changes, we will provide significant new levels of assistance. The United States and other developed countries should set an ambitious and specific target: to double the size of the world's poorest economies within a decade.

The United States Government will pursue these major strategies to achieve this goal:

- *Provide resources to aid countries that have met the challenge of national reform.* We propose a 50 percent increase in the core development assistance given by the United States. While continuing our present programs, including humanitarian assistance based on need alone, these billions of new dollars will form a new Millennium Challenge Account for projects in countries whose governments rule justly, invest in their people, and encourage economic freedom. Governments must fight corruption, respect basic human rights, embrace the rule of law, invest in health care and education, follow responsible economic policies, and enable entrepreneurship. The Millennium Challenge Account will reward countries that have demonstrated real policy change and challenge those that have not to implement reforms.

- *Improve the effectiveness of the World Bank and other development banks in raising living standards.* The United States is committed to a comprehensive reform agenda for making the World Bank and the other multilateral development banks more effective in improving the lives of the world's poor. We have reversed the downward trend in U.S. contributions and proposed an 18 percent increase in the U.S. contributions to the International Development Association (IDA)—the World Bank's fund for the poorest countries—and the African Development Fund. The key to raising living standards and reducing poverty around the world is increasing productivity growth, especially in the poorest countries. We will continue to press the multilateral development banks to focus on activities that increase economic productivity, such as improvements in education, health, rule of law, and private sector development. Every project, every loan, every grant must be judged by how much it will increase productivity growth in developing countries.

- *Insist upon measurable results to ensure that development assistance is actually making a difference in the lives of the world's poor.* When it comes to economic development, what really matters is that more children are getting a better education, more people have access to health care and clean water, or more workers can find jobs to make a better future for their families. We have a moral obligation to measure the success of our development assistance by whether it is delivering results. For this reason, we will continue to demand that our own development assistance as well as assistance from the multilateral development banks has measurable goals and concrete benchmarks for achieving those goals. Thanks to U.S. leadership, the recent IDA replenishment agreement will establish a monitoring and evaluation system that measures recipient countries' progress. For the first time, donors can link a portion of their contributions to IDA to the achievement of actual development results, and part of the U.S. contribution is linked in this way. We will strive to make sure that the World Bank and other multilateral development banks build on this progress so that a focus on results is an integral part of everything that these institutions do.
- *Increase the amount of development assistance that is provided in the form of grants instead of loans.* Greater use of results-based grants is the best way to help poor countries make productive investments, particularly in the social sectors, without saddling them with ever-larger debt burdens. As a result of U.S. leadership, the recent IDA agreement provided for significant increases in grant funding for the poorest countries for education, HIV/AIDS, health, nutrition, water, sanitation, and other human needs. Our goal is to build on that progress by increasing the use of grants at the other multilateral development banks. We will also challenge universities, nonprofits, and the private sector to match government efforts by using grants to support development projects that show results.
- *Open societies to commerce and investment.* Trade and investment are the real engines of economic growth. Even if government aid increases, most money for development must come from trade, domestic capital, and foreign investment. An effective strategy must try to expand these flows as well. Free markets and free trade are key priorities of our national security strategy.
- *Secure public health.* The scale of the public health crisis in poor countries is enormous. In countries afflicted by epidemics and pandemics like HIV/AIDS, malaria, and tuberculosis, growth and development will be threatened until these scourges can be contained. Resources from the developed world are necessary but will be effective only with honest governance, which supports prevention programs and provides effective local infrastructure. The United States has strongly backed the new global fund for HIV/AIDS

organized by U.N. Secretary General Kofi Annan and its focus on combining prevention with a broad strategy for treatment and care. The United States already contributes more than twice as much money to such efforts as the next largest donor. If the global fund demonstrates its promise, we will be ready to give even more.

- *Emphasize education.* Literacy and learning are the foundation of democracy and development. Only about 7 percent of World Bank resources are devoted to education. This proportion should grow. The United States will increase its own funding for education assistance by at least 20 percent with an emphasis on improving basic education and teacher training in Africa. The United States can also bring information technology to these societies, many of whose education systems have been devastated by HIV/AIDS.
- *Continue to aid agricultural development.* New technologies, including biotechnology, have enormous potential to improve crop yields in developing countries while using fewer pesticides and less water. Using sound science, the United States should help bring these benefits to the 800 million people, including 300 million children, who still suffer from hunger and malnutrition.

Develop Agendas for Cooperative Action with the Other Main Centers of Global Powers

America will implement its strategies by organizing coalitions—as broad as practicable—of states able and willing to promote a balance of power that favors freedom. Effective coalition leadership requires clear priorities, an appreciation of others' interests, and consistent consultations among partners with a spirit of humility.

There is little of lasting consequence that the United States can accomplish in the world without the sustained cooperation of its allies and friends in Canada and Europe. Europe is also the seat of two of the strongest and most able international institutions in the world: the North Atlantic Treaty Organization (NATO), which has, since its inception, been the fulcrum of transatlantic and inter-European security, and the European Union (EU), our partner in opening world trade.

The attacks of September 11 were also an attack on NATO, as NATO itself recognized when it invoked its Article V self-defense clause for the first time. NATO's core mission—collective defense of the transatlantic alliance of democracies—remains, but NATO must develop new structures and capabilities to carry out that mission under new circumstances. NATO must build a capability to field, at short notice, highly mobile, specially trained forces whenever they are needed to respond to a threat against any member of the alliance.

The alliance must be able to act wherever our interests are threatened, creating coalitions under NATO's own mandate, as well as contributing to mission-based coalitions. To achieve this, we must:

- expand NATO's membership to those democratic nations willing and able to share the burden of defending and advancing our common interests;
- ensure that the military forces of NATO nations have appropriate combat contributions to make in coalition warfare;
- develop planning processes to enable those contributions to become effective multinational fighting forces;
- take advantage of the technological opportunities and economies of scale in our defense spending to transform NATO military forces so that they dominate potential aggressors and diminish our vulnerabilities;
- streamline and increase the flexibility of command structures to meet new operational demands and the associated requirements of training, integrating, and experimenting with new force configurations; and
- maintain the ability to work and fight together as allies even as we take the necessary steps to transform and modernize our forces.

If NATO succeeds in enacting these changes, the rewards will be a partnership as central to the security and interests of its member states as was the case during the Cold War. We will sustain a common perspective on the threats to our societies and improve our ability to take common action in defense of our nations and their interests. At the same time, we welcome our European allies' efforts to forge a greater foreign policy and defense identity with the EU, and commit ourselves to close consultations to ensure that these developments work with NATO. We cannot afford to lose this opportunity to better prepare the family of transatlantic democracies for the challenges to come.

The attacks of September 11 energized America's Asian alliances. Australia invoked the ANZUS Treaty to declare [that] September 11 was an attack on Australia itself, following that historic decision with the dispatch of some of the world's finest combat forces for Operation Enduring Freedom. Japan and the Republic of Korea provided unprecedented levels of military logistical support within weeks of the terrorist attack. We have deepened cooperation on counterterrorism with our alliance partners in Thailand and the Philippines and received invaluable assistance from close friends like Singapore and New Zealand.

The war against terrorism has proven that America's alliances in Asia not only underpin regional peace and stability, but are flexible and ready to deal with new challenges. To enhance our Asian alliances and friendships, we will:

- look to Japan to continue forging a leading role in regional and global affairs based on our common interests, our common values, and our close defense and diplomatic cooperation;

- work with South Korea to maintain vigilance towards the North while preparing our alliance to make contributions to the broader stability of the region over the longer term;
- build on 50 years of U.S.-Australian alliance cooperation as we continue working together to resolve regional and global problems—as we have so many times from the Battle of the Coral Sea to Tora Bora;
- maintain forces in the region that reflect our commitments to our allies, our requirements, our technological advances, and the strategic environment; and
- build on stability provided by these alliances, as well as with institutions such as ASEAN and the Asia-Pacific Economic Cooperation forum, to develop a mix of regional and bilateral strategies to manage change in this dynamic region.

We are attentive to the possible renewal of old patterns of great power competition. Several potential great powers are now in the midst of internal transition—most importantly Russia, India, and China. In all three cases, recent developments have encouraged our hope that a truly global consensus about basic principles is slowly taking shape.

With Russia, we are already building a new strategic relationship based on a central reality of the twenty-first century: the United States and Russia are no longer strategic adversaries. The Moscow Treaty on Strategic Reductions is emblematic of this new reality and reflects a critical change in Russian thinking that promises to lead to productive, long-term relations with the Euro-Atlantic community and the United States. Russia's top leaders have a realistic assessment of their country's current weakness and the policies—internal and external—needed to reverse those weaknesses. They understand, increasingly, that Cold War approaches do not serve their national interests and that Russian and American strategic interests overlap in many areas.

United States policy seeks to use this turn in Russian thinking to refocus our relationship on emerging and potential common interests and challenges. We are broadening our already extensive cooperation in the global war on terrorism. We are facilitating Russia's entry into the World Trade Organization, without lowering standards for accession, to promote beneficial bilateral trade and investment relations. We have created the NATO-Russia Council with the goal of deepening security cooperation among Russia, our European allies, and ourselves. We will continue to bolster the independence and stability of the states of the former Soviet Union in the belief that a prosperous and stable neighborhood will reinforce Russia's growing commitment to integration into the Euro-Atlantic community.

At the same time, we are realistic about the differences that still divide us from Russia and about the time and effort it will take to build an enduring strategic partnership. Lingering distrust of our motives and policies by key Russian elites slows improvement in our relations. Russia's uneven commitment to the basic values of free-market democracy and dubious record in combating the proliferation of weapons of mass destruction remain matters of great concern. Russia's very weakness limits the opportunities for cooperation. Nevertheless, those opportunities are vastly greater now than in recent years—or even decades.

The United States has undertaken a transformation in its bilateral relationship with India based on a conviction that U.S. interests require a strong relationship with India. We are the two largest democracies, committed to political freedom protected by representative government. India is moving toward greater economic freedom as well. We have a common interest in the free flow of commerce, including through the vital sea lanes of the Indian Ocean. Finally, we share an interest in fighting terrorism and in creating a strategically stable Asia.

Differences remain, including over the development of India's nuclear and missile programs, and the pace of India's economic reforms. But while in the past these concerns may have dominated our thinking about India, today we start with a view of India as a growing world power with which we have common strategic interests. Through a strong partnership with India, we can best address any differences and shape a dynamic future.

The United States relationship with China is an important part of our strategy to promote a stable, peaceful, and prosperous Asia-Pacific region. We welcome the emergence of a strong, peaceful, and prosperous China. The democratic development of China is crucial to that future. Yet, a quarter century after beginning the process of shedding the worst features of the Communist legacy, China's leaders have not yet made the next series of fundamental choices about the character of their state. In pursuing advanced military capabilities that can threaten its neighbors in the Asia-Pacific region, China is following an outdated path that, in the end, will hamper its own pursuit of national greatness. In time, China will find that social and political freedom is the only source of that greatness.

The United States seeks a constructive relationship with a changing China. We already cooperate well where our interests overlap, including the current war on terrorism and in promoting stability on the Korean peninsula. Likewise, we have coordinated on the future of Afghanistan and have initiated a comprehensive dialogue on counterterrorism and similar transitional concerns. Shared health and environmental threats, such as the spread of HIV/AIDS, challenge us to promote jointly the welfare of our citizens.

Addressing these transnational threats will challenge China to become more open with information, promote the development of civil society, and enhance individual human rights. China has begun to take the road to political openness, permitting many personal freedoms and conducting village-level elections, yet remains strongly committed to national one-party rule by the Communist Party. To make that nation truly accountable to its citizen's needs and aspirations, however, much work remains to be done. Only by allowing the Chinese people to think, assemble, and worship freely can China reach its full potential.

Our important trade relationship will benefit from China's entry into the World Trade Organization, which will create more export opportunities and ultimately more jobs for American farmers, workers, and companies. China is our fourth largest trading partner, with over $100 billion in annual two-way trade. The power of market principles and the WTO's requirements for transparency and accountability will advance openness and the rule of law in China to help establish basic protections for commerce and for citizens. There are, however, other areas in which we have profound disagreements. Our commitment to the self-defense of Taiwan under the Taiwan Relations Act is one. Human rights is another. We expect China to adhere to its nonproliferation commitments. We will work to narrow differences where they exist, but not allow them to preclude cooperation where we agree.

The events of September 11, 2001, fundamentally changed the context for relations between the United States and other main centers of global power, and opened vast, new opportunities. With our long-standing allies in Europe and Asia, and with leaders in Russia, India, and China, we must develop active agendas of cooperation lest these relationships become routine and unproductive.

Every agency of the United States Government shares the challenge. We can build fruitful habits of consultation, quiet argument, sober analysis, and common action. In the long-term, these are the practices that will sustain the supremacy of our common principles and keep open the path of progress.

Transform America's National Security Institutions to Meet the Challenges and Opportunities of the Twenty-first Century

The major institutions of American national security were designed in a different era to meet different requirements. All of them must be transformed.

It is time to reaffirm the essential role of American military strength. We must build and maintain our defenses beyond challenge. Our military's highest priority is to defend the United States. To do so effectively, our military must:

- assure our allies and friends;
- dissuade future military competition;

- deter threats against U.S. interests, allies, and friends; and
- decisively defeat any adversary if deterrence fails.

The unparalleled strength of the United States armed forces, and their forward presence, have maintained the peace in some of the world's most strategically vital regions. However, the threats and enemies we must confront have changed, and so must our forces. A military structured to deter massive Cold War-era armies must be transformed to focus more on how an adversary might fight rather than where and when a war might occur. We will channel our energies to overcome a host of operational challenges.

The presence of American forces overseas is one of the most profound symbols of the U.S. commitments to allies and friends. Through our willingness to use force in our own defense and in defense of others, the United States demonstrates its resolve to maintain a balance of power that favors freedom. To contend with uncertainty and to meet the many security challenges we face, the United States will require bases and stations within and beyond Western Europe and Northeast Asia, as well as temporary access arrangements for the long-distance deployment of U.S. forces.

Before the war in Afghanistan, that area was low on the list of major planning contingencies. Yet, in a very short time, we had to operate across the length and breadth of that remote nation, using every branch of the armed forces. We must prepare for more such deployments by developing assets such as advanced remote sensing, long-range precision strike capabilities, and transformed maneuver and expeditionary forces. This broad portfolio of military capabilities must also include the ability to defend the homeland, conduct information operations, ensure U.S. access to distant theaters, and protect critical U.S. infrastructure and assets in outer space.

Innovation within the armed forces will rest on experimentation with new approaches to warfare, strengthening joint operations, exploiting U.S. intelligence advantages, and taking full advantage of science and technology. We must also transform the way the Department of Defense is run, especially in financial management and recruitment and retention. Finally, while maintaining near-term readiness and the ability to fight the war on terrorism, the goal must be to provide the President with a wider range of military options to discourage aggression or any form of coercion against the United States, our allies, and our friends.

We know from history that deterrence can fail; and we know from experience that some enemies cannot be deterred. The United States must and will maintain the capability to defeat any attempt by an enemy—whether a state or non-state actor—to impose its will on the United States, our allies, or our friends. We will maintain the forces sufficient to support our obligations, and to defend freedom.

Our forces will be strong enough to dissuade potential adversaries from pursuing a military build-up in hopes of surpassing, or equaling, the power of the United States.

Intelligence—and how we use it—is our first line of defense against terrorists and the threat posed by hostile states. Designed around the priority of gathering enormous information about a massive, fixed object—the Soviet bloc—the intelligence community is coping with the challenge of following a far more complex and elusive set of targets.

We must transform our intelligence capabilities and build new ones to keep pace with the nature of these threats. Intelligence must be appropriately integrated with our defense and law enforcement systems and coordinated with our allies and friends. We need to protect the capabilities we have so that we do not arm our enemies with the knowledge of how best to surprise us. Those who would harm us also seek the benefit of surprise to limit our prevention and response options and to maximize injury.

We must strengthen intelligence warning and analysis to provide integrated threat assessments for national and homeland security. Since the threats inspired by foreign governments and groups may be conducted inside the United States, we must also ensure the proper fusion of information between intelligence and law enforcement.

Initiatives in this area will include:

- strengthening the authority of the Director of Central Intelligence to lead the development and actions of the Nation's foreign intelligence capabilities;
- establishing a new framework for intelligence warning that provides seamless and integrated warning across the spectrum of threats facing the nation and our allies;
- continuing to develop new methods of collecting information to sustain our intelligence advantage;
- investing in future capabilities while working to protect them through a more vigorous effort to prevent the compromise of intelligence capabilities; and
- collecting intelligence against the terrorist danger across the government with all-source analysis.

As the United States Government relies on the armed forces to defend America's interests, it must rely on diplomacy to interact with other nations. We will ensure that the Department of State receives funding sufficient to ensure the success of American diplomacy. The State Department takes the lead in managing our bilateral relationships with other governments. And in this new era, its people and institutions must be able to interact equally adroitly with non-governmental organizations and international institutions. Officials trained mainly in international politics must also extend their reach to understand complex issues of domestic governance around the world, including public health, education, law enforcement, the judiciary, and public diplomacy.

Our diplomats serve at the front line of complex negotiations, civil wars, and other humanitarian catastrophes. As humanitarian relief requirements are better understood, we must also be able to help build police forces, court systems, and legal codes, local and provincial government institutions, and electoral systems. Effective international cooperation is needed to accomplish these goals, backed by American readiness to play our part.

Just as our diplomatic institutions must adapt so that we can reach out to others, we also need a different and more comprehensive approach to public information efforts that can help people around the world learn about and understand America. The war on terrorism is not a clash of civilizations. It does, however, reveal the clash inside a civilization, a battle for the future of the Muslim world. This is a struggle of ideas and this is an area where America must excel.

We will take the actions necessary to ensure that our efforts to meet our global security commitments and protect Americans are not impaired by the potential for investigations, inquiry, or prosecution by the International Criminal Court (ICC), whose jurisdiction does not extend to Americans and which we do not accept. We will work together with other nations to avoid complications in our military operations and cooperation, through such mechanisms as multilateral and bilateral agreements that will protect U.S. nationals from the ICC. We will implement fully the American Servicemembers Protection Act, whose provisions are intended to ensure and enhance the protection of U.S. personnel and officials.

We will make hard choices in the coming year and beyond to ensure the right level and allocation of government spending on national security. The United States Government must strengthen its defenses to win this war. At home, our most important priority is to protect the homeland for the American people.

Today, the distinction between domestic and foreign affairs is diminishing. In a globalized world, events beyond America's borders have a greater impact inside them. Our society must be open to people, ideas, and goods from across the globe. The characteristics we most cherish—our freedom, our cities, our systems of movement, and modern life—are vulnerable to terrorism. This vulnerability will persist long after we bring to justice those responsible for the September 11 attacks. As time passes, individuals may gain access to means of destruction that until now could be wielded only by armies, fleets, and squadrons. This is a new condition of life. We will adjust to it and thrive—in spite of it.

In exercising our leadership, we will respect the values, judgment, and interests of our friends and partners. Still, we will be prepared to act apart when our interests and unique responsibilities require. When we disagree on particulars, we will explain forthrightly the grounds for our concerns and strive to forge viable alternatives. We will not allow such disagreements to obscure our determination to secure together, with our allies and our friends, our shared fundamental interests and values.

Ultimately, the foundation of American strength is at home. It is in the skills of our people, the dynamism of our economy, and the resilience of our institutions. A diverse, modern society has inherent, ambitious, entrepreneurial energy. Our strength comes from what we do with that energy. That is where our national security begins.

Notes

Introduction

1. G. W. Bush, "Remarks by the President at the 20th Anniversary of the National Endowment for Democracy" (Washington, D.C., November 6, 2003).

2. G. W. Bush, "Remarks at the United States Military Academy" (June 2002).

3. G. W. Bush, "The National Security Strategy of the United States" (March 2006), 1.

4. Alas, a growing number of conservatives and even some neoconservatives have criticized the Bush Doctrine (the latter more on the issue of implementation than on conception). Although these neoconservative critics have a point about some of the shortcomings on the practical side, they betray a lack of proportion and lack of appreciation that politics is reconciling the desirable with the possible. For a nice rebuttal to the conservative critique, see Norman Podhoretz, "Is the Bush Doctrine Dead?" *Commentary* (September 2006): 17–31.

5. See, for example, J. L. Gaddis, *Surprise, Security, and the American Experience* (Cambridge: Harvard University Press, 2004), and W. R. Mead, *Power, Terror, Peace, and War: America's Grand Strategy in a World at Risk* (New York: Alfred A. Knopf, 2004).

6. National Security Council (NSC) 68, "United States Objectives and Programs for National Security" (April 14, 1950), in E. May, ed., *American Cold War Strategy: Interpreting NSC 68* (Boston: Bedford Books of St. Martin's Press, 1993), 26.

7. Thomas Aquinas, *Summa Theologica*, trans. Fathers of the English Dominican Province (Chicago: Encyclopedia Britannica, 1948), 2: 37–41. Aquinas's conception of prudence contrasts sharply with the mere cunning of Machiavelli; see N. Machiavelli, *The Prince*, 2nd ed., trans. H. C. Mansfield (Chicago: University of Chicago Press, 1998), 38.

8. J. Pieper, *The Four Cardinal Virtues* (Notre Dame, Ind.: University of Notre Dame Press, 1966), 10, 18.

9. Aquinas, *Summa Theologica,* 2: 37–41.

10. C. Krauthammer, *Democratic Realism: An American Foreign Policy for a Unipolar World* (Washington, D.C.: AEI Press, 2004).

11. W. Kristol and R. Kagan, "Toward a Neo-Reaganite Foreign Policy," *Foreign Affairs* (July/August 1996): 18–32.

12. G. Weigel, *The Cube and the Cathedral: Europe, America, and Politics without God* (New York: Basic Books, 2005), 99–107.

1. The Imprudence of Isolationism

1. N. Podhoretz, "The War against World War IV," *Commentary* 119, no. 5 (February 2005): 23; C. Krauthammer, "In Defense of Democratic Realism," *National Interest* 77 (Fall 2004): 15–25.

2. E. Rostow, *Toward Managed Peace: The National Security Interests of the United States, 1759 to the Present* (New Haven: Yale University Press, 1993), 53–251.

3. Isolationism comes, of course, in several variations. Eric Nordlinger represents the more liberal and academic tradition of isolationism. See, e.g., E. Nordlinger, *Isolationism Reconfigured: American Foreign Policy for a New Century* (Princeton: Princeton University Press, 1995). Unlike conservative isolationists, Nordlinger believes in promoting democracy and human rights. His policy prescriptions, however, would yield the same disasters as those of conservative isolationists, because he and they overestimate the cost of America's role in the world and the catastrophic consequences of the strategic withdrawal isolationists urge.

4. Buchanan's two major books on American foreign policy are the most deliberate, detailed, and extensive expositions of his views. P. J. Buchanan, *A Republic, Not an Empire: Reclaiming America's Destiny* (Washington, D.C.: Regnery Publishing, 1999); P. J. Buchanan, *Where the Right Went Wrong: How Neoconservatives Subverted the Reagan Revolution and Hijacked the Bush Presidency* (New York: Thomas Dunne Books, 2004).

5. P. Kennedy, *The Rise and Fall of the Great Powers* (1987; rept., New York: Vintage, 1989).

6. For an excellent recent account of the Founders' idealism in the realm of foreign affairs, see B. Bailyn, *To Begin the World Anew: The Genius and Ambiguities of the American Founders* (New York: Alfred A. Knopf, 2003), 60–99.

7. J. Q. Adams, "4th of July Address" (1821).

8. A. DeConde, *A History of American Foreign Policy,* 2nd ed. (New York: Charles Scribner's Sons, 1962), 40–71.

9. G. Washington, "Farewell Address," in M. Spalding and P. J. Garrity, *A Sacred Union of Citizens: George Washington's Farewell Address and the American Character* (Lanham, Md.: Rowman and Littlefield, 1996), 175–88. This book really surpasses Felix Gilbert's work as the definitive interpretation of the Farewell

Address. See also F. Gilbert, *To the Farewell Address: Ideas in Early American Foreign Policy* (Princeton: Princeton University Press, 1961).

10. For an authoritative explanation of the contingent nature of the European balance of power, see E. V. Gulick, *Europe's Classical Balance of Power* (Ithaca: Cornell University Press, 1955).

11. W. S. Churchill, "British Foreign Policy in Europe" (March 1936), in R. R. James, ed., *Winston Churchill: His Complete Speeches, 1897–1963* (London: Chelsea House, 1974), 6: 5694–97.

12. For one of the very best books on the diplomacy of the formative years, see R. W. Tucker and D. C. Hendrickson, *Empire of Liberty: The Statecraft of Thomas Jefferson* (New York: Oxford University Press, 1990). For an excellent account of the Washington administration's diplomacy, see F. McDonald, *The Presidency of George Washington* (Lawrence: University Press of Kansas, 1974), 67–186.

13. S. F. Bemis, *A Diplomatic History of the United States,* 2nd ed. (New York: Henry Holt, 1942), 137.

14. Rostow, *Toward Managed Peace,* 115–23.

15. Quoted in Tucker and Hendrickson, *Empire of Liberty,* 329.

16. For an outstanding new book on American diplomacy during the formative period that is congenial to my interpretation, see Robert Kagan, *Dangerous Nation: America's Place in the World from Its Earliest Days to the Dawn of the Twentieth Century* (New York: Alfred A. Knopf, 2006), esp. 104–29.

17. For an extended account of his theories and policy implications, see H. J. Mackinder, *Democratic Ideals and Reality* (New York: Norton, 1962).

18. For the most respectable revisionist accounts of American entry into World War I, see N. Ferguson, *The Pity of War: Explaining World War I* (New York: Basic Books, 2000), and T. Fleming, *The Illusion of Victory: America in World War I* (New York: Basic Books, 2004).

19. F. Fischer, *Germany's Aims in the First World War* (New York: Norton, 1967); D. Fromkin, *Europe's Last Summer: Who Started the Great War in 1914?* (New York: Alfred A. Knopf, 2004); D. Kagan, *On the Origins of War and the Preservation of Peace* (New York: Doubleday, 1995).

20. M. Howard, "The Great War: Mystery or Error," *National Interest* 64 (Summer 2001): 83.

21. J. M. Cooper Jr., *The Warrior and the Priest: Woodrow Wilson and Theodore Roosevelt* (Cambridge: Belknap Press of Harvard University Press, 1983); H. A. Kissinger, *Diplomacy* (New York: Simon and Schuster, 1994), 29–55.

22. Quoted in R. E. Osgood, *Ideals and Self-Interest in America's Foreign Relations* (Chicago: University of Chicago Press, 1953), 136.

23. For one of the best books on Theodore Roosevelt that is more critical of him than I am here, see Cooper, *The Warrior and the Priest.*

24. Ibid., 151.

25. For the definitive account of the tragedy of the Treaty of Versailles, see M.

MacMillan, *Paris 1919: Six Months That Changed the World* (New York: Random House, 2002). For the two most reliable guides to Wilson's flawed vision, see A. Link, *Wilson the Diplomatist: A Look at His Major Foreign Policies* (Baltimore: Johns Hopkins University Press, 1957), and T. Knock, *To End All Wars: Woodrow Wilson and the Quest for a New World Order* (1992; rept., Princeton: Princeton University Press, 1995).

26. For two recent histories more reputable but no more persuasive than Buchanan's on American entry into World War II, see J. Doenecke, *Storm on the Horizon: The Challenge to American Interventionism, 1939–1941* (Lanham, Md.: Rowman and Littlefield, 2000); T. Fleming, *The New Dealers' War: FDR and the War within World War II* (New York: Basic Books, 2002).

27. A. J. P. Taylor, *The Origins of the Second World War* (1961; rept., New York: Simon and Schuster, 1996).

28. Buchanan, *A Republic, Not an Empire,* 278.

29. Buchanan's flawed assessment of Hitler owes much to Taylor's *Origins of the Second World War.*

30. See, for example, G. Weinberg, *A World at Arms: A Global History of World War II* (New York: Cambridge University Press, 1994), 171–86; I. Kershaw, *Hitler, 1936–1945: Nemesis* (New York: Norton, 2000), 336, 340–43; J. Keegan, "How Hitler Could Have Won the War," in R. Cowley, ed., *What If? The World's Foremost Military Historians Imagine What Might Have Been* (New York: Putnam, 1999), 295–305.

31. For the most compelling critique of FDR from this more plausible perspective, see F. W. Marks III, *Wind over Sand: The Diplomacy of Franklin Roosevelt* (Athens: University of Georgia Press, 1988).

32. For a generally convincing defense of FDR's diplomacy leading up to World War II, see C. Black, *Franklin Delano Roosevelt: Champion of Freedom* (New York: Public Affairs, 2003), 455–680. For two accounts more sympathetic to FDR, see R. Dallek, *Franklin D. Roosevelt and American Foreign Policy, 1932–1945* (New York: Oxford University Press, 1979), and W. F. Kimball, *The Juggler: Franklin Roosevelt as Wartime Statesman* (Princeton: Princeton University Press, 1991).

33. Black, *Franklin Delano Roosevelt,* 180.

34. For the definitive account of how the democracies squandered an enormous material advantage by not fighting sooner rather than later, see W. Murray, *The Change in the European Balance of Power, 1938–1939: The Path to Ruin* (Princeton: Princeton University Press, 1984).

35. Although Mark Stoler goes too far in the other direction, he makes a good case that FDR was a better strategist than his critics recognize. M. Stoler, *Allies and Adversaries: The Joint Chiefs of Staff, the Grand Alliance, and U.S. Strategy in World War II* (Chapel Hill: University of North Carolina Press, 2000). In his memoirs Churchill also exaggerates his support for a cross-channel invasion

even in 1944. See D. Reynolds, *In Command of History: Churchill Fighting and Writing the Second World War* (New York: Random House, 2005).

36. For the German aspect of this strategy, see M. Beschloss, *The Conquerors: Roosevelt, Truman, and the Destruction of Hitler's Germany, 1941–1945* (New York: Simon and Schuster, 2002).

37. A splendid account of Roosevelt's illusions about the Soviet Union and its baleful consequences is in A. Perlmutter, *FDR and Stalin: The Not So Grand Alliance, 1943–1945* (Columbia: University of Missouri Press, 1993).

38. National Security Council (NSC) 68; J. L. Gaddis, *Strategies of Containment* (New York: Oxford University Press, 1982), 25–88.

39. C. E. Wunderlin, *Robert A. Taft: Ideas, Tradition, and Party in U.S. Foreign Policy* (Lanham, Md.: Rowman and Littlefield, 2005), 33–66, 147–72.

40. For a more respectable criticism of the Iraq War from isolationist premises, minus Buchanan's Zionist conspiracy theories, see C. Preble, ed., *Exiting Iraq: Why the United States Must End the Military Occupation and Resume the War against Al Qaeda* (Washington, D.C.: Cato Institute, 2004).

41. Kissinger, *Diplomacy,* 813.

42. Nordlinger, *Isolationism Reconfigured,* 142–59.

43. P. Kennedy, "The Eagle Has Landed," *Financial Times,* February 2, 2002, I, IV.

44. For a splendid analysis of why Europe is unlikely to challenge the United States soon, which also emphasizes the moral dimension of Europe's malaise, see Weigel, *The Cube and the Cathedral.*

45. U.S. Department of Defense, FY 2007, briefing slides, Department of Defense Budget, February 6, 2006, at www.defenselink.mil/news/Feb2006/d200606slides pdf (February 22, 2006).

46. Josef Joffe, *Uberpower: The Imperial Temptation of America* (New York: Norton, 2006), 165–66.

47. D. H. Levy and S. S. Brown, "The Overstretch Myth, or How We Learned to Stop Worrying and Love the Current Account Deficit," *Foreign Affairs* (March/April 2005): 2–3.

2. The Perils of Neorealism

1. Many prominent voices in the debate take hybrid positions. For instance, it is best to classify Richard Haass as a realist/multilateralist. On the one hand, he is intensely skeptical about promoting democratic regime change; on the other, he stresses the importance of multilateralism largely from realist premises. See R. H. Haass, *The Opportunity: America's Moment to Alter History's Course* (New York: Public Affairs, 2005). Similarly, Francis Fukuyama criticizes neoconservatism and embraces multilateralism, but he concedes that the neoconservatives were right about the Cold War and about the organic inability of the United

Nations to operate effectively as the arbiter of international legitimacy on when to use force. See F. Fukuyama, *America at the Crossroads: Democracy, Power, and the Neoconservative Legacy* (New Haven: Yale University Press, 2006).

2. For two decades neorealism has vied with liberal institutionalism as the dominant paradigm for studying international relations. The discussion here focuses on the best work of the three leading scholars of neorealism: K. M. Waltz, *Theory of International Politics* (Reading, Mass.: Addison-Wesley, 1979); S. M. Walt, *The Origins of Alliances* (Ithaca: Cornell University Press, 1987); J. J. Mearsheimer, *The Tragedy of Great Power Politics* (New York: Norton, 2001).

3. S. M. Walt, "Never Say Never: Wishful Thinking on Democracy and War," *Foreign Affairs* (January/February 1999): 146–51; J. Mearsheimer, "Back to the Future: Instability in Europe after the Cold War," *International Security* 15, no. 1 (Summer 1990): 5–56; Waltz, *Theory of International Politics*, 77–78.

4. The tenets of defensive neorealism and their policy implications are articulated nicely in F. Zakaria, "Realism and Domestic Politics," *International Security* 17, no. 1 (Summer 1992): 177–98.

5. Walt, *The Origins of Alliances*, 6, 262–85; S. M. Walt, "The Case for Finite Containment: Analyzing U.S. Grand Strategy," *International Security* 14, no. 1 (Summer 1989): 5–49.

6. See, e.g., S. Van Evera, "The Case against Intervention," *Atlantic Monthly*, July 1990, 72–80; C. Layne, "Why the Gulf War Was Not in the National Interest," *Atlantic Monthly*, July 1991, 54–81.

7. J. J. Mearsheimer, "Guns Won't Win the Afghan War," *New York Times*, November 4, 2001, sec. 4, 13.

8. J. J. Mearsheimer et al., "War with Iraq Is Not in America's National Interest," paid advertisement, *New York Times*, September 26, 2002.

9. J. J. Mearsheimer and S. M. Walt, "An Unnecessary War," *Foreign Policy* (January/February 2003): 51–60.

10. S. M. Walt, *Taming American Power: The Global Response to U.S. Primacy* (New York: Norton, 2005).

11. S. M. Walt, "The Blame Game," *Foreign Policy* 151 (November/December 2005): 45.

12. Walt, *Taming American Power*, 218–47.

13. Ibid., 208–20.

14. R. J. Lieber, "Foreign Policy Realists Are Unrealistic on Iraq," *Chronicle of Higher Education* 49, no. 8 (October 18, 2002): B15; R. J. Lieber, "The Folly of Containment," *Commentary* 115, no. 4 (April 2003): 15–21.

15. Lieber has also made a compelling case for the defense of American primacy in general and the overall approach of the Bush administration in particular. R. J. Lieber, *The American Era: Power and Strategy for the 21st Century* (Cambridge: Cambridge University Press, 2005).

16. Of course, states sometimes overestimate threats as well. See R. Jervis,

Perception and Misperception in International Politics (Princeton: Princeton University Press, 1976). Jervis sees overestimation of threat as more common than I do, particularly among stable, liberal democracies. I argue that stable, liberal democracies have a propensity to underestimate threats in peacetime. For an excellent analysis of this phenomenon with regard to the Nazi threat, see A. Groth, *Democracies against Hitler: Myth, Reality, and Prologue* (Brookfield, Vt.: Ashgate, 1979).

17. S. M. Walt, "Alliances, Threats, and U.S. Grand Strategy: A Reply to Kaufman and Labs," *Security Studies* 2, no. 3 (Spring 1992): 444–82.

18. There is a vast literature demolishing any plausible defense of appeasement. Virtually all of it emphasizes domestic motives, constraints, and misperceptions, as well as external conditions. See, for example, A. L. Rowse, *Appeasement: A Study in Political Decline, 1933–1939* (New York: Norton, 1963), 3–30; M. George, *The Warped Vision: British Foreign Policy, 1933–1939* (Pittsburgh: University of Pittsburgh Press, 1965), 24–41; M. S. Gilbert and R. Gott, *The Appeasers* (Boston: Houghton Mifflin, 1963), 3–25; R. K. Middlemas, *The Strategy of Appeasement: The British Government and Germany, 1937–39* (Chicago: Quadrangle, 1972), 12–19; W. R. Rock, *British Appeasement in the 1930s* (New York: Norton, 1977), 22–84; G. Stewart, *Burying Caesar: The Churchill-Chamberlain Rivalry* (Woodstock, N.Y.: Overlook Press, 2001); M. S. Gilbert, *Winston S. Churchill: The Prophet of Truth, 1922–1939* (Boston: Houghton Mifflin, 1963), 3–25.

19. W. S. Churchill, *The Gathering Storm* (Boston: Houghton Mifflin, 1948), 345–47.

20. Ibid., ix.

21. A. Hanby, *Man of the People: A Life of Harry Truman* (New York: Oxford University Press, 1995).

22. Quoted in R. Conquest, *Reflections on a Ravaged Century* (New York: Norton, 2000), 154.

23. There is a vast literature on the Cold War, divided into three categories. Traditionalist scholars, including this writer, identify implacable Soviet aggressiveness, fueled by an interaction of ideology, the totalitarian nature of the Soviet regime, geopolitics, and the perception of its leaders, as the main cause of the Cold War. Revisionists blame the United States primarily for initiating and perpetuating the Cold War; postrevisionists blame both sides. For examples of traditionalist scholarship, see R. G. Kaufman, *Henry M. Jackson: A Life in Politics* (Seattle: University of Washington Press, 2000); A. B. Ulam, *Expansion and Coexistence: Soviet Foreign Policy, 1917–73*, 2nd ed. (New York: Praeger, 1974); A. B. Ulam, *The Communists: The Story of Power and Lost Illusions* (New York: Charles Scribner's Sons, 1992); R. Pipes, *Survival Is Not Enough: Soviet Realities and America's Future* (New York: Simon and Schuster, 1984); M. Malia, *The Soviet Tragedy: A History of Socialism in Russia, 1917–1991* (New York: Free Press, 1994); R. Conquest, *Reflections on a Ravaged Century*. A long and compelling

literature also links totalitarian domestic structures to aggressive foreign policies, especially for powerful states. For the classics on this subject, see H. Arendt, *The Origins of Totalitarianism* (New York: Harcourt, Brace, 1951); C. J. Friedrich and Z. K. Brzezinski, *Totalitarian Dictatorship and Autocracy* (Cambridge: Harvard University Press, 1956); J. L. Talmon, *The Origins of Totalitarian Democracy* (New York: Praeger, 1960); R. Pipes, *Russia under the Bolshevik Regime* (New York: Alfred A. Knopf, 1993), chap. 5. For an excellent analysis of the concept of totalitarianism and its application to foreign policy analysis, see A. Gleason, *Totalitarianism: The Inner History of the Cold War* (New York: Oxford University Press, 1995). For a superior analysis of the reason the totalitarian model applied to the Soviet Union throughout the Cold War, see W. Odom, "Soviet Politics and After: Old and New Concepts," *World Politics* 45, no. 1 (October 1992): 66–98.

For examples of revisionist scholarship, see W. A. Williams, *The Tragedy of American Diplomacy*, 2nd ed. (New York: Dell, 1972); W. LaFeber, *America, Russia, and the Cold War, 1945–1992*, 7th ed. (New York: McGraw-Hill, 1993). The writings of Daniel Yergin, Raymond Garthoff, Richard Ned Lebow, and Janice Gross Stein are more nuanced but sympathetic to the revisionist point of view. See, for example, D. Yergin, *Shattered Peace: The Origins of the Cold War and the National Security State* (Boston: Houghton Mifflin, 1977); R. Garthoff, *Détente and Confrontation: American-Soviet Relations from Nixon to Reagan* (Washington, D.C.: Brookings Institution Press, 1985); R. Garthoff, *The Great Transition: Soviet-American Relations and the End of the Cold War* (Washington, D.C.: Brookings Institution Press, 1994).

The major postrevisionist interpretations include the following: J. L. Gaddis, *The United States and the Origins of the Cold War, 1941–1947* (New York: Columbia University Press, 1972); J. L. Gaddis, *Strategies of Containment*; and M. P. Leffler, *A Preponderance of Power: National Security, the Truman Administration, and the Cold War* (Stanford: Stanford University Press, 1992). Leffler is actually closer to the revisionists than to the middle in apportioning blame for the Cold War. Although Gaddis began as a postrevisionist in the works cited above, he has moved to embrace the traditionalist viewpoint. See J. L. Gaddis, *We Now Know: Rethinking Cold War History* (New York: Oxford University Press, 1997); J. L. Gaddis, *The Cold War: A New History* (New York: Penguin Press, 2005).

What we have learned from the Soviet archives has significantly bolstered the already powerful case of the traditionalists. See, for example, H. J. Ellison, "Messengers to Moscow," parts 1–4 (PBS documentary, Fall 1994); W. Wohlforth, ed., *Cold War Endgame: Oral History, Analysis, Debates* (University Park: Pennsylvania State University Press, 2003); R. Pipes, ed., *The Unknown Lenin: From the Secret Archive* (New Haven: Yale University Press, 1996); R. Pipes, "Misinterpreting the Cold War," *Foreign Affairs* 74, no. 1 (January/February 1995): 154–60; and see, of course, the magisterial Gaddis, *We Now Know*. Melvyn Leffler has tried to rebut the traditionalists but failed, in my estimation. See M. P. Leffler, "Inside Enemy Archives," *Foreign Affairs* 75, no. 4 (July/August 1996): 120–35. Among other things, he rests much of his dubious arguments on the conclusion drawn by Zubok and Pleshakov that Stalin had limited aims and ambitions. See V. Zubok and C. Pleshakov, *Inside the Kremlin's Cold War: From Stalin to Khrushchev* (Cambridge: Harvard University Press, 1996). Yet Robert Legvold, no hard-liner himself, admits that even the Zubok and Pleshakov book provides much evidence to support the hard-line position rather than the position that the authors intend to defend. See R. Legvold, "Eastern Europe and the Former Soviet Republics," *Foreign Affairs* (July/August 1996): 153–56.

24. J. Joffe, "Europe's American Pacifier," *Foreign Policy* 54 (Spring 1984): 64–82; J. Joffe, *The Limited Partnership: Europe, the United States, and the Burdens of Alliance* (Cambridge: Ballinger, 1987), 186–88.

25. R. Cooper, *The Breaking of Nations: Order and Chaos in the Twenty-first Century* (New York: Atlantic Monthly Press, 2003), 34–35.

26. T. Smith, *America's Mission: The United States and the Worldwide Struggle for Democracy in the Twentieth Century* (Princeton: Princeton University Press, 1994), 146–76. For a splendid account of President Truman's more enlarged, enlightened conception of containment, which rested on the belief in the virtues of a democratic peace and the need for American power to sustain it, see E. E. Spalding, *The First Cold Warrior: Harry Truman, Containment, and the Remaking of Liberal Internationalism* (Lexington: University Press of Kentucky, 2006).

27. There is a vast literature demonstrating the higher realism of the democratic peace. See, e.g., S. Weart, *Never at War: Why Democracies Will Not Fight One Another* (New Haven: Yale University Press, 1998); J. M. Owen, *Liberal Peace, Liberal War: American Politics and International Security* (Ithaca: Cornell University Press, 1997); M. W. Doyle, "Kant, Liberal Legacies, and Foreign Affairs, Part 1," *Journal of Philosophy and Public Affairs* 12, no. 3 (Summer 1983): 205–335, and "Kant, Liberal Legacies, and Foreign Affairs, Part 2," *Journal of Philosophy and Public Affairs* 12, no. 4 (Autumn 1983): 323–53; M. W. Doyle, "Liberalism and World Politics," *American Political Science Review* 80, no. 4 (December 1986): 1151–69; B. Russett, *Grasping the Democratic Peace: Principles for a Post–Cold War World* (Princeton: Princeton University Press, 1993).

28. N. Sharansky, with Ron Dermer, *The Case for Democracy: The Power of Freedom to Overcome Tyranny and Terror* (New York: Public Affairs, 2004).

29. F. Zakaria, *The Future of Freedom: Illiberal Democracy at Home and Abroad* (New York: Norton, 2003); J. L. Snyder, *From Voting to Violence: Democratization and Nationalist Conflict* (New York: Norton, 2000).

30. For a prime example of democratic triumphalism, see F. Fukuyama, *The End of History and the Last Man* (New York: Free Press, 1992).

31. A. M. Schlesinger Jr., *A Thousand Days: John F. Kennedy in the White House* (Boston: Houghton Mifflin, 1965), 769.

32. J. J. Kirkpatrick, *Dictatorships and Double Standards: Rationalism and Reason in Politics* (New York: Simon and Schuster, 1982).

33. For the best account of the evolution of U.S. policy toward China since the 1970s and the underlying strategic rationale for it, see J. Mann, *About Face: A History of America's Curious Relationship with China, from Nixon to Clinton* (New York: Alfred A. Knopf, 1999).

34. F. Zakaria, "India Rising," *Newsweek,* March 6, 2006, 40–41.

35. R. G. Kaufman, "A Two-Level Interaction: Structure, Stable Liberal Democracy, and U.S. Grand Strategy," *Security Studies* 3, no. 4 (Summer 1994): 679–717.

36. For the classic account of the insidious interaction, see Churchill, *The Gathering Storm.* See also S. Lee, *The European Dictatorships, 1918–1945* (New York: Methuen, 1987).

37. Cooper, *The Breaking of Nations,* 143.

38. See R. G. Kaufman, *Arms Control during the Pre-nuclear Era* (New York: Columbia University Press, 1990); M. Peattie, *Ishiwara Kanji and Japan's Confrontation with the West* (Princeton: Princeton University Press, 1975); H. Borton, *Japan's Modern Century* (New York: Ronald Press, 1955); Y. Maxton, *Control of Japan's Foreign Policy: A Study in Civilian Military Rivalry, 1930–1945* (Berkeley: University of California Press, 1957); R. Scalapino, *Democracy and the Party Movement in Prewar Japan* (Berkeley: University of California Press, 1953); R. Scalapino, "Democratizing Dragons: South Korea and Taiwan," *Journal of Democracy* 4, no. 3 (Summer 1993): 70–84; J. Dower, *Embracing Defeat: Japan in the Wake of World War II* (New York: Norton, 1999).

39. S. P. Huntington, *American Politics: The Promise of Disharmony* (Cambridge: Belknap Press of Harvard University Press, 1981), 240–59.

40. S. P. Huntington, *The Third Wave: Democratization in the Late Twentieth Century* (Norman: University of Oklahoma Press, 1993).

41. Mearsheimer, "Back to the Future."

42. R. Pipes, "The Soviet Union Adrift," *Foreign Affairs: America and the World* 70, no. 1 (1990/1991): 70–87.

43. For an excellent account on the insidious linkage between Vladimir Putin's repression of freedom at home and growing Russian belligerence abroad, see P. Baker and S. Glasser, *Kremlin Rising: Vladimir Putin's Russia and the End of Revolution* (New York: Scribner, 2005).

44. C. Menges, *China: The Gathering Threat* (Nashville: Nelson Current, 2005), 167–289.

45. J. J. Mearsheimer and S. M. Walt, "Can Saddam Be Contained? History Says Yes" (paper delivered at the Belfer Center for Science and International Affairs, John F. Kennedy School of Government, Cambridge, November 12, 2002).

46. For an analysis that claims, as I do not, that the Osirak strike may have

expedited the Iraqi nuclear program, see B. Posen, "U.S. Security Policy in a Nuclear Armed World," *Security Studies* 6, no. 3 (Spring 1997): 1–31.

47. W. Shawcross, *Allies: The U.S., Britain, Europe, and the War in Iraq* (New York: Public Affairs, 2004), 37.

48. For an assessment more optimistic than mine of whether deterrence could operate reliably against Saddam, see R. Jervis, *American Foreign Policy in a New Era* (New York: Routledge, 2005), 59–78.

49. Charles Duelfer, "Comprehensive Report of the Special Advisor to the DCI on Iraq's WMD" (September 30, 2004), available at www.cia.gov/cia/reports /iraq_wmd_2004.

50. E. Karsh, *Islamic Imperialism: A History* (New Haven: Yale University Press, 2006), 234.

51. There is a vast literature on this subject as well. For the definitive account of the Israeli-Palestinian dispute since the Oslo Accords of 1993, see D. Ross, *The Missing Peace: The Inside Story of the Fight for Middle East Peace* (New York: Farrar, Straus and Giroux, 2004). Ross started with the premise that Arafat was interested in a genuine peace, but he concluded that Arafat and the tyrannical nature of the PLO constituted the primary obstacles. See also E. Karsh, *Arafat's War: The Man and His Battle for Israeli Conquest* (New York: Grove, 2003). For assessments of the Oslo Accords that blame the Palestinians less and the Israelis more than I do, see H. Agha and R. O'Malley, "Camp David: The Tragedy of Errors," *New York Review of Books,* August 9, 2001; J. Slater, "What Went Wrong: The Collapse of the Israeli-Palestinian Peace Process," *Political Science Quarterly* 16, no. 2 (Summer 2001): 171–99. For the most compelling general statement on the linkage between tyranny and aggression in the Middle East, and the need for regime change in the region, see B. Lewis, *What Went Wrong: The Clash between Islam and Modernity in the Middle East* (New York: Harper Perennial, 2003).

52. Gabriel Schoenfeld makes this point powerfully in Schoenfeld, "Dual Loyalty and the 'Israel Lobby,' " *Commentary* (November 2006): 33–40.

53. Walter Russell Mead, "God's Country," *Foreign Affairs* (September/October 2006): 40–41.

54. J. Joffe, "A World without Israel," *Foreign Policy* 146 (January/February 2005): 36–43.

55. M. Habeck, *Knowing the Enemy: Jihadist Ideology and the War on Terror* (New Haven: Yale University Press, 2006), 177.

56. I. Buruma and A. Margalit, *Occidentalism: The West in the Eyes of Its Enemies* (New York: Penguin Press, 2004).

57. Ross, *The Missing Peace,* 768.

58. Osama bin Laden, "Declaration of War against Americans Occupying the Land of Two Holy Places," *Al-Quds Al-'Arabi,* August 1996.

59. See F. Ajami, "The Autumn of the Autocrats," *Foreign Affairs* 84, no. 3

(May/June 2005): 20–35; B. Lewis, "Freedom and Justice in the Modern Middle East," *Foreign Affairs* 84, no. 3 (May/June 2005): 36–51; and D. Makovsky, "Gaza: Moving Forward by Pulling Back," *Foreign Affairs* 84, no. 3 (May/June 2005): 52–62.

60. G. W. Bush, "Call for a New Palestinian Leadership" (West Point, N.Y., June 24, 2002).

61. V. D. Hanson, "Hope amid Despair," *National Review Online*, August 18, 2006, available at http://article.nationalreview.com/?q=MWE4NDBjNzNjNjE4 YzklNTU2YWQ0ZjE3N2I5ZWE5NWY=.

62. For an excellent critique of offshore balancing as insufficiently vigilant and prudent, see R. J. Art, *A Grand Strategy for America* (Ithaca: Cornell University Press, 2003), 172–97.

63. S. G. Brooks and W. C. Wohlforth, "American Primacy in Perspective," *Foreign Affairs* 81, no. 4 (July/August 2002): 20–34.

64. For an excellent argument along these lines, see A. L. Friedberg, *In the Shadow of the Garrison State* (Princeton: Princeton University Press, 2000).

65. R. Kagan, *Of Paradise and Power: America and Europe in a New World Order* (2003; rept, New York: Vintage, 2004), 73–74.

66. W. Wohlforth, "The Stability of a Unipolar World," *International Security* 24, no. 1 (Summer 1999): 5–41.

67. M. Mandelbaum, *The Case for Goliath: How America Acts as the World's Government in the Twenty-first Century* (New York: Public Affairs, 2005), 195.

3. The Unrealistic Realism of Classical Realists

1. For a more scholarly critique along these lines, see R. M. Merry, *Sands of Empire: Missionary Zeal, American Foreign Policy, and the Hazards of Global Ambition* (New York: Simon and Schuster, 2005); A. Bacevich, *The New American Militarism: How Americans Are Seduced by War* (New York: Oxford University Press, 2005). For Henry Kissinger's take on the war, which is different from that of most classical realists, see H. A. Kissinger, "Intervention with a Vision," in G. Rosen, ed., *The Right War? The Conservative Debate on Iraq* (New York: Cambridge University Press, 2005), 49–53.

2. For examples of stark realism, see N. Machiavelli, *The Prince, and The Discourses* (New York: Modern Library, 1950); T. Hobbes, *Leviathan* (1651; rept., London: Penguin, 1985); E. H. Carr, *The Twenty Years' Crisis, 1919–1939: An Introduction to the Study of International Relations* (London: Macmillan, 1940). For American versions of classical realism, less stark but still intensely critical of legalism and moralism in foreign policy, see G. F. Kennan, *American Diplomacy: 1900–1950* (Chicago: University of Chicago Press, 1951); H. J. Morgenthau, *Politics among Nations: The Struggle for Power and Peace*, 6th ed., rev. Kenneth Thompson (New York: Alfred A. Knopf, 1985).

3. Of course, some realists take into account domestic variables and ideology more than others. Explaining the largely successful operation of the European balance of power, Edward Gulick, Raymond Aron, and Henry Kissinger stress the importance of common aims, assumptions, self-conscious moderation, and ideological homogeneity among the major powers. E. Gulick, *Europe's Classical Balance of Power;* R. Aron, *Peace and War* (Garden City, N.Y.: Doubleday, 1962); H. A. Kissinger, *A World Restored: Metternich, Castlereagh, and the Problems of Peace, 1812–1822* (Boston: Houghton Mifflin, 1957); Kissinger, *Diplomacy,* 78–102, 133–67. Arnold Wolfers draws a critical distinction among status quo, revisionist, and self-abnegating states. A. Wolfers, *Discord and Collaboration: Essays on International Politics* (Baltimore: Johns Hopkins University Press, 1962), 181–204.

4. Morgenthau, *Politics among Nations,* 5.

5. Carr, *The Twenty Years' Crisis,* 123.

6. G. F. Kennan, *Realities of American Foreign Policy* (Princeton: Princeton University Press, 1954), 47. For a more recent statement, see G. F. Kennan, "Morality and Foreign Policy," *Foreign Affairs* 64, no. 2 (Winter 1985–1986): 205–18.

7. H. J. Morgenthau, *Scientific Man vs. Power Politics* (Chicago: University of Chicago Press, 1946), 191–201.

8. G. Russell, *Hans J. Morgenthau and the Ethics of American Statecraft* (Baton Rouge: Louisiana State University Press, 1990), 169–70.

9. H. A. Kissinger, *American Foreign Policy* (London: Weidenfeld and Nicolson, 1969), 12.

10. Quoted in J. Goldberg, "Breaking Ranks: What Turned Brent Scowcroft against the Bush Administration," *New Yorker,* October 31, 2005, 60.

11. J. Derbyshire, "Management or Confrontation? The Brent Scowcroft Problem," *National Review Online,* August 20, 2002, available at www.nationalreview. com/derbyshire/derbyshire082002.asp; B. Scowcroft, "Don't Attack Saddam," *Wall Street Journal,* August 15, 2002, A12; G. Kessler, "Scowcroft Critical of Bush, Cheney," *Washington Post,* October 16, 2004, A2.

12. Quoted in Goldberg, "Breaking Ranks," 60.

13. B. Scowcroft, "A Modest Proposal," *National Interest* 83 (Spring 2006): 13–15.

14. R. Niebuhr, *The Children of Light and the Children of Darkness: A Vindication of Democracy and a Critique of Its Traditional Defense* (New York: Charles Scribner's Sons, 1944), 176.

15. A. de Tocqueville, *Democracy in America,* trans. and ed. Harvey C. Mansfield and Delba Winthrop (1835, 1840; rept., Chicago: University of Chicago Press, 2000), 502.

16. For an important book on different schools of thought on American foreign policy, and the constituencies they represent, see W. R. Mead, *Special Providence: American Foreign Policy and How It Changed the World* (New York: Routledge,

2002). In my view, Mead's four schools do not capture all the alternatives, or adequately express the range of opinion, but it is a very good start to thinking about public opinion and American foreign policy.

17. R. Aron, *Peace and War: A Theory of International Relations*, trans. Richard Howard and Annette B. Fox (Malabar, Fla.: Robert Krieger, 1981), 597–98.

18. Gaddis, *Strategies of Containment*, 25–127; W. L. Hixson, *George F. Kennan: Cold War Iconoclast* (New York: Columbia University Press, 1989), 73–80, 139–141.

19. E. E. Spalding, *The First Cold Warrior*; Cooper, *The Breaking of Nations*, 142–44.

20. A. Puddington, "The Wages of Durban," *Commentary* 112, no. 4 (November 2001): 29.

21. Carr, *The Twenty Years' Crisis*, 282, 284.

22. E. H. Carr, *The Soviet Impact on the Western World* (New York: Macmillan, 1947), 3.

23. G. F. Kennan, *From Prague after Munich: Diplomatic Papers, 1938–1940* (Princeton: Princeton University Press, 1968).

24. W. S. Churchill, "A Total and Unmitigated Defeat" (October 5, 1938), in R. R. James, ed., *Winston S. Churchill: His Complete Speeches, 1897–1963* (New York: Atheneum, 1983), 7: 6011.

25. W. S. Churchill, "An Open Letter to a Communist" (August 25, 1934), in M. Gilbert, ed., *Winston Churchill: The Wilderness Years* (Boston: Houghton Mifflin, 1982), 859–60.

26. W. S. Churchill, "Constituent Meeting" (September 12, 1947), in R. Churchill, ed., *Speeches by Winston Churchill, 1947–48* (London: Cassell, 1950), 144.

27. W. S. Churchill, "A Congress of Europe—A Speech at the Hague" (May 7, 1948), in James, *Winston Churchill: His Complete Speeches*, 318–19.

28. G. H. W. Bush and B. Scowcroft, *A World Transformed* (New York: Alfred A. Knopf, 1998), 449–87.

29. P. Zelikow and C. Rice, *Germany Unified and Europe Transformed: A Study in Statecraft* (Cambridge: Harvard University Press, 1995).

30. Goldberg, "Breaking Ranks," 63.

31. Derbyshire, "Management or Confrontation."

32. W. Safire, "Putin's Chicken Kiev," *New York Times*, December 6, 2004, 23.

33. Goldberg, "Breaking Ranks," 60. For an example of a prominent realist Arabist worried that the spread of democracy in the Middle East would make terrorism even worse, an argument that is untenable in the long run, see F. G. Gause, "Can Democracy Stop Terrorism?" *Foreign Affairs* 84, no. 5 (September/October 2005): 62–76.

34. Bush and Scowcroft, *A World Transformed*, 16–17.

35. Kaufman, *Henry M. Jackson*, 291–94.

36. B. Scowcroft, Memorandum, June 26, 1975 (Henry Martin Jackson Papers, University of Washington, Seattle, series 3560-6, box 38, folder 1).

4. The Perils of Liberal Multilateralism

1. Krauthammer, "In Defense of Democratic Realism," 16.

2. J. S. Nye Jr., *The Paradox of American Power: Why the World's Only Superpower Can't Go It Alone* (New York: Oxford University Press, 2002).

3. C. H. Kupchan, *The End of the American Era: U.S. Foreign Policy and the Geopolitics of the Twenty-first Century* (2002; rept., New York: Vintage, 2003); G. J. Ikenberry, "America's Imperial Ambitions," *Foreign Affairs* 77 (September/ October 2002): 44.

4. Fukuyama, *America at the Crossroads,* 155–80.

5. Cooper, *The Breaking of Nations,* 47–48.

6. Kaufman, *Henry M. Jackson,* 175, 444–47; R. Radosh, *Divided They Fell: The Demise of the Democratic Party, 1964–1996* (New York: Free Press, 1996).

7. See, for example, D. Halberstam, *War in a Time of Peace: Bush, Clinton, and the Generals* (New York: Charles Scribner's Sons, 2001); W. Clark, *Waging Modern War: Bosnia, Kosovo, and the Future of Combat* (New York: Public Affairs, 2001).

8. J. S. Nye Jr., *Soft Power: The Means to Success in World Politics* (New York: Public Affairs, 2004).

9. G. J. Ikenberry and C. A. Kupchan, "Liberal Realism: The Foundations of a Democratic Foreign Policy," *National Interest* 77 (Fall 2004): 38–49.

10. For Nye's stringent conditions on using force unilaterally, see Nye, *Paradox of American Power,* 154–63.

11. Nye, *Soft Power.*

12. Joffe, *Uncertain Partnership,* 186–88.

13. N. Ferguson, *Colossus: The Rise and Fall of the American Empire* (New York: Penguin, 2005); A. J. Bacevich, *American Empire: The Realities and Consequences of American Diplomacy* (Cambridge: Harvard University Press, 2004); C. Johnson, *The Sorrows of Empire: Militarism, Secrecy, and the End of the Republic* (New York: Metropolitan Books, 2004). Ferguson atypically does not consider empire a bad thing, but he does not believe the United States has the wherewithal to maintain it. Bacevich and Johnson are more typical in using the term negatively.

14. Cooper, *The Breaking of Nations,* 47–48.

15. G. Lundestad, "Empire by Invitation? The United States and Western Europe, 1945–1952," *Journal of Peace Research* 23, no. 3 (September 1986): 262–77.

16. Some professed realists also equate consensus with legitimacy in their criticism of President Bush. See R. W. Tucker and D. D. Hendrickson, "The

Sources of American Legitimacy," *Foreign Affairs* 83, no. 6 (November/December 2004): 18–32; R. Kagan, "A Matter of Record," *Foreign Affairs* 84, no. 1 (January/February 2005): 170–73; R. W. Tucker and D. D. Hendrickson, "The Flip Side of the Record," *Foreign Affairs* 84, no. 2 (March/April 2005): 139–41. Kagan gets the better of this exchange in chiding Tucker and Hendrickson for their inconsistency and mistake in viewing consensus as the arbiter of legitimacy.

17. For the classic statement on the daunting requirement of collective security, see A. Wolfers, "Collective Defense versus Collective Security," in Wolfers, *Discord and Collaboration*, 181–204.

18. Kissinger, *Diplomacy*, 53–55.

19. S. Power, *A Problem from Hell: America and the Age of Genocide* (New York: Basic Books, 2002), xx.

20. M. Meredith, *The Fate of Africa: From the Hopes of Freedom to the Heart of Despair: A History of Fifty Years of Independence* (New York: Public Affairs, 2005), 517–18.

21. For the source of this history, see R. G. Kaufman, "The UN Record," *The World and I* 16, no. 9 (September 2001): 34–39.

22. Meredith, *The Fate of Africa*, 518–19. For a scathing account of the UN's role in Rwanda, see M. Barnett, *Eyewitness to a Genocide: The United Nations and Rwanda* (Ithaca: Cornell University Press, 2002).

23. Shawcross, *Allies*.

24. P. Kennedy, *The Parliament of Man: The Past, Present, and Future of the United Nations* (New York: Random House, 2006), 110.

25. Shawcross, *Allies*.

26. For a fine account of the UN's disreputable record in the realms of human rights and international security, see J. Muravchik, *The Future of the United Nations: Understanding the Past to Chart a Way Forward* (Washington, D.C.: AEI Press, 2005), 117–72.

27. For the best book on this subject, see M. A. Glendon, *A World Made New: Eleanor Roosevelt and the Universal Declaration of Human Rights* (New York: Random House, 2001).

28. This story is best told in D. P. Moynihan with Suzanne Weaver, *A Dangerous Place* (Boston: Little, Brown, 1978).

29. Puddington, "The Wages of Durban."

30. J. A. Rabkin, *The Case for Sovereignty: Why the World Should Welcome American Independence* (Washington, D.C.: AEI Press, 2004), 182–84.

31. Osgood, *Ideals and Self Interest in America's Foreign Relations*, 90–91.

32. For example, see I. H. Daalder and J. M. Lindsay, *America Unbound: The Bush Revolution in Foreign Policy* (Washington, D.C.: Brookings Institution Press, 2003); these authors and countless others who criticize the president vastly exaggerate the degree of consensus that existed during the final stages of the Cold War.

33. J. Lacouture, *De Gaulle: The Ruler, 1945–1970* (New York: Norton, 1992), 383–86.

34. J.-F. Revel with Branko Lazitch, *How Democracies Perish*, trans. William Byron (Garden City, N.Y.: Doubleday, 1984), 260.

35. For a similar criticism of de Gaulle and French foreign policy along these lines, see R. Aron, *Memoirs: Fifty Years of Political Reflection* (New York: Holmes and Meier, 1990), 286–300, 347–48.

36. P. Roger, *The American Enemy: A Story of French Anti-Americanism*, trans. Sharon Bowman (Chicago: University of Chicago Press, 2005), x–xi. For an excellent study on the deep roots of anti-Americanism in Europe generally and its contemporary manifestations, see P. Hollander, ed., *Understanding Anti-Americanism: Its Origins and Impact at Home and Abroad* (Chicago: Ivan R. Dee, 2004).

37. D. L. Bark and D. R. Gress, *Democracy and Its Discontents, 1963–1988*, vol. 2 of *A History of West Germany* (Oxford: Basil Blackwell, 1989), 151–513.

38. M. E. Sarotte, *Dealing with the Devil: East Germany, Détente, and Ostpolitik, 1969–1973* (Chapel Hill: University of North Carolina Press, 2001); W. F. Hanrieder, *Germany, America, Europe: Forty Years of German Foreign Policy* (New Haven: Yale University Press, 1989), 195–219.

39. J. Herf, *War by Other Means: Soviet Power, West German Resistance, and the Battle of the Euromissiles* (New York: Free Press, 1991).

40. For the very best account of Ostpolitik and the deep controversies surrounding it, see T. Garton Ash, *In Europe's Name: Germany and the Divided Continent* (New York: Random House, 1993).

41. Quoted in J. Hoagland, "Germany's New Outlook," *Washington Post*, October 16, 2005, B07.

42. For an excellent account of the many difficulties the United States had in Europe during the Cold War, and how precarious things were at the beginning of it, see T. Judt, *Postwar: A History of Europe since 1945* (New York: Penguin Books, 2005), 13–225.

43. Ulam, *Expansion and Coexistance*, 584–89.

44. N. Safran, *Israel, the Embattled Ally* (Cambridge: Belknap Press of Harvard University Press, 1981), 477–95.

45. G. P. Shultz, *Turmoil and Triumph: My Years as Secretary of State* (New York: Charles Scribner's Sons, 1993), 685–88.

46. Kagan, *Of Paradise and Power*.

47. J.-F. Revel, *Anti-Americanism*, trans. Diarmid Cammell (San Francisco: Encounter Books, 2003).

48. K. R. Timmerman, *The French Betrayal of America* (New York: Crown Forum, 2004).

49. M. Boot, "A Transatlantic Truce: Isn't It Pragmatic?" *Los Angeles Times*, February 17, 2005, B13.

50. K. M. Pollack, *The Persian Puzzle: The Conflict between Iran and America* (New York: Random House, 2004), 266–424.

51. Washington, "Farewell Address."

5. Moral Democratic Realism

1. R. Niebuhr, *Christianity and Power Politics* (New York: Charles Scribner's Sons, 1940), 125.

2. Churchill, "Dictators and the Covenant," in R. R. James, ed., *Winston Churchill: His Complete Speeches, 1897–1963*, 6: 5717–21.

3. Niebuhr, *Children of Light and the Children of Darkness*, xi–xii.

4. For an excellent analysis of the successes and failures of American commitment to promoting reform abroad among allies, see D. J. Macdonald, *Adventures in Chaos: American Intervention for Reform in the Third World* (Cambridge: Harvard University Press, 1992).

5. R. Lowry, "Reaganites v. Neo-Reaganites," *National Interest* 79 (Spring 2005): 36.

6. For an excellent recent study arguing that the United States has done a much better job with nation building than critics concede, see J. Dobbins, J. G. McGinn, K. Crane, S. G. Jones, R. Lal, A. Rathmell, R. Swanger, and A. Timilsina, *America's Role in Nation-Building: From Germany to Iraq* (Santa Monica, Calif.: Rand, 2003).

7. C. Krauthammer, "The Power of Faith," *Washington Post*, April 4, 2005, A21.

8. C. Krauthammer, "In Defense of Democratic Realism."

9. This framework is congenial not only with Krauthammer's reasonable distinctions, but also with Robert Art's grand strategy of selective engagement and the logic behind it, though he would probably reach different conclusions about the application of this framework to specific cases than I do. R. Art, *A Grand Strategy for America*, 223–48.

10. For an authoritative account of the Rwandan genocide and how the West could have stopped it without major effort or risk, see S. Powers, *A Problem from Hell*, 329–90.

11. See, for, example, C. Weinberger, "Speech at the National Press Club" (Washington, D.C., November 28, 1984), and C. Powell, "U.S. Forces: Challenges Ahead," *Foreign Affairs* 71, no. 5 (Winter 1992–1993): 32–45. In an otherwise splendid book, Jean Bethke Elshtain made the same error in imposing the requirement that force be used as a last resort. J. B. Elshtain, *Just War against Terror: The Burden of American Power in a Violent World* (New York: Basic Books, 2003), 46–58. For a splendid history of the Catholic just-war tradition and the disturbing trend of many Catholic theologians to abandon it, see G. Weigel, *Tranquillitas Ordinis: The Present Failure and Future Promise of American Catho-*

lic Thought on War and Peace (New York: Oxford University Press, 1987). For excellent treatments of just-war theory historically, see J. T. Johnson, *Just War Tradition and the Restraint of War: A Moral and Historical Inquiry* (Princeton: Princeton University Press, 1981), and J. T. Johnson, *Can Modern War Be Just?* (New Haven: Yale University Press, 1984). For the standard secular-liberal versions of just-war theory, which reach different conclusions on specifics from those I do, see M. Walzer, *Just and Unjust Wars: A Moral Argument with Historical Illustrations,* 3rd ed. (New York: Basic Books, 2000), and M. Walzer, *Arguing about War* (New Haven: Yale University Press, 2004). For another good, balanced account, see P. S. Temes, *The Just War: An American Reflection on the Morality of War in Our Time* (Chicago: Ivan R. Dee, 2003).

12. For a superb strategic critique of the Weinberger-Powell guidelines, see M. I. Handel, *Masters of War: Classical Strategic Thought,* 2nd ed. (London: Frank Cass, 1996), 185–203.

13. Churchill, *The Gathering Storm,* 348.

14. A. Hillgruber, *Germany and the Two World Wars,* trans. William C. Kirby (Cambridge: Harvard University Press, 1981), 57.

15. W. S. Churchill, *Their Finest Hour* (Boston: Houghton Mifflin, 1949), 224–41.

16. For a contrary view, see Posen, "U.S. Security Policy in a Nuclear Armed World."

17. For the standard interpretation of the Cuban missile crisis, highly complimentary of President Kennedy, see M. Frankel, *High Noon in the Cold War: Kennedy, Khrushchev, and the Cuban Missile Crisis* (2004; rept., San Francisco: Presidio Press, 2005). For a more critical and compelling account that still agrees with Frankel that Kennedy ultimately would have used force preemptively had the Soviet Union not removed the missiles, see D. Kagan, *On the Origins of War,* 437–573.

18. J. Carter, "Just War—or a Just War," *New York Times,* March 9, 2003, 13.

19. J. T. Johnson, "Just War, as It Was and Is," *First Things* 149 (January 2005): 14–24. For an excellent extended account, see J. T. Johnson, *The War to Oust Saddam Hussein: Just War and the New Face of Conflict* (Lanham, Md.: Rowman and Littlefield, 2005).

20. Aquinas, *Summa Theologica,* 2: 577–81.

21. V. D. Hanson, *The Soul of Battle: From Ancient Times to the Present Day, How Three Great Liberators Vanquished Tyranny* (1999; rept., New York: Anchor Books, 2001); G. Blainey, *The Causes of War,* 3rd ed. (New York: Free Press, 1988).

22. For an excellent analysis of how the ethic of the lesser evil applies to the current war on terror, see M. Ignatieff, *The Lesser Evil: Political Ethics in an Age of Terror* (Princeton: Princeton University Press, 2004).

23. R. Evans, *The Coming of the Third Reich* (New York: Penguin Press, 2004),

1–153; M. Burleigh, *The Third Reich: A New History* (New York: Hill and Wang, 2001), 1–145.

24. Beschloss, *The Conquerors,* 13–19.

25. See Chen J., *Mao's China and the Cold War* (Chapel Hill: University of North Carolina Press, 2001); J. Chang and J. Halliday, *Mao: The Unknown Story* (New York: Alfred A. Knopf, 2005).

26. Ulam, *The Communists,* 80–107.

27. For an excellent analysis of the Iranian danger and how to deal with it, see I. I. Berman, *Tehran Rising: Iran's Challenge to the United States* (Lanham, Md.: Rowman and Littlefield, 2005).

28. Quoted in J. Hoagland, "Iran's Useful Reminder," *Washington Post,* October 30, 2005, B07.

29. For an excellent short statement on the conventional costs of preemption in Iran, see the analysis of one of its more compelling advocates, Charles Krauthammer, "The Tehran Calculus," *Washington Post,* September 15, 2006, A9.

30. Pollack, *The Persian Puzzle,* 375–424; C. Krauthammer, "Syria and the New Axis of Evil," *Washington Post,* April 4, 2005, A27.

31. E. N. Luttwak, "Three Reasons Not to Bomb Iran—Yet," *Commentary* 121, no. 5 (May 2006): 21–28. For an analysis that opposes preemption in Iran, which I disagree with but desire be taken seriously, see R. R. Betts, "The Osirak Fallacy," *National Interest* 83 (Spring 2006): 22–25. For an argument that Washington can and should relinquish the goal of regime change in exchange for stopping Iran's nuclear program, a policy this author considers undesirable and implausible, see Scott Sagan, "How to Keep the Bomb from Iran," *Foreign Affairs* (September/October 2006): 45–59.

32. For the best account of the North Korean problem, see J. Becker, *Rogue Regime: Kim Jong Il and the Looming Threat of North Korea* (New York: Oxford University Press, 2005). For the best analysis more sympathetic to President Clinton's policy of accommodation, see M. O'Hanlon and M. Mochizuki, *Crisis on the Korean Peninsula: How to Deal with a Nuclear North Korea* (New York: McGraw-Hill, 2003).

33. N. Eberstadt, "North Korea's Weapons Quest," *National Interest* 80 (Summer 2005): 49–52.

34. "Pyongyang Highlight Reel" (editorial), *Wall Street Journal,* July 8, 2006, A10.

35. M. G. Franc, "Korean Threat Launches Senate into the Next Phase of Missile Defense," *Human Events Online,* July 1, 2006, available at www.humanevents.com/article.php?id=15836.

36. Ibid.

37. Sun T., *The Art of War,* trans. Lionel Giles (Mineola, N.Y.: Dover, 2002), 48.

38. D. H. Fischer, *Washington's Crossing* (New York: Oxford University Press, 2004), 375–76.

39. For a recent analysis that accepts the importance of moral reasoning in American foreign policy but reaches conclusions on Iraq the antithesis of my own, see P. Schroeder, "Mirror, Mirror, on the War," *American Interest* 1, no. 3 (Spring 2006): 41–55.

6. Moral Democratic Realism and the Endgame of the Cold War

1. See, for example, R. Garthoff, *The Great Transition,* and R. N. Lebow and J. G. Stein, eds., *We All Lost the Cold War* (Princeton: Princeton University Press, 1994).

2. P. Johnson, *Modern Times: The World from the 1920s to the 1990s,* rev. ed. (New York: HarperCollins, 1991), 612–96.

3. S. F. Hayward, *The Real Jimmy Carter* (Washington, D.C.: Regnery, 2004), 157–68.

4. A. B. Ulam, *Dangerous Relations: The Soviet Union in World Politics, 1970–1982* (New York: Oxford University Press, 1983), 83–144.

5. For an incisive and authoritative account of the political climate and cleavages of the final two decades of the Cold War, see M. Barone, *Our Country: The Shaping of America from Roosevelt to Reagan* (New York: Free Press, 1990), 383–670.

6. Kaufman, *Henry M. Jackson,* 161–442; Radosh, *Divided They Fell;* D. Leebaert, *The Fifty-Year Wound: The True Price of America's Cold War Victory* (Boston: Little, Brown, 2002), 377–487; S. Gillon, *The Democrats' Dilemma: Walter F. Mondale and the Liberal Legacy* (New York: Columbia University Press, 1992); R. B. Woods, *Fulbright: A Biography* (New York: Cambridge University Press, 1995), 463–672.

7. J. Muravchik, "In the Cold War: Kerry Froze," *Los Angeles Times,* August 10, 2004, B13.

8. C. Hagel, "A Republican Foreign Policy," *Foreign Affairs* 83, no. 4 (July/ August 2004): 64.

9. H. Kissinger, *Years of Renewal* (New York: Simon and Schuster, 1999), 92–135; H. Kissinger, *Years of Upheaval* (Boston: Little, Brown, 1982), 980–95; Kissinger, *Diplomacy,* 751–54; R. M. Nixon, *RN: The Memoirs of Richard Nixon* (1978; rept., New York: Touchstone, 1990); Gaddis, *Strategies of Containment,* 274–344.

10. For an interpretation of Nixon's détente that considers it far more robust than I do, see Garthoff, *Détente and Confrontation,* chaps. 1–16.

11. H. Kissinger, *The White House Years* (Boston: Little, Brown, 1979), 7–309.

12. Ibid., 162, 193.

13. Gaddis, *Strategies of Containment,* 298–306.

14. Kissinger, *White House Years,* 820–21.

15. Kaufman, *Henry M. Jackson,* 245–48.

16. Kissinger, *Diplomacy,* 733–61; R. M. Nixon, interview by R. G. Kaufman, June 1993.

17. R. Pipes, interview by R. G. Kaufman, September 26, 1995.

18. Woods, *Fulbright,* 651, 669.

19. Malia, *The Soviet Tragedy,* 376.

20. For the classic statement of the sensibilities of the New Left on foreign policy, see J. W. Fulbright, *The Arrogance of Power* (New York: Random House, 1966).

21. Kaufman, *Henry M. Jackson,* 351–57; C. Johnson, "McGovernism without McGovern," *Commentary* 65, no. 1 (January 1978): 36–39.

22. Zbigniew Brzezinski, interview by R. G. Kaufman, December 8, 1994; Z. Brzezinksi, *Power and Principle: Memoirs of the National Security Adviser, 1977–1981* (New York: Farrar, Straus and Giroux, 1983), 459. For anybody who doubts that dovishness is President Carter's dominant instinct, see J. Carter, *Our Endangered Values: America's Moral Crisis,* 99–145.

23. A. Dobrynin, *In Confidence: Moscow's Ambassador to America's Six Cold War Presidents (1962–1986)* (New York: Times Books, 1995), 387–90.

24. R. Schuettinger, "The New Foreign Policy Network," *Policy Review* (July 1977): 95–119; D. P. Moynihan, interview by R. G. Kaufman, July 28, 1996.

25. M. Abram, interview by R. G. Kaufman, January 8, 1995.

26. Marshall Shulman set forth the dominant paradigm of the Carter administration in his widely read article "On Learning to Live with Authoritarian Regimes," *Foreign Affairs* 55, no. 3 (January 1977): 325–38. Shulman argued not only that the Soviet Union was not totalitarian, but that Soviet communist expansion no longer constituted a major threat to U.S. security.

27. P. Warnke, "Apes on a Treadmill," *Foreign Policy* 18 (Spring 1975): 25–29.

28. Barone, *Our Country,* 559–68.

29. P. G. Bourne, *Jimmy Carter: A Comprehensive Biography from Plains to Post-Presidency* (New York: Scribner's, 1997), 385–86.

30. C. Gershman, "The World According to Andrew Young," *Commentary* 66, no. 2 (August 1978): 28–29; J. Muravchik, *Uncertain Crusade: Jimmy Carter and the Dilemmas of Human Rights Policies* (Washington, D.C.: AEI Press, 1988), 210.

31. "Vance: Man on the Move," *Time,* April 24, 1978, 20.

32. Shulman, "On Learning to Live with Authoritarian Regimes," 333–34.

33. Kaufman, *Henry M. Jackson,* 354.

34. P. Glynn, *Closing Pandora's Box: Arms Races, Arms Control, and the History of the Cold War* (New York: Basic Books, 1992), 289; Herf, *War by Other Means,* 45–66.

35. U.S. Office of Management and Budget, *Budget of the United States: FY 1978–82* (Washington, D.C.: Government Printing Office, 1979–1983), 5–6; *Wall Street Journal,* January 24, 1980, 11.

36. For an excellent analysis along these lines, see C. Gray and J. Barlow, "Inexcusable Restraint: The Decline of American Military Policy in the 1970s," *International Security* 10, no. 2 (Autumn 1985): 27–69.

37. D. Brinkley, *The Unfinished Presidency: Jimmy Carter's Journey beyond the White House* (New York: Viking Press, 1998), 333–43.

38. Carter, "Just War—or a Just War."

39. Henry M. Jackson, "Virginia General Assembly Address" (Williamsburg, Va., February 4, 1980; Henry M. Jackson Papers, University of Washington, Seattle, series 3560-6, box 13, folder 68).

40. Johnson, *Modern Times*, 674.

41. Hayward, *The Real Jimmy Carter*, 141–56.

42. For an excellent analysis of this dimension of Reagan, see P. Kengor, *God and Ronald Reagan: A Spiritual Life* (New York: Regan Books, 2004).

43. R. Reagan, "Losing Freedoms by Installments" (address to the Long Beach Rotary Club, June 6, 1962; Ronald Reagan Presidential Papers, Ronald Reagan Presidential Library, Simi Valley, Calif. [hereafter cited as RRPL], box 43).

44. R. Reagan to Victor Krulak, June 6, 1983 (RRPL, Presidential Handwriting File, series 2).

45. R. Reagan, *An American Life* (New York: Simon and Schuster, 1990), 410.

46. R. Reagan, "Speech at Westminster Cold War Memorial" (Fulton, Mo., November 19, 1990).

47. Ibid.

48. R. Reagan, "How Do You Fight Communism?" *Fortnight*, 1951, 13.

49. R. Reagan, *Reagan in His Own Hand: The Writings of Ronald Reagan That Reveal His Revolutionary Vision for America*, ed. A. Anderson and M. Anderson (New York: Free Press, 2001), 23–218.

50. For six excellent books demonstrating Reagan's consistency and coherence in foreign affairs and demolishing the myth of Reagan as a creature of his advisors, see P. Schweizer, *Victory: The Reagan Administration's Secret Strategy That Hastened the Collapse of the Soviet Union* (New York: Atlantic Monthly Press, 1994); P. Schweizer, *Reagan's War: The Epic Story of His Forty-Year Struggle and Final Triumph over Communism* (New York: Doubleday, 2002); P. Lettow, *Ronald Reagan and His Quest to Abolish Nuclear Weapons* (New York: Random House, 2005); D. D'Souza, *Ronald Reagan: How an Ordinary Man Became an Extraordinary President* (New York: Free Press, 1997); J. Arquilla, *The Reagan Imprint: Ideas in American Foreign Policy from the Collapse of Communism to the War on Terror* (Chicago: Ivan R. Dee, 2006); P. Kengor, *The Crusader: Ronald Reagan and the Fall of Communism* (New York: Regan Books, 2006).

51. There are of course many scholars and commentators who give Reagan much less credit than I do, though the archival evidence that I have seen firsthand is running in the direction of my interpretation of Reagan's decisive influence

and the reasons for it. For accounts that give much more credit to Gorbachev and other factors, see Garthoff, *The Great Transition;* A. Brown, *The Gorbachev Factor* (New York: Oxford University Press, 1997); J. F. Matlock, *Reagan and Gorbachev: How the Cold War Ended* (New York: Random House, 2004); K. L. Shimko, *Images and Arms Control: Perceptions of the Soviet Union in the Reagan Administration* (Ann Arbor: University of Michigan Press, 1991). For others the Cold War ended in spite of Reagan. See D. W. Larson, *Anatomy of Mistrust: U.S.–Soviet Relations during the Cold War* (Ithaca: Cornell University Press, 2000); F. Fitzgerald, *Way Out There in the Blue: Reagan, Star Wars, and the End of the Cold War* (New York: Simon and Schuster, 2000). For a debate among academics over the end of the Cold War that misses Reagan's pivotal positive importance because the realists underestimate the importance of ideas and the constructivists underestimate the importance of power, see W. C. Wohlforth, "Realism and the End of the Cold War," *International Security* 19, no. 3 (Winter 1994–1995): 91–129; S. G. Brooks and W. C. Wohlforth, "Power, Globalization, and the End of the Cold War: Reevaluating the Landmark Case for Ideas," *International Security* 25, no. 3 (Winter 2000–2001): 5–53; R. D. English, "Power, Ideas, and the New Evidence on the Cold War's End: A Reply to Brooks and Wohlforth," *International Security* 26, no. 4 (Spring 2002): 70–92; Larson, *Anatomy of Mistrust,* chaps. 6–7; R. N. Lebow and T. Risse-Kappen, eds., *International Relations Theory and the End of the Cold War* (New York: Columbia University Press, 1995).

52. R. G. Powers, *Not without Honor: The History of American Anticommunism* (New York: Free Press, 1995).

53. Johnson, *Modern Times,* 744–53.

54. G. Weigel, *The Final Revolution: The Resistance Church and the Collapse of Communism* (New York: Oxford University Press, 1992).

55. R. Reagan, "Commencement Address at Notre Dame" (May 1981, RRPL).

56. George Shultz, originally one of the skeptics, tells this story authoritatively in *Turmoil and Triumph,* 463–780.

57. Ibid., 879–900, 983–1015.

58. National Security Decision Directive (hereafter cited as NSDD) 75, "U.S. Relations with the U.S.S.R," January 19, 1983, Records Declassified and Released by the National Security Council, RRPL; NSSD 11–82, August 21, 1982, RRPL; R. Pipes, *Vixi: Memoirs of a Non-Belonger* (New Haven: Yale University Press, 2003), 125–211.

59. R. Reagan, "Address to the British Parliament" (June 8, 1982, RRPL).

60. Quoted in D'Souza, *Ronald Reagan,* 2–3.

61. R. Reagan, "Remarks at the Annual Convention of the National Association of Evangelicals" (Orlando, Fla., March 8, 1983, RRPL).

62. Sharansky, *The Case for Democracy,* 138.

63. For example, see Fitzgerald, *Way Out There in the Blue.* Although more

positively inclined to Reagan and more reliable in his analysis, Jack Matlock also succumbs to the error of giving too much credit to Gorbachev and too little to Reagan; Matlock, *Reagan and Gorbachev.*

64. B. Fischer, *The Reagan Reversal: Foreign Policy and the End of the Cold War* (Columbia: University of Missouri Press, 1997).

65. NSDD 172, "Strategic Defense Initiative" (May 30, 1985); NSDD 192, "The ABM Treaty" (October 11, 1985); NSDD 209, "Implementing the Decisions of the Geneva Summit" (February 4, 1986); NSDD 227, "U.S. Interim Restraint Policy" (August 25, 1986); NSDD 245, "Reagan-Gorbachev Preparatory Meeting" (October 7, 1986); NSDD 248, "Central America" (October 22, 1986); NSDD 250, "Post-Reykjavik Followup" (November 3, 1986); NSDD 288, "My Objectives at the Summit" (November 10, 1987); NSDD 305, "Objectives of the Moscow Summit" (April 26, 1988); all in RRPL.

66. R. Reagan, "Speech before the Brandenburg Gate" (West Berlin, June 12, 1987, RRPL).

67. P. Rodman, *More Precious Than Peace: The Cold War and the Struggle for the Third World* (New York: Charles Scribner's, 1994), 412–32; Shultz, *Turmoil and Triumph,* 608–42, 969–75.

68. S. Courtois, N. Werth, J.-L. Panné, A. Paczkowski, K. Bartosek, and J. L. Margolin, *The Black Book of Communism: Crimes, Terror, Repression* (Cambridge: Harvard University Press, 1999); A. Applebaum, *Gulag: A History* (New York: Doubleday, 2003): R. Pipes, *Communism: The Vanished Specter* (New York: Oxford University Press, 1994). .

69. B. Yeltsin quoted in the *Washington Post,* January 30, 1995, A09.

70. Pipes, "Misinterpreting the Cold War."

71. A. Garfinkle, *Telltale Hearts: The Origins and Impact of the Vietnam Antiwar Movement* (New York: St. Martin's Press, 1995), 209–35.

72. R. Bartley, *The Seven Fat Years: And How to Do It Again* (New York: Free Press, 1992).

73. G. Troy, *Morning in America: How Ronald Reagan Invented the 1980s* (Princeton: Princeton University Press, 2005), 324–47.

74. J. Ehrman, *The Eighties: America in the Age of Reagan* (New Haven: Yale University Press, 2005), 2.

7. The Bush Doctrine and Iraq

1. Buchanan, *Where the Right Went Wrong;* S. Halper and J. Clarke, *America Alone: The Neo-Conservatives and the Global Order* (New York: Cambridge University Press, 2004), 172–78; B. Bartlett, *Impostor: How George W. Bush Bankrupted America and Betrayed the Reagan Legacy* (New York: Doubleday, 2006).

2. Fukuyama, *America at the Crossroads,* 45–46.

3. D. Henninger, "The Weekend Interview with George Shultz: Father of the Bush Doctrine," *Wall Street Journal*, April 29, 2006, A08.

4. Ibid.

5. Quoted in ibid.

6. R. Reagan, "Address to the British Parliament."

7. G. W. Bush, Second Inaugural Address (January 20, 2005).

8. For an incisive analysis of the depth and extent of European anti-Americanism in general and the more virulent French version in particular, see Joffe, *Uberpower*, 67–94.

9. Bush, "Address to the American Legion National Convention" (Salt Lake City, August 31, 2006).

10. For the most balanced critique of the Iraq War, which still concludes the United States can succeed, see M. R. Gordon and B. E. Trainor, *Cobra II: The Inside Story of the Invasion and Occupation of Iraq* (New York: Pantheon Books, 2006). For another recent weighty but ultimately unconvincing critique, see P. Galbraith, *The End of Iraq: How American Incompetence Created a War without End* (New York: Simon and Schuster, 2006).

11. The field of Middle East studies does not have an outstanding track record, to say the least. Ideological bias has produced a conventional wisdom within it that has underestimated the Islamic threat and overestimated the moderation of much of the Arab world. See M. Kramer, *Ivory Towers on Sand: The Failure of Middle Eastern Studies in America* (Washington, D.C.: Washington Institute for Near East Policy, 2001), and R. Kaplan, *The Arabists: The Romance of an American Elite* (New York: Free Press, 1993). The dissenters from this consensus are much more reliable, in my estimation. See B. Lewis, *What Went Wrong*; B. Lewis, *The Crisis of Islam: Holy War and Unholy Terror* (New York: Modern Library, 2003); B. Lewis, *From Babel to Dragomans: Interpreting the Middle East* (New York: Oxford University Press, 2004); D. Pipes, *In the Path of God: Islam and Political Power* (New Brunswick, N.J.: Transaction Books, 2002); F. Ajami, *The Foreigners' Gift: The Americans, the Arabs, and the Iraqis in Iraq* (New York: Free Press, 2006); Karsh, *Islamic Imperialism*. For assessments somewhat different from my own but which deserve to be taken quite seriously, see O. Roy, *The Failure of Political Islam*, trans. Carol Volk (Cambridge: Harvard University Press, 1996); O. Roy, *Globalized Islam: The Search for a New Ummah* (New York: Columbia University Press, 2004); G. Kepel, *Jihad: The Trail of Political Islam*, trans. Anthony F. Roberts (Cambridge: Belknap Press of Harvard University Press, 2003); G. Kepel, *The War for Muslim Minds: Islam and the West*, trans. Pascale Ghazaleh (Cambridge: Belknap Press of Harvard University Press, 2004).

12. W. I. Hitchcock, *The Struggle for Europe: The Turbulent History of a Divided Continent, 1945 to the Present* (New York: Anchor Books, 2004), 13–39, 69–97.

13. Quoted in J. Hoagland, "Middle East Surprises," *Washington Post*, November 27, 1995, B07.

14. Fukuyama, *America at the Crossroads,* 114–54.

15. F. Zakaria, "What Bush Got Right," *Newsweek,* March 14, 2005, 24–26; V. D. Hanson, "The Bush Doctrine's Next Test," *Commentary* 119, no. 5 (May 2005): 21.

16. Ajami, *The Foreigners' Gift,* 108.

17. For an excellent argument along these lines, see "The Case for Democracy" (editorial), *Washington Post,* March 5, 2006, B06.

18. For a thoughtful analysis of why Hamas cannot be restrained, see M. Herzog, "Can Hamas Be Tamed?" *Foreign Affairs* 85, no. 2 (March/April 2006): 83–94.

19. For two authoritative defenses of applying the Bush Doctrine to Iraq, see K. Pollack, *The Threatening Storm: The Case for Invading Iraq* (New York: Random House, 2002), and J. Keegan, *The Iraq War* (New York: Alfred A. Knopf, 2004).

20. For an excellent polemic, in the best sense, making this case, see L. Kaplan and W. Kristol, *The War over Iraq: Saddam's Tyranny and America's Mission* (San Francisco: Encounter Books, 2003).

21. The claim that the administration unwisely disbanded the Iraqi Army is just one of the many untenable claims in Ricks, *Fiasco: The American Military Adventure in Iraq* (New York: Penguin Press, 2006), 12–28.

22. For an excellent analysis of the North Korean regime, its malevolence, and the strategic options for dealing with it, see Becker, *Rogue Regime,* 249–74.

23. Amir Taheri, "Getting Serious about Iran: For Regime Change," *Commentary,* November 2006, 23.

24. P. Berman et al., "Defending and Advancing Freedom: A Symposium," *Commentary* 120, no. 4 (November 2005): 24.

25. C. Krauthammer, "Man for a Glass Booth," *Washington Post,* December 9, 2005, A31.

26. For an excellent analysis and account of the Nuremberg trials, see T. Taylor, *The Anatomy of the Nuremberg Trials: A Personal Memoir* (New York: Alfred A. Knopf, 1992).

27. National Security Council, *National Strategy for Victory in Iraq* (Washington, D.C.: Government Printing Office, November 2005), 1–38.

28. For a thoughtful assessment of what has gone wrong in Iraq after American troops occupied Baghdad from a critic of the war, see J. Record, *Dark Victory: America's Second War against Iraq* (Annapolis: Naval Institute Press, 2004); see also L. Diamond, *Squandered Victory: The American Occupation and the Bungled Effort to Bring Democracy to Iraq* (New York: Times Books, 2005). For a thoughtful analysis of the dangers of giving a Shiite-dominated Iraqi army too much discretion in combating Sunni violence in Iraq, see S. Biddle, "Seeing Baghdad, Thinking Saigon," *Foreign Affairs* 85, no. 2 (March/April 2006): 2–14.

29. W. Kristol and R. Lowry, "Reinforce Baghdad," *Washington Post,* September 12, 2006, A23.

30. For an excellent account of the brilliance of the battlefield phase of the Iraq war by one of the world's preeminent military historians, see Keegan, *The Iraq War*.

31. M. Boot, *The Savage Wars of Peace: Small Wars and the Rise of American Power* (New York: Basic Books, 2002), 125.

32. NSC, *National Strategy for Victory in Iraq*, 10.

33. F. Zakaria, "Why Iraq Is Still Worth the Effort," *Washington Post*, March 22, 2006, A21.

34. Quoted in Ajami, *The Foreigners' Gift*, 155.

35. This applies as well to some of the president's conservative and neoconservative critics. For a robust defense of the president against such disproportionate criticism from conservative quarters, see Podhoretz, "Is the Bush Doctrine Dead?"

36. R. Holbrooke, "The Guns of August," *Washington Post*, August 10, 2006, A23.

37. Ross, *The Missing Peace*, 768.

38. See M. Albright, *The Mighty and the Unmighty* (New York: HarperCollins, 2006), 109–54.

39. G. F. Will, "The Triumph of Unrealism," *Washington Post*, August 15, 2006, A13.

40. See, for example, J. A. Baker III, with T. M. DeFrank, *The Politics of Diplomacy: Revolution, War, and Peace, 1989–1992* (New York: Putnam, 1995). He has reprised this flawed outlook in his latest book, Baker, with S. Fiffer, *Work Hard, Study—and Keep Out of Politics!* (New York: Putnam, 2006).

41. George F. Will, "Questions to Guide an Exit Policy," *Washington Post*, October 22, 2006, B7.

42. For an example of this flawed critique, which is widely accepted among the president's critics, see Ricks, *Fiasco*, 158–64.

43. J. Stobart, "Blair Defends Foreign Policy of Intervention," *Los Angeles Times*, March 22, 2006, A3.

44. J. Lieberman, "Our Troops Must Stay," *Wall Street Journal*, November 29, 2005, A18.

45. Quoted in A. Charlton, "World Leaders Offer Sharon Compassion," Associated Press, January 5, 2006, available at www.sfgate.com/cgi-bin/article.cgi?file=/n/a/2006/01/05/international/i090207S43.DTL&type=printable.

46. Ibid.

47. Shawcross, *Allies*.

8. Conclusion

1. Baker and Glasser, *Kremlin Rising*, 375.

2. D. Twining, "Putin's Power Politics," *Weekly Standard*, January 16, 2006, 17–24.

3. M. McFaul and J. M. Goldgeier, "Putin's Authoritarian Soul," *Weekly Standard*, February 28, 2005, 14–17; M. McFaul, N. Petrov, and A. Ryabov, *Between Dictatorship and Democracy: Russian Post-Communist Political Reform* (Washington, D.C.: Carnegie Endowment for International Peace, 2004); J. M. Goldgeier and M. McFaul, *Power and Purpose: U.S. Policy toward Russia after the Cold War* (Washington, D.C.: Brookings Institution Press, 2003).

4. D. Trenin, "Russia Leaves the West," *Foreign Affairs* 85, no. 4 (July/August 2006): 95.

5. R. Lim, *The Geopolitics of East Asia* (London: Routledge/Curzon, 2003); J. Hoge, "A Global Power Shift in the Making: Is the United States Ready?" *Foreign Affairs* 83, no. 4 (July 2004): 2–7.

6. H. Kissinger, *Does America Need a Foreign Policy? Toward a Diplomacy for the 21st Century* (New York: Simon and Schuster, 2001), 110–63. Avery Goldstein and Boston College's Robert Ross are two of the most thoughtful and prolific of the soft-liners. A. Goldstein, *Rising to the Challenge: China's Grand Strategy and International Security* (Stanford: Stanford University Press, 2005); R. Ross, "Beijing as a Conservative Power," *Foreign Affairs* 76, no. 2 (March/April 1997): 33–44; R. Ross, "Why Our Hardliners Are Wrong," *National Interest* 49 (Fall 1997): 42; R. Ross, "The Stability of Deterrence in the Taiwan Strait," *National Interest* 65 (Fall 2001): 67; A. Nathan and R. Ross, *The Great Wall and the Empty Fortress: China's Search for Security* (New York: Norton, 1997). Ross discounts the importance of regime type in analyzing Chinese foreign policy. For a recent article on how the PRC portrays its ambitions—peacefully—see Zheng B., "China's Peaceful Rise to Great Power Status," *Foreign Affairs* 84, no. 5 (September/October 2005): 18–24.

7. Mann, *About Face*, 273–361; B. Clinton, *My Life* (New York: Alfred A. Knopf, 2004), 956–57, 1231–33, 1272–74, 1370–71, 1413–14; M. Albright, with B. Woodward, *Madam Secretary: A Memoir* (New York: Miramax Books, 2003), 446–54.

8. Quoted in Menges, *China*, 129.

9. For analysis along these lines, see A. I. Johnston and R. Ross, eds., *New Directions in the Study of China's Foreign Policy* (Stanford: Stanford University Press, 2006); D. Shambaugh, ed., *Power Shift: China and Asia's New Dynamics* (Berkeley: University of California Press, 2005).

10. Arthur Waldron at the University of Pennsylvania and Aaron Friedberg at Princeton are the leading academic hard-liners on the subject of China. See, for example, A. Friedberg, "Arming China against Ourselves," *Commentary* 108, no. 1 (July/August 1999): 27–33; A. L. Friedberg, "Will We Abandon Taiwan?" *Commentary* 109, no. 5 (May 2000): 26–32; A. L. Friedberg, "The Struggle for Mastery in Asia," *Commentary* 110, no. 4 (November 2000): 17–27; A. L. Friedberg, "Asian Allies: True Strategic Partners," in R. Kagan and W. Kristol, eds., *Present Dangers: Crisis and Opportunity in American Foreign and Defense Policy*

(San Francisco: Encounter Books, 2000); A. Waldron, "Deterring China," *Commentary* 100, no. 4 (October 1995): 17–21; A. Waldron, "How Not to Deal with China," *Commentary* 103, no. 3 (March 1997): 44–49; A. L. Waldron, "Bowing to Beijing," *Commentary* 106, no. 3 (September 1998): 15–20; A. Waldron, "A Free and Democratic China," *Commentary* 110, no. 4 (November 2000): 27–32; A. Waldron, "The Chinese Sickness," *Commentary* 116, no. 1 (July 2003): 36–42; A. Waldron, "Hong Kong and the Future of Freedom," *Commentary* 116, no. 2 (September 2003): 21–25; A. Waldron, "Our Game with North Korea," *Commentary* 117, no. 2 (September 2004): 27–32.

11. E. McVaden and R. Fisher Jr. are both quoted in "China's Growing Navy Worries U.S." *International Herald Tribune*, December 31, 2004.

12. M. Pillsbury, *China Debates the Future Security Environment* (Washington, D.C.: National Defense University Press, 2000); M. Pillsbury, ed., *Chinese Views of Future Warfare* (Washington, D.C.: National Defense University Press, 1998). For a good assessment of Pillsbury's prominence and his influence on the Bush administration's conception of China, see N. King, Jr., "Inside the Pentagon: A Scholar Shapes Views of China," *Wall Street Journal,* September 8, 2005, 1.

13. D. Zweig and B. Jianhai, "China's Global Hunt for Energy," *Foreign Affairs* 84, no. 5 (September/October 2005): 30.

14. Mearsheimer, *The Tragedy of Great Power Politics,* 375–402.

15. R. Terrill, *The New Chinese Empire, and What It Means for the United States* (New York: Basic Books, 2003), 3–4.

16. Waldron, "Deterring China," 17–21.

17. Menges, *China;* see also note 10, above.

18. Waldron, "The Chinese Sickness," 42.

19. Goldstein, *Rising to the Challenge,* 204–19.

20. For a magisterial and definitive account of how the illiberal, authoritarian nature of Wilhelmine Germany ultimately drove German foreign policy in an aggressive direction, see G. A. Craig, *Germany, 1866–1945* (New York: Oxford University Press, 1978), 1–339.

21. R. G. Sutter, *China's Rise in Asia: Promises and Perils* (Lanham, Md.: Rowman and Littlefield, 2005). For a much more optimistic view, which I do not share, see R. S. Ross, "Taiwan's Fading Independence Movement," *Foreign Affairs* 85, no. 2 (March/April 2006): 141–48.

22. For a good recent assessment of Sino-Japanese competition, see K. E. Calder, "China and Japan's Simmering Rivalry," *Foreign Affairs* 85, no. 2 (March/April 2006): 129–39.

23. Zakaria, "India Rising," 40.

24. R. D. Blackwill, "The India Imperative," *National Interest* 80 (Summer 2005): 10.

25. Gurcharan Das, "The Indian Model," *Foreign Affairs* 85, no. 4 (July/August 2006): 2–16.

26. T. Donnelly, "Going Out for Indian," *Daily Standard,* March 31, 2005, available at www.weeklystandard.com/Utilities/printer_preview.asp?idArticle=5420.

27. R. Kagan, "India Is Not a Precedent," *Washington Post,* March 12, 2006, B07.

28. C. R. Mojan, "India and the Balance of Power," *Foreign Affairs* 85, no. 4 (July/August 2006): 32.

29. For arguments advocating strategic ambiguity regarding Taiwan, see N. B. Tucker, ed., *Dangerous Strait: The U.S.-Taiwan-China Crisis* (New York: Columbia University Press, 2005).

30. Menges, *China,* xxiii–xxiv.

Epilogue

1. Charles Krauthammer, "Why Iraq Is Crumbling," *Washington Post,* November 17, 2006, A25.

2. For an excellent analysis of the chimera of withdrawal as a panacea for avoiding defeat and an alternative strategy with a plausible chance of succeeding, see Frederick W. Kagan, "No Third Way in Iraq," *Weekly Standard,* November 13, 2006, 23–29.

3. See, for example, Fareed Zakaria, "Don't Punt on the Troops Issue," *Newsweek,* November 20, 2006, 48.

4. Doyle McManus, "Kissinger Says Iraq Isn't Ripe for Democracy," *Los Angeles Times,* November 15, 2006, A1.

5. Peter Spiegel, "Perle Says He Should Not Have Backed the Iraq War," *Los Angeles Times,* November 5, 2006, A1.

6. This point is made very well by Jim Hoagland, "Right Vision, Wrong Policy—And a Middle East Price to Pay," *Washington Post,* November 12, 2006, B07.

7. Mark Steyn, *America Alone: The End of the World as We Know It* (Washington, D.C.: Regnery, 2006), 169–70.

8. John M. Broder, "In Call for More Troops, McCain Places His Bet on Iraq," *New York Times Online,* November 13, 2006.

Bibliography

Abram, Morris. Interview by Robert G. Kaufman, January 8, 1995.

Adams, John Q. "4th of July Address." 1821.

Agha, Hussein, and Robert Malley. "Camp David: The Tragedy of Errors." *New York Review of Books,* August 9, 2001, available at www.nybooks.com/articles /14380.

Ajami, Fouad. "The Autumn of Autocrats." *Foreign Affairs* 84, no. 3 (May/June 2005): 20–35.

———. *The Foreigners' Gift: The Americans, the Arabs, and the Iraqis in Iraq.* New York: Free Press, 2006.

Albright, Madeleine. *The Mighty and the Unmighty.* New York: HarperCollins, 2006.

Albright, Madeleine, with Bill Woodward. *Madam Secretary: A Memoir.* New York: Miramax Books, 2003.

Applebaum, Anne. *Gulag: A History.* New York: Doubleday, 2003.

Arendt, Hannah. *The Origins of Totalitarianism.* New York: Harcourt, Brace, 1951.

Aron, Raymond. *Memoirs: Fifty Years of Political Reflection.* Trans. George Holoch. New York: Holmes and Meier, 1990.

———. *Peace and War.* Trans. Richard Howard and Annette B. Fox. Garden City, N.Y.: Doubleday, 1962.

———. *Peace and War: A Theory of International Relations.* Trans. Richard Howard and Annette B. Fox. Malabar, Fla.: Robert Krieger, 1981.

Arquilla, John. *The Reagan Imprint: Ideas in American Foreign Policy from the Collapse of Communism to the War on Terror.* Chicago: Ivan R. Dee, 2006.

Art, Robert J. *A Grand Strategy for America.* Ithaca: Cornell University Press, 2003.

Bacevich, Andrew J. *American Empire: The Realities and Consequences of American Diplomacy.* Cambridge: Harvard University Press, 2004.

———. *The New American Militarism: How Americans Are Seduced by War.* New York: Oxford University Press, 2005.

Bailyn, Bernard. *To Begin the World Anew: The Genius and Ambiguities of the American Founders.* New York: Alfred A. Knopf, 2003.

Baker, James A., III, with Thomas M. DeFrank. *The Politics of Diplomacy: War, Revolution, and Peace, 1989–1992.* New York: Putnam, 1995.

Baker, James A., III, with Steve Fiffer. *Work Hard, Study—and Keep Out of Politics!* New York: Putnam, 2006.

Baker, Peter, and Susan Glasser. *Kremlin Rising: Vladimir Putin's Russia and the End of Revolution.* New York: Scribner, 2005.

Bark, Dennis L., and David R. Gress. *Democracy and Its Discontents, 1963–1988,* vol. 2 of *A History of West Germany.* Oxford: Basil Blackwell, 1989.

Barnett, Michael. *Eyewitness to a Genocide: The United Nations and Rwanda.* Ithaca: Cornell University Press, 2002.

Barone, Michael. *Our Country: The Shaping of America from Roosevelt to Reagan.* New York: Free Press, 1990.

Bartlett, Bruce. *Impostor: How George W. Bush Bankrupted America and Betrayed the Reagan Legacy.* New York: Doubleday, 2006.

Bartley, Robert L. *The Seven Fat Years: And How to Do It Again.* New York: Free Press, 1992.

Becker, Jasper. *Rogue Regime: Kim Jong Il and the Looming Threat of North Korea.* New York: Oxford University Press, 2005.

Bemis, Samuel F. *A Diplomatic History of the United States.* New York: Henry Holt, 1946.

Berman, Ilan. *Tehran Rising: Iran's Challenge to the United States.* Lanham, Md.: Rowman and Littlefield, 2005.

Berman, Paul, et al. "Defending and Advancing Freedom: A Symposium." *Commentary* 120, no. 4 (November 2005): 21–68.

Beschloss, Michael. *The Conquerors: Roosevelt, Truman, and the Destruction of Hitler's Germany. 1941–1945.* New York: Simon and Schuster, 2002.

Betts, Richard K. "The Osirak Fallacy." *National Interest* 83 (Spring 2006): 22–25.

Biddle, Stephen. "Seeing Baghdad, Thinking Saigon." *Foreign Affairs* 85, no. 2 (March/April 2006): 2–14.

bin Laden, Osama. "Declaration of War against Americans Occupying the Land of Two Holy Places." *Al-Quds Al-'Arabi,* August 1996.

Black, Conrad. *Franklin Delano Roosevelt: Champion of Freedom.* New York: Public Affairs, 2003.

Blainey, Geoffrey. *The Causes of War.* 3rd ed. New York: Free Press, 1988.

Boot, Max. *The Savage Wars of Peace: Small Wars and the Rise of American Power.* New York: Basic Books, 2002.

———. "A Transatlantic Truce: Isn't It Pragmatic?" *Los Angeles Times,* February 17, 2005, B13.

Borton, Hugh. *Japan's Modern Century.* New York: Ronald Press, 1955.

Bourne, Peter G. *Jimmy Carter: A Comprehensive Biography from Plains to Post-Presidency.* New York: Scribner's, 1997.

Brinkley, Douglas. *The Unfinished Presidency: Jimmy Carter's Journey beyond the White House.* New York: Viking Press, 1998.

Broder, John M. "In Call for More Troops, McCain Places His Bet on Iraq." *New York Times Online,* November 13, 2006.

Brooks, Stephen G., and William C. Wohlforth. "American Primacy in Perspective." *Foreign Affairs* 81, no. 4 (July/August 2002): 20–34.

———. "Power, Globalization, and the End of the Cold War: Reevaluating the Landmark Case for Ideas." *International Security* 25, no. 3 (Winter 2000–2001): 5–53.

Brown, Archie. *The Gorbachev Factor.* New York: Oxford, 1996.

Brzezinksi, Zbigniew. Interview by Robert G. Kaufman, December 8, 1994.

———. *Power and Principle: Memoirs of the National Security Adviser, 1977–1981.* New York: Farrar, Straus and Giroux, 1983.

Buchanan, Patrick J. *A Republic, Not an Empire: Reclaiming America's Destiny.* Washington, D.C.: Regnery Publishing, 1999.

———. *Where the Right Went Wrong: How Neoconservatives Subverted the Reagan Revolution and Hijacked the Bush Presidency.* New York: Thomas Dunne Books, 2004.

Burleigh, Michael. *The Third Reich: A New History.* New York: Hill and Wang, 2001.

Buruma, Ian, and Avishai Margalit. *Occidentalism: The West in the Eyes of Its Enemies.* New York: Penguin Press, 2004.

Bush, George H. W., and Brent Scowcroft. *A World Transformed.* New York: Alfred A. Knopf, 1998.

Bush, George W. "Call for a New Palestinian Leadership." Washington, D.C., June 24, 2002.

———. "The National Security Strategy of the United States." March 2006.

———. "Remarks at the United States Military Academy." June 2002.

———. "Remarks by the President at the 20th Anniversary of the National Endowment for Democracy." Washington, D.C., November 6, 2003.

———. Second Inaugural Address. January 20, 2005.

Calder, Kent E. "China and Japan's Simmering Rivalry." *Foreign Affairs* 85, no. 2 (March/April 2006): 129–39.

Carr, Edward Hallett. *The Soviet Impact on the Western World.* New York: Macmillan, 1947.

———. *The Twenty Years' Crisis, 1919–1939: An Introduction to the Study of International Relations.* London: Macmillan, 1940.

Carter, Ashton. "America's New Strategic Partner." *Foreign Affairs* 85, no. 4 (July/August 2006): 33–45.

Carter, Jimmy. "Just War—or a Just War." *New York Times,* March 9, 2003, 13.

————. *Our Endangered Values: America's Moral Crisis.* New York: Simon and Schuster, 2005.

"The Case for Democracy" (editorial). *Washington Post,* March 5, 2006, B06.

Chang, Jung, and Jon Halliday. *Mao: The Unknown Story.* New York: Alfred A. Knopf, 2005.

Charlton, Angela. "World Leaders Offer Sharon Compassion." Associated Press, January 5, 2006, available at www.sfgate.com/cgi-bin/article.cgi?file=/n/a/2006/01/05/international/i090207S43.DTL&type=printable.

Chen Jian. *Mao's China and the Cold War.* Chapel Hill: University of North Carolina Press, 2001.

"China's Growing Navy Worries U.S." *International Herald Tribune,* December 31, 2004.

Churchill, Winston. "British Foreign Policy in Europe." March 1936. In R. R. James, ed., *Winston S. Churchill: His Complete Speeches, 1897–1963.* Vol. 6. London: Chelsea House, 1974.

————. "A Congress of Europe—A Speech at the Hague." May 7, 1948.

————. "Constituent Meeting." September 12, 1947. In R. Churchill, ed., *Speeches by Winston Churchill, 1947–48.* London: Cassell, 1950.

————. "Dictators and the Covenant." December 21, 1937. In R. R. James, ed., *Winston Churchill: His Complete Speeches, 1897–1963.* Vol. 6. London: Chelsea House, 1974.

————. *The Gathering Storm.* Boston: Houghton Mifflin, 1948.

————. "An Open Letter to a Communist." August 25, 1934. In M. Gilbert, ed., *Winston S. Churchill, The Wilderness Years.* Boston: Houghton Mifflin, 1982.

————. *Their Finest Hour.* Boston: Houghton Mifflin, 1949.

————. "A Total and Unmitigated Defeat." October 5, 1938. In R. R. James, ed., *Winston S. Churchill: His Complete Speeches, 1897–1963.* Vol. 7. New York: Atheneum, 1983.

Clark, Wesley K. *Waging Modern War: Bosnia, Kosovo, and the Future of Combat.* New York: Public Affairs, 2002.

Clinton, Bill. *My Life.* New York: Alfred A. Knopf, 2004.

Conquest, Robert. *Reflections on a Ravaged Century.* New York: Norton, 2000.

Cooper, John Milton, Jr. *The Warrior and the Priest: Woodrow Wilson and Theodore Roosevelt.* Cambridge: Belknap Press of Harvard University Press, 1985.

Cooper, Robert. *The Breaking of Nations: Order and Chaos in the Twenty-first Century.* New York: Atlantic Monthly Press, 2003.

Courtois, Stéphane, Nicolas Werth, Jean-Louis Panné, Andrzej Paczkowski, Karel Bartošek, and Jean-Louis Margolin. *The Black Book of Communism: Crimes, Terror, Repression.* Trans. Jonathan Murphy and Mark Kramer. Cambridge: Harvard University Press, 1999.

Craig, Gordon A. *Germany, 1866–1945.* New York: Oxford University Press, 1978.

Daalder, Ivo H., and James M. Lindsay. *America Unbound: The Bush Revolution in Foreign Policy.* Washington, D.C.: Brookings Institution Press, 2003.

Dallek, Robert. *Franklin D. Roosevelt and American Foreign Policy, 1932–1945.* New York: Oxford University Press, 1979.

Das, Gurucharan. "The Indian Model." *Foreign Affairs* 85, no. 4 (July/August 2006): 2–16.

DeConde, Alexander. *A History of American Foreign Policy.* 2nd ed. New York: Charles Scribner's Sons, 1962.

Derbyshire, John. "Management or Confrontation? The Brent Scowcroft Problem." *National Review Online,* August 20, 2002, www.nationalreview.com/derbyshire/derbyshire082002.asp.

Dershowitz, Alan. "Debunking the Newest—and Oldest—Jewish Conspiracy: A Reply to the Mearsheimer-Walt Working Paper." Paper delivered at the John F. Kennedy School of Government, April 2006.

Diamond, Larry. *Squandered Victory: The American Occupation and the Bungled Effort to Bring Democracy to Iraq.* New York: Times Books, 2005.

Dobbins, James, Seth G. Jones, Keith Crane, Andrew Rathmell, Brett Steele, Richard Teltschik, and Anga Timilsina. *America's Role in Nation-Building: From Germany to Iraq.* Santa Monica, Calif.: Rand, 2003.

Dobrynin, Anatoly. *In Confidence: Moscow's Ambassador to America's Six Cold War Presidents (1962–1986).* New York: Times Books, 1995.

Doenecke, Justus D. *Storm on the Horizon: The Challenge to American Interventionism, 1939–1941.* Lanham, Md.: Rowman and Littlefield, 2000.

"Does the Israeli Lobby Have Too Much Power?" *Foreign Policy* 155 (July/August 2006): 56–68.

Donnelly, Tom. "Going Out for Indian." *Weekly Standard,* March 30, 2005, available at www.weeklystandard.com/Content/Public/Articles/000/000/005/420lqluy.asp.

Dower, John W. *Embracing Defeat: Japan in the Wake of World War II.* New York: Norton, 1999.

Doyle, Michael W. "Kant, Liberal Legacies, and Foreign Affairs, Part 1." *Journal of Philosophy and Public Affairs* 12, no. 3 (Summer 1983): 205–335.

———. "Kant, Liberal Legacies, and Foreign Affairs, Part 2." *Journal of Philosophy and Public Affairs* 12, no. 4 (Autumn 1983): 323–53.

———. "Liberalism and World Politics." *American Political Science Review* 80, no. 4 (December 1986): 1151–69.

D'Souza, Dinesh. *Ronald Reagan: How an Ordinary Man Became an Extraordinary President.* New York: Free Press, 1997.

Duelfer, Charles. "Comprehensive Report of the Special Advisor to the DCI on Iraq's WMD." September 30, 2004, available at www.cia.gov/cia/reports/iraq_wmd_2004.

Eberstadt, Nicholas. "North Korea's Weapons Quest." *National Interest* 80 (Summer 2005): 49–52.

Ehrman, John. *The Eighties: America in the Age of Reagan.* New Haven: Yale University Press, 2005.

Ellison, Herbert J. "Messengers from Moscow, Parts 1–4." PBS documentary, Fall 1994.

Elshtain, Jean Bethke. *Just War against Terror: The Burden of American Power in a Violent World.* New York: Basic Books, 2003.

English, Robert D. "Power, Ideas, and the New Evidence on the Cold War's End: A Reply to Brooks and Wohlforth." *International Security* 26, no. 4 (Spring 2002): 70–92.

Evans, Richard. *The Coming of the Third Reich.* New York: Penguin Press, 2004.

Ferguson, Niall. *Colossus: The Rise and Fall of the American Empire.* New York: Penguin, 2005.

———. *The Pity of War: Explaining World War I.* New York: Basic Books, 2000.

Fischer, Beth. *The Reagan Reversal: Foreign Policy and the End of the Cold War.* Columbia: University of Missouri Press, 1997.

Fischer, David Hackett. *Washington's Crossing.* New York: Oxford University Press, 2004.

Fischer, Fritz. *Germany's Aims in the First World War.* New York: Norton, 1967.

Fitzgerald, Frances. *Way Out There in the Blue: Reagan, Star Wars, and the End of the Cold War.* New York: Simon and Schuster, 2000.

Fleming, Thomas. *The Illusion of Victory: America in World War I.* New York: Basic Books, 2004.

———. *The New Dealers' War: FDR and the War within World War II.* New York: Basic Books, 2002.

Franc, M. G. "Korean Threat Launches Senate into the Next Phase of Missile Defense." *Human Events Online,* July 1, 2006.

Frankel, Max. *High Noon in the Cold War: Kennedy, Khrushchev, and the Cuban Missile Crisis.* 2004; rept., San Francisco: Presidio Press, 2005.

Friedberg, Aaron L. "Arming China against Ourselves." *Commentary* 108, no. 1 (July/August 1999): 27, available at www.heritage.org/Press/Commentary/ed070106d.cfm.

———. "Asian Allies: True Strategic Partners." In Robert Kagan and William Kristol, eds., *Present Dangers: Crisis and Opportunity in American Foreign and Defense Policy.* San Francisco: Encounter Books, 2000.

———. *In the Shadow of the Garrison State.* Princeton: Princeton University Press, 2000.

———. "The Struggle for Mastery in Asia." *Commentary* 110, no. 4 (November 2000): 17–27.

———. "Will We Abandon Taiwan?" *Commentary* 109, no. 5 (May 2000): 26–32.

Friedrich, Carl J., and Zbigniew K. Brzezinski. *Totalitarian Dictatorship and Autocracy.* Cambridge: Harvard University Press, 1956.

Fromkin, David. *Europe's Last Summer: Who Started the Great War of 1914?* New York: Alfred A. Knopf, 2004.

Fukuyama, Francis. *America at the Crossroads: Democracy, Power, and the Neoconservative Legacy.* New Haven: Yale University Press, 2006.

———. *The End of History and the Last Man.* New York: Free Press, 1992.

Fulbright, James William. *The Arrogance of Power.* New York: Random House, 1966.

Gaddis, John L. *The Cold War: A New History.* New York: Penguin Press, 2005.

———. *Strategies of Containment.* New York: Oxford University Press, 1982.

———. *Surprise, Security, and the American Experience.* Cambridge: Harvard University Press, 2004.

———. *The United States and the Origins of the Cold War, 1941–1947.* New York: Columbia University Press, 1972.

———. *We Now Know: Rethinking Cold War History.* New York: Oxford University Press, 1997.

Galbraith, Peter. *The End of Iraq: How American Incompetence Created a War without End.* New York: Simon and Schuster, 2006.

Garfinkle, Adam. *Telltale Hearts: The Origins and Impact of the Vietnam Antiwar Movement.* New York: St. Martin's Press, 1995.

Garthoff, Raymond L. *Détente and Confrontation: American-Soviet Relations from Nixon to Reagan.* Washington, D.C.: Brookings Institution Press, 1985.

———. *The Great Transition: American-Soviet Relations and the End of the Cold War.* Washington, D.C.: Brookings Institution Press, 1994.

Garton Ash, Timothy. *In Europe's Name: Germany and the Divided Continent.* New York: Random House, 1993.

Gause, F. Gregory, III. "Can Democracy Stop Terrorism?" *Foreign Affairs* 84, no. 5 (September/October 2005): 62–76.

George, Margaret. *The Warped Vision: British Foreign Policy, 1933–1939.* Pittsburgh: University of Pittsburgh Press, 1963.

Gershman, Carl. "The World According to Andrew Young." *Commentary* 66, no. 2 (August 1978): 28–29.

Gilbert, Felix. *To the Farewell Address: Ideas of Early American Foreign Policy.* Princeton: Princeton University Press, 1961.

Gilbert, Martin S. *Winston S. Churchill: The Prophet of Truth, 1922–1939.* Boston: Houghton Mifflin, 1963.

Gilbert, Martin S., and Richard Gott. *The Appeasers.* Boston: Houghton Mifflin, 1963.

Gillon, Steven M. *The Democrats' Dilemma: Walter F. Mondale and the Liberal Legacy.* New York: Columbia University Press, 1992.

Gleason, Abbot. *Totalitarianism: The Inner History of the Cold War.* New York: Oxford University Press, 1995.

Glendon, Mary Ann. *A World Made New: Eleanor Roosevelt and the Universal Declaration of Human Rights.* New York: Random House, 2001.

Glynn, Patrick. *Closing Pandora's Box: Arms Races, Arms Control, and the History of the Cold War*. New York: Basic Books, 1992.

Goldberg, Jeffrey. "Breaking Ranks: What Turned Brent Scowcroft against the Bush Administration." *New Yorker*, October 31, 2005, available at www.newyorker.com/fact/content/articles/051031fa_fact2.

Goldgeier, James M., and Michael McFaul. *Power and Purpose: U.S. Policy toward Russia after the Cold War*. Washington, D.C.: Brookings Institution Press, 2003.

Goldstein, Avery. *Rising to the Challenge: China's Grand Strategy and International Security*. Stanford: Stanford University Press, 2005.

Gordon, Michael R., and Bernard E. Trainor. *Cobra II: The Inside Story of the Invasion and Occupation of Iraq*. New York: Pantheon Books, 2006.

Gray, Colin, and Jeffrey Barlow. "Inexcusable Restraint: The Decline of American Military Power in the 1970s." *International Security* 10, no. 2 (Autumn 1985): 27–69.

Groth, Alex. *Democracies against Hitler: Myth, Reality, and Prologue*. Brookfield, Vt.: Ashgate, 1979.

Gulick, Edward V. *Europe's Classical Balance of Power*. New York: Norton, 1955.

Haass, Richard N. *The Opportunity: America's Moment to Alter History's Course*. New York: Public Affairs, 2005.

Habeck, Mary. *Knowing the Enemy: Jihadist Ideology and the War on Terror*. New Haven, Conn.: Yale University Press, 2006.

Hagel, Chuck. "A Republican Foreign Policy." *Foreign Affairs* 83, no. 4 (July/August 2004): 64.

Halberstam, David. *War in a Time of Peace: Bush, Clinton, and the Generals*. New York: Scribner, 2001.

Halper, Stefan, and Jonathan Clarke. *America Alone: The Neo-Conservatives and the Global Order*. Cambridge: Cambridge University Press, 2004.

Hanby, Alonzo. *Man of the People: A Life of Harry S. Truman*. New York: Oxford University Press, 1995.

Handel, Michael I. *Masters of War: Classical Strategic Thought*. 2nd ed. London: Frank Cass, 1996.

Hanrieder, Wolfram F. *Germany, America, Europe: Forty Years of German Foreign Policy*. New Haven: Yale University Press, 1989.

Hanson, Victor Davis. "The Bush Doctrine's Next Test." *Commentary* 119, no. 5 (May 2005): 21.

———. "Hope amid Despair." *National Review Online*, August 18, 2006, http://article.nationalreview.com/q=MWE4NDBjNzNjNjE4Yzk1NTU2YWQ0Zj E3N2I5ZWE5NWY=.

———. *The Soul of Battle: From Ancient Times to the Present Day, How Three Great Liberators Vanquished Tyranny*. 1999; rept., New York: Anchor Books, 2001.

Hayward, Steven F. *The Real Jimmy Carter*. Washington, D.C.: Regnery, 2004.

Henninger, Daniel. "Father of the Bush Doctrine: George Shultz on Pre-emption and the Revolt of the Generals." *Wall Street Journal,* April 29, 2006, A08.

Herf, Jeffrey. *War by Other Means: Soviet Power, West German Resistance, and the Battle of the Euromissiles.* New York: Free Press, 1991.

Herzog, Michael. "Can Hamas Be Tamed?" *Foreign Affairs* 85, no. 2 (March/April 2006): 83–94.

Hillgruber, Andreas. *Germany and the Two World Wars.* Trans. William C. Kirby. Cambridge: Harvard University Press, 1981.

Hitchcock, William I. *The Struggle for Europe: The Turbulent History of a Divided Continent, 1945 to the Present.* New York: Anchor Books, 2004.

Hixson, Walter L. *George Kennan: Cold War Iconoclast.* New York: Columbia University Press, 1989.

Hoagland, Jim. "Germany's New Outlook." *Washington Post,* October 16, 2005, B07.

———. "Iran's Useful Reminder." *Washington Post,* October 30, 2005, B07.

———. "Middle East Surprises." *Washington Post,* November 27, 1995, B07.

———. "Right Vision, Wrong Policy—And a Middle East Price to Pay." *Washington Post,* November 12, 2006, B07.

Hobbes, Thomas. *Leviathan.* 1651; rept., London: Penguin, 1985.

Hoge, James F. "A Global Power Shift in the Making: Is the United States Ready?" *Foreign Affairs* 83, no. 4 (July 2004): 2–7.

Holbrooke, Richard. "The Guns of August." *Washington Post,* August 10, 2006, A23.

Hollander, Paul, ed. *Understanding Anti-Americanism: Its Origins and Impact at Home and Abroad.* Chicago: Ivan R. Dee, 2004.

Howard, Michael. "The Great War: Mystery or Error." *National Interest* 64 (Summer 2001): 78–85.

Huntington, Samuel P. *American Politics: The Promise of Disharmony.* Cambridge: Belknap Press of Harvard University Press, 1981.

———. *The Third Wave: Democratization in the Late Twentieth Century.* Norman: University of Oklahoma Press, 1993.

Ignatieff, Michael. *The Lesser Evil: Political Ethics in an Age of Terror.* Princeton: Princeton University Press, 2004.

Ikenberry, G. John. "America's Imperial Ambitions." *Foreign Affairs* 77 (September/October 2002): 44.

Ikenberry, G. John, and Charles A. Kupchan. "Liberal Realism: The Foundations of a Democratic Foreign Policy." *National Interest* 77 (Fall 2004): 38–49.

Jackson, Henry M. "Virginia General Assembly Address." Williamsburg, Va., February 4, 1980. Henry M. Jackson Papers, University of Washington, series 3560-6, box 13, folder 68.

James, Robert R., ed. *Winston S. Churchill: His Complete Speeches 1897–1963,* vol. 6. London: Chelsea House, 1943.

Jervis, Robert. *American Foreign Policy in a New Era.* New York: Routledge, 2005.

——. *Perception and Misperception in International Politics.* Princeton: Princeton University Press, 1976.

Joffe, Josef. "Europe's American Pacifier." *Foreign Policy* 54 (Spring 1984): 64–82.

——. *The Limited Partnership: Europe, the United States, and the Burdens of Alliance.* Cambridge: Ballinger, 1987.

——. *Uberpower: The Imperial Temptation of America.* New York: Norton, 2006.

——. "A World without Israel." *Foreign Policy* 146 (January/February 2005): 36–42.

Johnson, Chalmers. "Carter in Asia: McGovernism without McGovern." *Commentary* 65, no. 1 (January 1978): 36–39.

——. *The Sorrows of Empire: Militarism, Secrecy, and the End of the Republic.* New York: Metropolitan Books, 2004.

Johnson, James Turner. *Can Modern War Be Just?* New Haven: Yale University Press, 1984.

——. "Just War, as It Was and Is." *First Things* 149 (January 2005): 14–24.

——. *Just War Tradition and the Restraint of War: A Moral and Historical Inquiry.* Princeton: Princeton University Press, 1981.

——. *The War to Oust Saddam Hussein: Just War and the New Face of Conflict.* Lanham, Md.: Rowman and Littlefield, 2005.

Johnson, Paul. *Modern Times: The World from the Twenties to the Nineties.* Rev. ed. New York: HarperCollins, 1991.

Johnston, Alastair Iain, and Robert S. Ross, eds. *New Directions in the Study of China's Foreign Policy.* Stanford: Stanford University Press, 2006.

Judt, Tony. *Postwar: A History of Europe since 1945.* New York: Penguin Books, 2005.

Kagan, Donald. *On the Origins of War and the Preservation of Peace.* New York: Doubleday, 1995.

Kagan, Frederick W. "No Third Way in Iraq." *Weekly Standard,* November 13, 2006, 23–29.

Kagan, Robert. *Dangerous Nation: America's Place in the World from Its Earliest Days to the Dawn of the Twentieth Century* (New York: Alfred A. Knopf, 2006).

——. "India Is Not a Precedent." *Washington Post,* March 12, 2006, B07.

——. "A Matter of Record." *Foreign Affairs* 84, no. 1 (January/February 2005): 170–73.

——. *Of Paradise and Power: America and Europe in the New World Order.* New York: Vintage, 2004.

Kaplan, Lawrence F., and William Kristol. *The War over Iraq: Saddam's Tyranny and America's Mission.* San Francisco: Encounter Books, 2003.

Kaplan, Robert D. *The Arabists: The Romance of an American Elite.* New York: Free Press, 1993.

Karsh, Efraim. *Arafat's War: The Man and His Battle for Israeli Conquest.* New York: Grove, 2003.

———. *Islamic Imperialism: A History.* New Haven: Yale University Press, 2006.

Kaufman, Robert G. *Arms Control during the Pre-nuclear Era.* New York: Columbia University Press, 1990.

———. *Henry M. Jackson: A Life in Politics.* Seattle: University of Washington Press, 2000.

———. "A Two-Level Interaction: Structure, Stable Liberal Democracy, and U.S. Grand Strategy." *Security Studies* 3, no. 4 (Summer 1994): 678–717.

———. "The UN Record." *The World and I* 16, no. 9 (September 2001): 34–39.

Keegan, J. "How Hitler Could Have Won the War." In R. Cowley, ed., *What If? The World's Foremost Military Historians Imagine What Might Have Been.* New York: Putnam, 1999.

———. *The Iraq War.* New York: Alfred A. Knopf, 2004.

Kengor, Paul. *The Crusader: Ronald Reagan and the Fall of Communism.* New York: Regan Books, 2006.

———. *God and Ronald Reagan: A Spiritual Life.* New York: Regan Books, 2004.

Kennan, George Frost. *American Diplomacy: 1900–1950.* Chicago: University of Chicago Press, 1951.

———. *From Prague after Munich: Diplomatic Papers, 1938–1940.* Princeton: Princeton University Press, 1968.

———. "Morality and Foreign Policy." *Foreign Affairs 64,* no. 2 (Winter 1985–1986): 205–18.

———. *Realities of American Foreign Policy.* Princeton: Princeton University Press, 1954.

Kennedy, Paul. "The Eagle Has Landed." *Financial Times,* February 2, 2002, I, IV.

———. *The Parliament of Man: The Past, Present, and Future of the United Nations.* New York: Random House, 2006.

———. *The Rise and Fall of the Great Powers: Economic Change and Military Conflict from 1500 to 2000.* New York: Vintage, 1989 (paperback edition).

Kepel, Gilles. *The War for Muslim Minds: Islam and the West.* Trans. Pascale Ghazaleh. Cambridge: Belknap Press of Harvard University Press, 2004.

Kepel, Gilles, and Anthony F. Roberts. *Jihad: The Trail of Political Islam.* Trans. Anthony F. Roberts. Cambridge: Belknap Press of Harvard University Press, 2002.

Kershaw, Ian. *Hitler, 1936–1945: Nemesis.* New York: Norton, 2000.

Kessler, Glenn. "Scowcroft Critical of Bush, Cheney." *Washington Post,* October 16, 2004, A02.

Kimball, Warren F. *The Juggler: Franklin Roosevelt as Wartime Statesman.* Princeton: Princeton University Press, 1991.

King, Neil, Jr. "A Scholar Shapes Views of China." *Wall Street Journal,* September 8, 2005, 1.

Kirkpatrick, Jeane J. *Dictatorships and Double Standards: Rationalism and Reason in Politics.* New York: Simon and Schuster, 1982.

Kissinger, Henry A. *American Foreign Policy.* London: Weidenfeld and Nicolson, 1969.

———. *Diplomacy.* New York: Simon and Schuster, 1994.

———. *Does America Need a Foreign Policy? Toward a Diplomacy for the 21st Century.* New York: Simon and Schuster, 2001.

———. "Intervention with a Vision." In G. Rosen, ed., *The Right War? The Conservative Debate on Iraq.* New York: Cambridge University Press, 2005.

———. *The White House Years.* Boston: Little, Brown, 1979.

———. *A World Restored: Metternich, Castlereagh, and the Problems of Peace, 1812–1822.* Boston: Houghton Mifflin, 1957.

———. *Years of Renewal.* New York: Simon and Schuster, 1999.

———. *Years of Upheaval.* Boston: Little, Brown, 1982.

Knock, Thomas J. *To End All Wars: Woodrow Wilson and the Quest for a New World Order.* 1992; rept., Princeton: Princeton University Press, 1995.

Kramer, Martin. *Ivory Towers on Sand: The Failure of Middle Eastern Studies in America.* Washington, D.C.: Washington Institute for Near East Policy, 2001.

Krauthammer, Charles. *Democratic Realism: An American Foreign Policy for a Unipolar World.* Washington, D.C.: AEI Press, 2004.

———. "In Defense of Democratic Realism." *National Interest* 77 (Fall 2004): 15–25.

———. "Man for a Glass Booth." *Washington Post,* December 9, 2005, A31.

———. "The Power of Faith." *Washington Post,* April 4, 2005, A21.

———. "Syria and the New Axis of Evil." *Washington Post,* April 4, 2005, A27.

———. "The Tehran Calculus." *Washington Post,* September 15, 2006, A9.

———. "Why Iraq Is Crumbling." *Washington Post,* November 17, 2006, A25.

Kristol, William, and Robert Kagan. "Toward a Neo-Reaganite Foreign Policy." *Foreign Affairs* 75, no. 4 (July/August 1996): 18–32.

Kupchan, Charles H. *The End of the American Era: U.S. Foreign Policy and the Geopolitics of the Twenty-first Century.* 2002; rept., New York: Vintage, 2003.

Lacouture, Jean. *De Gaulle: The Ruler, 1945–1970.* New York: Norton, 1992.

LaFeber, Walter. *America, Russia, and the Cold War, 1945–1992.* 7th ed. New York: McGraw-Hill, 1993.

Larson, Deborah Welch. *Anatomy of Mistrust: U.S.–Soviet Relations during the Cold War.* Ithaca: Cornell University Press, 1997.

Layne, Christopher. "Why the Gulf War Was Not in the National Interest." *Atlantic Monthly,* July 1991, 54–81.

Lebow, Richard Ned, and Janice Gross Stein, eds. *We All Lost the Cold War.* Princeton: Princeton University Press, 1994.

Lebow, Richard Ned, and Thomas Risse-Kappen, eds. *International Relations Theory and the End of the Cold War.* New York: Columbia University Press, 1995.

Lee, Stephen J. *The European Dictatorships, 1918–1945.* London: Methuen, 1987.

Leebaert, Derek. *The Fifty-Year Wound: The True Price of America's Cold War Victory.* Boston: Little, Brown, 2002.

Leffler, Melvyn P. "Inside Enemy Archives." *Foreign Affairs* 75, no. 4 (July/August 1996): 120–35.

———. *A Preponderance of Power: National Security, the Truman Administration, and the Cold War.* Stanford: Stanford University Press, 1992.

Legvold, Robert. "Eastern Europe and the Former Soviet Republics." *Foreign Affairs* (July/August 1996): 153–56.

Lettow, Paul. *Ronald Reagan and His Quest to Abolish Nuclear Weapons.* New York: Random House, 2005.

Levy, David H., and Stuart S. Brown. "The Overstretch Myth, or How We Learned to Stop Worrying and Love the Current Account Deficit." *Foreign Affairs* 84, no. 2 (March/April 2005): 2–7.

Lewis, Bernard. *The Crisis of Islam: Holy War and Unholy Terror.* New York: Modern Library, 2003.

———. "Freedom and Justice in the Modern Middle East." *Foreign Affairs* 84, no. 3 (May/June 2005): 36–51.

———. *From Babel to Dragomans: Interpreting the Middle East.* New York: Oxford University Press, 2004.

———. *What Went Wrong: The Clash between Islam and Modernity in the Middle East.* New York: Harper Perennial, 2003.

Lieber, Robert J. *The American Era: Power and Strategy for the 21st Century.* Cambridge: Cambridge University Press, 2005.

———. "The Folly of Containment." *Commentary* 115, no. 4 (April 2003): 15–21.

———. "Foreign Policy Realists Are Unrealistic on Iraq." *Chronicle of Higher Education* 49, no. 8 (October 18, 2002): B15.

Lieberman, Joe. "Our Troops Must Stay." *Wall Street Journal,* November 29, 2005, A18.

Lim, Robyn. *The Geopolitics of East Asia: Search for Equilibrium.* New York: Routledge/Curzon, 2003.

Link, Arthur S. *Wilson the Diplomatist: A Look at His Major Foreign Policies.* Baltimore: Johns Hopkins University Press, 1957.

Lowry, Richard. "Reaganism v. Neo-Reaganism." *National Interest* 79 (Spring 2005): 35–41.

Lundestad, Geir. "Empire by Invitation? The United States and Western Europe, 1945–1952." *Journal of Peace Research* 23, no. 3 (September 1986): 262–77.

Luttwak, Edward N. "Three Reasons Not to Bomb Iran—Yet." *Commentary* 121, no. 5 (May 2006): 21–28.

Macdonald, Douglas J. *Adventures in Chaos: American Intervention for Reform in the Third World.* Cambridge: Harvard University Press, 1992.

Machiavelli, Niccolo. *The Prince.* 2nd ed. Trans. Harvey C. Mansfield. Chicago: University of Chicago Press, 1998.

———. *The Prince, and The Discourses.* New York: Modern Library, 1950.

Mackinder, Halford John. *Democratic Ideals and Reality.* New York: Norton, 1962.

MacMillan, Margaret. *Paris 1919: Six Months That Changed the World.* New York: Random House, 2002.

Makovsky, David. "Gaza: Moving Forward by Pulling Back." *Foreign Affairs* 84, no. 3 (May/June 2005): 52–62.

Malia, Martin. *The Soviet Tragedy: A History of Socialism in Russia, 1917–1991.* New York: Free Press, 1994.

Mandelbaum, Michael. *The Case for Goliath: How America Acts as the World's Government in the Twenty-first Century.* New York: Public Affairs, 2005.

Mann, James. *About Face: A History of America's Curious Relationship with China, from Nixon to Clinton.* New York: Alfred A. Knopf, 1999.

Marks, Frederick W., III. *Wind over Sand: The Diplomacy of Franklin Roosevelt.* Athens: University of Georgia Press, 1988.

Matlock, Jack F. *Reagan and Gorbachev: How the Cold War Ended.* New York: Random House, 2004.

Maxton, Yale Candee. *Control of Japan's Foreign Policy: A Study in Civilian Military Rivalry, 1930–1945.* Berkeley: University of California Press, 1957.

McDonald, Forrest. *The Presidency of George Washington.* Lawrence: University Press of Kansas, 1974.

McFaul, Michael, and James M. Goldgeier. "Putin's Authoritarian Soul." *Weekly Standard,* February 28, 2005, 14–17.

McFaul, Michael, Nikolai Petrov, and Andrei Riabov. *Between Dictatorship and Democracy: Russian Post-Communist Political Reform.* Washington, D.C.: Carnegie Endowment for International Peace, 2004.

McManus, Doyle. "Kissinger Says Iraq Isn't Ripe for Democracy." *Los Angeles Times,* November 15, 2006, A1.

Mead, Walter Russell. "God's Country." *Foreign Affairs* (September/October 2006): 40–41.

———. *Power, Terror, Peace, and War: America's Grand Strategy in a World at Risk.* New York: Alfred A. Knopf, 2004.

———. *Special Providence: American Foreign Policy and How It Changed the World.* New York: Routledge, 2002.

Mearsheimer, John J. "Back to the Future: Instability in Europe after the Cold War." *International Security* 15, no. 1 (Summer 1990): 5–56.

———. "Guns Won't Win the Afghan War." *New York Times,* November 4, 2001, sect. 4, 13.

———. "The Israel Lobby and U.S. Foreign Policy." Working paper no. RPW06–011, John F. Kennedy School of Government, Harvard University, 2006.

———. *The Tragedy of Great Power Politics.* New York: Norton, 2001.

Mearsheimer, John J., and Stephen M. Walt. "Can Saddam Be Contained? History Says Yes." Paper presented at the Belfer Center for Science and International Affairs, John F. Kennedy School of Government, Harvard University, November 12, 2002.

———. "Guns Won't Win the Afghan War." *New York Times,* November 4, 2001, 13.

———. "An Unnecessary War." *Foreign Policy* 134 (January/February 2003): 51–60.

Mearsheimer, John J., et al. "War with Iraq Is Not in America's National Interest." Paid advertisement. *New York Times,* September 26, 2002.

Menges, Constantine C. *China: The Gathering Threat.* Nashville, Tenn.: Nelson Current, 2005.

Meredith, Martin. *The Fate of Africa: From the Hopes of Freedom to the Heart of Despair.* New York: Public Affairs, 2005.

Merry, Robert M. *Sands of Empire: Missionary Zeal, American Foreign Policy, and the Hazards of Global Ambition.* New York: Simon and Schuster, 2005.

Middlemas, Keith. *Strategy of Appeasement: The British Government and Germany, 1937–39.* Chicago: Quadrangle, 1972.

Mojan, C. Raja. "India and the Balance of Power." *Foreign Affairs* 85, no. 4 (July/August 2006): 17–32.

Morgenthau, Hans J. *Politics among Nations: The Struggle for Power and Peace.* 6th ed. Rev. Kenneth Thompson. New York: Alfred A. Knopf, 1985.

———. *Scientific Man vs. Power Politics.* Chicago: University of Chicago Press, 1946.

Moynihan, Daniel Patrick. Interview by Robert G. Kaufman, July 28, 1996.

Moynihan, Daniel Patrick, with Suzanne Weaver. *A Dangerous Place.* Boston: Little, Brown, 1978.

Muravchik, Joshua. *The Future of the United Nations: Understanding the Past to Chart a Way Forward.* Washington, D.C.: AEI Press, 2005.

———. "In the Cold War: Kerry Froze." *Los Angeles Times,* August 10, 2004, B13.

———. *Uncertain Crusade: Jimmy Carter and the Dilemmas of Human Rights Policy.* Washington D.C.: AEI Press, 1988.

Murray, Williamson. *The Change in the European Balance of Power, 1938–1939: The Path to Ruin.* Princeton: Princeton University Press, 1984.

Nathan, Andrew J., and Robert S. Ross. *The Great Wall and the Empty Fortress: China's Search for Security.* New York: Norton, 1997.

National Security Council. "National Strategy for Victory in Iraq." Washington, D.C.: Government Printing Office, 2005.

National Security Council (NSC) 68. "United States Objectives and Programs for National Security." April 14, 1950. In Ernest May, ed., *American Cold War Strategy: Interpreting NSC 68*. Boston: Bedford Books of St. Martin's Press, 1993.

National Security Decision Directive (NSDD) 75. "U.S. Relations with the U.S.S.R." January 19, 1983. Records Declassified and Released by the National Security Council, Ronald Reagan Presidential Library.

——— 172. "Strategic Defense Initiative." May 30, 1985. Ronald Reagan Presidential Library.

——— 192. "The ABM Treaty." October 11, 1985. Ronald Reagan Presidential Library.

——— 209. "Implementing the Decisions of the Geneva Summit." February 4, 1986. Ronald Reagan Presidential Library.

——— 227. "U.S. Interim Restraint Policy." August 25, 1986. Ronald Reagan Presidential Library.

——— 245. "Reagan-Gorbachev Preparatory Meeting." October 7, 1986. Ronald Reagan Presidential Library.

——— 248. "Central America." October 22, 1986. Ronald Reagan Presidential Library.

——— 250. "Post-Reykjavik Followup." November 3, 1986. Ronald Reagan Presidential Library.

——— 288. "My Objectives at the Summit." November 10, 1987. Ronald Reagan Presidential Library.

——— 305. "Objectives of the Moscow Summit." April 26, 1988. Ronald Reagan Presidential Library.

National Security Study Directive (NSSD) 11–82. August 21, 1982. Ronald Reagan Presidential Library.

Niebuhr, Reinhold. *The Children of Light and the Children of Darkness: A Vindication of Democracy and a Critique of Its Traditional Defense*. New York: Charles Scribner's Sons, 1944.

———. *Christianity and Power Politics*. New York: Charles Scribner's Sons, 1940.

Nixon, Richard M. Interview by Robert G. Kaufman, June 1993.

———. *RN: The Memoirs of Richard Nixon*. 1978; rept., New York: Touchstone, 1990.

Nordlinger, Eric. *Isolationism Reconfigured: American Foreign Policy for a New Century*. Princeton: Princeton University Press, 1995.

Nye, Joseph S., Jr. *The Paradox of American Power: Why the World's Only Superpower Can't Go It Alone*. New York: Oxford University Press, 2002.

———. *Soft Power: The Means to Success in World Politics*. New York: Public Affairs, 2004.

Odom, William. "Soviet Politics and After: Old and New Concepts." *World Politics* 45, no. 1 (October 1992): 66–98.

O'Hanlon, Michael, and Mike M. Mochizuki. *Crisis on the Korean Peninsula: How to Deal with a Nuclear North Korea*. New York: McGraw-Hill, 2003.

Osgood, Robert E. *Ideals and Self-Interest in America's Foreign Relation*. Chicago: University of Chicago Press, 1953.

Owen, John M. *Liberal Peace, Liberal War: American Politics and International Security*. Ithaca: Cornell University Press, 1997.

Peattie, Mark R. *Ishiwara Kanji and Japan's Confrontation with the West*. Princeton: Princeton University Press, 1975.

Perlmutter, Amos. *FDR and Stalin: The Not So Grand Alliance, 1943–1945*. Columbia: University of Missouri Press, 1993.

Pieper, Josef. *The Four Cardinal Virtues*. Notre Dame, Ind.: University of Notre Dame Press, 1966.

Pillsbury, Michael. *China Debates the Future Security Environment*. Washington, D.C.: National Defense University Press, 2000.

———, ed. *Chinese Views of Future Warfare*. Washington, D.C.: National Defense University Press, 1998.

Pipes, Daniel. *In the Path of God: Islam and Political Power*. 1983; rept., New Brunswick, N.J.: Transaction Books, 2002.

Pipes, Richard. *Communism: The Vanished Specter*. New York: Oxford University Press, 1994.

———. Interview by Robert G. Kaufman, September 26, 1995.

———. "Misinterpreting the Cold War." *Foreign Affairs* 74, no. 1 (January/February 1995): 154–60.

———. *Russia under the Bolshevik Regime*. New York: Alfred A. Knopf, 1993.

———. "The Soviet Union Adrift." *Foreign Affairs: America and the World* 70, no. 1 (1990–1991): 70–87.

———. *Survival Is Not Enough: Soviet Realities and America's Future*. New York: Simon and Schuster, 1984.

———. *Vixi: Memoirs of a Non-Belonger*. New Haven: Yale University Press, 2003.

———, ed. *The Unknown Lenin: From the Secret Archive*. New Haven: Yale University Press, 1996.

Podhoretz, Norman. "Is the Bush Doctrine Dead?" *Commentary* 122, no. 2 (September 2006): 17–31.

———. "The War against World War IV." *Commentary* 119, no. 2 (February 2005): 23.

Pollack, Kenneth M. *The Persian Puzzle: The Conflict between Iran and America*. New York: Random House, 2004.

———. *The Threatening Storm: The Case for Invading Iraq*. New York: Random House, 2002.

Posen, Barry. "U.S. Security Policy in a Nuclear Armed World." *Security Studies* 6, no. 3 (Spring 1997): 1–31.

Powell, Colin. "U.S. Forces: Challenges Ahead." *Foreign Affairs* 71, no. 5 (Winter 1992): 32–45.

Power, Samantha. *A Problem from Hell: America and the Age of Genocide.* New York: Basic Books, 2002.

Powers, Richard G. *Not Without Honor: The History of American Anticommunism.* New York: Free Press, 1995.

Preble, Chris, ed. *Exiting Iraq: Why the U.S. Must End the Military Occupation and Renew the War against Al Qaeda.* Washington, D.C.: Cato Institute, 2004.

Puddington, Arch. "The Wages of Durban." *Commentary* 112, no. 4 (November 2001): 29.

Rabkin, Jeremy A. *The Case for Sovereignty: Why the World Should Welcome American Independence.* Washington, D.C.: AEI Press, 2004.

Radosh, Ronald. *Divided They Fell: The Demise of the Democratic Party, 1964–1996.* New York: Free Press, 1996.

Reagan, Ronald. "Address to the British Parliament." June 8, 1982.

———. *An American Life.* New York: Simon and Schuster, 1990.

———. "Commencement Address at Notre Dame." May 1981.

———. "How Do You Fight Communism?" *Fortnight* (1951). Ronald Reagan Presidential Library.

———. "Losing Freedoms by Installments." Speech to Long Beach Rotary Club, June 6, 1962. Ronald Reagan Presidential Library, Ronald Reagan Presidential Papers, box 43.

———. *Reagan in His Own Hand: The Writings of Ronald Reagan That Reveal His Revolutionary Vision for America.* Ed. Annelise Anderson and Martin Anderson. New York: Free Press, 2001.

———. "Remarks at the Annual Convention of the National Association of Evangelicals." Orlando, Fla., March 8, 1983.

———. Ronald Reagan to Victor Krulak, June 6, 1983. Ronald Reagan Presidential Library, Presidential Handwriting File, series 2.

———. "Speech at Westminster Cold War Memorial." Fulton, Mo., November 19, 1990.

———. "Speech before the Brandenburg Gate." West Berlin, June 12, 1987.

Record, Jeffrey. *Dark Victory: America's Second War against Iraq.* Annapolis: Naval Institute Press, 2004.

Revel, Jean-François. *Anti-Americanism.* Trans. Diarmid Cammell. New York: Encounter Books, 2003.

Revel, Jean-François, with Branko Lazitch. *How Democracies Perish.* Trans. William Byron. Garden City, N.Y.: Doubleday, 1984.

Reynolds, David. *In Command of History: Churchill Fighting and Writing the Second World War.* New York: Random House, 2005.

Rock, William R. *British Appeasement in the 1930s.* New York: Norton, 1977.

Rodman, Peter W. *More Precious Than Peace: The Cold War and the Struggle for the Third World.* New York: Charles Scribner's, 1994.

Roger, Philippe. *The American Enemy: The History of French Anti-Americanism.* Trans. Sharon Bowman. Chicago: University of Chicago Press, 2005.

Ross, Dennis. *The Missing Peace: The Inside Story of the Fight for Middle East Peace.* New York: Farrar, Straus and Giroux, 2004.

Ross, Robert S. "Beijing as a Conservative Power." *Foreign Affairs* 76, no. 2 (March/April 1997): 33–44.

———. "The Stability of Deterrence in the Taiwan Strait." *National Interest* 65 (Fall 2001): 67.

———. "Taiwan's Fading Independence Movement." *Foreign Affairs* (March/April 2006): 141–48.

———. "Why Our Hardliners Are Wrong." *National Interest* 49 (Fall 1997): 42.

Rostow, Eugene V. *Toward Managed Peace: The National Security Interests of the United States, 1759 to the Present.* New Haven: Yale University Press, 1993.

Rowse, A. L. *Appeasement: A Study of Political Decline.* New York: Norton, 1963.

Roy, Olivier. *The Failure of Political Islam.* Trans. Carol Volk. Cambridge: Harvard University Press, 1996.

———. *Globalized Islam: The Search for a New Ummah.* New York: Columbia University Press, 2004.

Russell, Greg. *Hans J. Morgenthau and the Ethics of American Statecraft.* Baton Rouge: Louisiana State University Press, 1990.

Russett, Bruce. *Grasping the Democratic Peace: Principles for a Post–Cold War World.* Princeton: Princeton University Press, 1993.

Safire, William. "Putin's Chicken Kiev." *New York Times,* December 6, 2004, 23.

Safran, Bezalel. *Israel, the Embattled Ally.* Cambridge: Harvard University Press, 1981.

Sarotte, M. E. *Dealing with the Devil: East Germany, Détente, and Ostpolitik, 1969–1973.* Chapel Hill: University of North Carolina Press, 2001.

Scalapino, Robert. *Democracy and the Party Movement in Prewar Japan: The Failure of the First Attempt.* Berkeley: University of California Press, 1953.

———. "Democratizing Dragons: South Korea and Taiwan." *Journal of Democracy* 4, no. 3 (Summer 1993): 70–84.

Schlesinger, Arthur M., Jr. *A Thousand Days: John F. Kennedy in the White House.* Boston: Houghton Mifflin, 1965.

Schoenfeld, Gabriel. "Dual Loyalty and the 'Israel Lobby.'" *Commentary* (November 2006): 33–40.

Schroeder, Paul. "Mirror, Mirror, on the War." *American Interest* 1, no. 3 (Spring 2006): 41–55.

Schuettinger, Robert. "The New Foreign Policy Network." *Policy Review* (July 1977): 95–119.

Schweizer, Peter. *Reagan's War: The Epic Story of His Forty-Year Struggle and Final Triumph over Communism.* New York: Doubleday, 2002.

——. *Victory: The Reagan Administration's Secret Strategy That Hastened the Collapse of the Soviet Union.* New York: Atlantic Monthly Press, 1994.

Scowcroft, Brent. "Don't Attack Saddam." *Wall Street Journal,* August 15, 2002, A12.

——. Memorandum. June 26, 1975. Henry Martin Jackson Papers, University of Washington, Seattle, series 3560-6, box 38, folder 1.

——. "A Modest Proposal." *National Interest* 83 (Spring 2006): 13–15.

Shambaugh, David, ed. *Power Shift: China and Asia's New Dynamics.* Berkeley: University of California Press, 2005

Sharansky, Natan, with Ron Dermer. *The Case for Democracy: The Power of Freedom to Overcome Tyranny and Terror.* New York: Public Affairs, 2004.

Shawcross, William. *Allies: The U.S., Britain, Europe, and the War in Iraq.* New York: Public Affairs, 2004.

Shimko, Keith L. *Images and Arms Control: Perceptions of the Soviet Union in the Reagan Administration.* Ann Arbor: University of Michigan Press, 1991.

Shulman, Marshall D. "On Learning to Live with Authoritarian Regimes." *Foreign Affairs* 55, no. 3 (January 1977): 325–38.

Shultz, George P. *Turmoil and Triumph: My Years as Secretary of State.* New York: Charles Scribner's Sons, 1993.

Simes, Dimitri. "The Unrealists." *National Interest* 84 (Summer 2006): 5–7.

Slater, Jerome. "What Went Wrong: The Collapse of the Israeli-Palestinian Peace Process." *Political Science Quarterly* 16, no. 2 (Summer 2001): 171–99.

Smith, Tony. *America's Mission: The United States and the Worldwide Struggle for Democracy in the Twentieth Century.* Princeton: Princeton University Press, 1994.

Snyder, Jack L. *From Voting to Violence: Democratization and Nationalist Conflict.* New York: Norton, 2000.

Spalding, Elizabeth E. *The First Cold Warrior: Harry Truman, Containment, and the Remaking of Liberal Internationalism.* Lexington: University Press of Kentucky, 2006.

Spiegel, Peter. "Perle Says He Should Not Have Backed the Iraq War." *Los Angeles Times,* November 5, 2006, A1.

Stewart, Graham. *Burying Caesar: The Churchill-Chamberlain Rivalry.* Woodstock, N.Y.: Overlook Press, 2001.

Steyn, Mark. *America Alone: The End of the World as We Know It.* Washington, D.C.: Regnery, 2006.

Stobart, Janet. "Blair Defends Foreign Policy of Intervention." *Los Angeles Times,* March 22, 2006, A3.

Stoler, Mark A. *Allies and Adversaries: The Joint Chiefs of Staff, the Grand Alliance, and U.S. Strategy in World War II.* Chapel Hill: University of North Carolina Press, 2000.

Sun Tzu. *The Art of War.* Trans. Lionel Giles. Mineola, N.Y.: Dover, 2002.

Sutter, Robert G. *China's Rise in Asia: Promises and Perils.* Lanham, Md.: Rowman and Littlefield, 2005.

Taheri, Amir. "Getting Serious about Iran: For Regime Change," *Commentary* (November 2006): 21–27.

Talmon, Jacob Leib. *The Origins of Totalitarian Democracy.* New York: Praeger, 1960.

Taylor, Alan John Percivale. *Origins of the Second World War.* 1961; rept., New York: Simon and Schuster, 1996.

Taylor, Telford. *The Anatomy of the Nuremberg Trials: A Personal Memoir.* New York: Alfred A. Knopf, 1992.

Temes, Peter S. *The Just War: An American Reflection on the Morality of War in Our Time.* Chicago: Ivan R. Dee, 2003.

Terrill, Ross. *The New Chinese Empire, and What It Means for the United States.* New York: Basic Books, 2003.

Thomas Aquinas. *Summa Theologica,* Vol. 2. Trans. The Fathers of the English Dominican Province. Chicago and London: Encyclopedia Britannica, 1948.

Timmerman, Kenneth R. *The French Betrayal of America.* New York: Crown Forum, 2004.

Tocqueville, Alexis de. *Democracy in America.* Trans. and ed. Harvey C. Mansfield and Delba Winthrop. 1835, 1840; rept., Chicago: University of Chicago Press, 2000.

Trenin, Dmitri. "Russia Leaves the West." *Foreign Affairs* 85, no. 4 (July/August 2006): 87–96.

Troy, Gil. *Morning in America: How Ronald Reagan Invented the 1980s.* Princeton: Princeton University Press, 2005.

Tucker, Nancy B., ed. *Dangerous Strait: The U.S.–Taiwan–China Crisis.* New York: Columbia University Press, 2005.

Tucker, Robert W., and David C. Hendrickson. *Empire of Liberty: The Statecraft of Thomas Jefferson.* New York: Oxford University Press, 1990.

———. "The Flip Side of the Record." *Foreign Affairs* 84, no. 2 (March/April 2005): 139–41.

———. "The Sources of American Legitimacy." *Foreign Affairs* 83, no. 6 (November/December 2004): 18–32.

Twining, Daniel. "Putin's Power Politics." *Weekly Standard,* January 16, 2006, 17–24.

Ulam, Adam B. *The Communists: The Story of Power and Lost Illusions, 1948–1991.* New York: Charles Scribner's Sons, 1992.

———. *Dangerous Relations: The Soviet Union in World Politics, 1970–1982.* New York: Oxford University Press, 1983.

———. *Expansion and Coexistence: Soviet Foreign Policy, 1917–73.* 2nd ed. New York: Praeger, 1974.

U.S. Office of Management and Budget. *Budget of the United States: FY 1978–1982*. Washington, D.C.: Government Printing Office, 1979–1983.

Van Evera, Stephen. "The Case against Intervention." *Atlantic Monthly*, July 1990, 72.

"Vance: Man on the Move." *Time*, April 24, 1978, available at www.time.com/time/magazine/article/0,9171,916105,00.html.

Waldron, Arthur. "Bowing to Beijing." *Commentary* 106, no. 3 (September 1998): 15–20.

———. "The Chinese Sickness." *Commentary* 116, no. 1 (July 2003): 36–42.

———. "Deterring China." *Commentary* 100, no. 4 (October 1995): 17–21.

———. "A Free and Democratic China." *Commentary* 110, no. 4 (November 2000): 27–32.

———. "Hong Kong and the Future of Freedom." *Commentary* 116, no. 2 (September 2003): 21–25.

———. "How Not to Deal with China." *Commentary* 103, no. 3 (March 1997): 44–49.

———. "Our Game with North Korea." *Commentary* 117, no. 2 (September 2004): 27–32.

Walt, Stephen M. "Alliances, Threats, and U.S. Grand Strategy: A Reply to Kaufman and Labs." *Security Studies* 2, no. 3 (Spring 1992): 444–82.

———. "The Blame Game." *Foreign Policy* 151 (November/December 2005): 44–46.

———. "The Case for Finite Containment: Analyzing U.S. Grand Strategy." *International Security* 14, no. 1 (Summer 1989): 5–49.

———. "Never Say Never." *Foreign Affairs* 78, no. 1 (January/February 1999): 146–51.

———. *The Origins of Alliances*. Ithaca: Cornell University Press, 1987.

———. *Taming American Power: The Global Response to U.S. Primacy*. New York: Norton, 2005.

Waltz, Kenneth M. *Theory of International Politics*. Reading, Mass.: Addison-Wesley, 1979.

Walzer, Michael. *Arguing about War*. New Haven: Yale University Press, 2004.

———. *Just and Unjust Wars: A Moral Argument with Historical Illustrations*. 3rd ed. New York: Basic Books, 2000.

Warnke, Paul. "Apes on a Treadmill." *Foreign Policy* 18 (Spring 1975): 12–29.

Washington, George. "Farewell Address." In Matthew Spalding and Patrick J. Garrity, eds., *A Sacred Union of Citizens: George Washington's Farewell Address and the American Character*. Lanham, Md.: Rowman and Littlefield, 1996.

Weart, Spencer. *Never at War: Why Democracies Will Not Fight One Another*. New Haven: Yale University Press, 1998.

Weigel, George. *The Cube and the Cathedral: Europe, America, and Politics without God*. New York: Basic Books, 2005.

———. *The Final Revolution: The Resistance Church and the Collapse of Communism*. New York: Oxford University Press, 1992.

———. *Tranquillitas Ordinis: The Present Failure and Future Promise of American Catholic Thought on War and Peace*. New York: Oxford University Press, 1987.

Weinberg, Gerhard. *A World at Arms: A Global History of World War II*. Cambridge: Cambridge University Press, 1994.

Weinberger, Casper. "Speech at the National Press Club." Washington, D.C., November 28, 1984.

Will, George F. "Questions to Guide an Exit Policy." *Washington Post*, October 22, 2006, B7.

———. "The Triumph of Unrealism." *Washington Post*, August 15, 2006.

Williams, William A. *The Tragedy of American Diplomacy*. 2nd ed. New York: Dell, 1972.

Wohlforth, William C. "Realism and the End of the Cold War." *International Security* 19, no. 3 (Winter 1994): 91–129.

———. "The Stability of a Unipolar World." *International Security* 24, no. 1 (Summer 1999): 5–41.

———, ed. *Cold War Endgame: Oral History, Analysis, Debates*. University Park: Pennsylvania State University Press, 2003.

Wolfers, Arnold. *Discord and Collaboration: Essays on International Politics*. Baltimore: Johns Hopkins University Press, 1962.

Woods, Randall B. *Fulbright: A Biography*. Cambridge: Cambridge University Press, 1995.

Wunderlin, Clarence E. *Robert A. Taft: Ideas, Tradition, and Party in U.S. Foreign Policy*. Lanham, Md.: Rowman and Littlefield Publishers, 2005.

Yeltsin, Boris. *Washington Post*, January 30, 1995, A09.

Yergin, Daniel. *Shattered Peace: The Origins of the Cold War and the National Security State*. Boston: Houghton Mifflin, 1977.

Zakaria, Fareed. "Don't Punt on the Troops Issue." *Newsweek*, November 20, 2006, 48.

———. *The Future of Freedom: Illiberal Democracy at Home and Abroad*. New York: Norton, 2004.

———. "India Rising." *Newsweek*, March 6, 2006, 32–42.

———. "Realism and Domestic Politics: A Review Essay." *International Security* 17, no. 1 (Summer 1992): 177–98.

———. "What Bush Got Right." *Newsweek*, March 14, 2005, 22–26.

———. "Why Iraq Is Still Worth the Effort." *Washington Post*, March 22, 2006, A21.

Zelikow, Phillip D., and Condoleezza Rice. *Germany Unified and Europe Transformed: A Study in Statecraft*. Cambridge: Harvard University Press, 1995.

Zheng Bijian. "China's Peaceful Rise to Great Power Status." *Foreign Affairs* 84, no. 5 (September/October 2005): 18.

Zubok, Vladislav, and Constantin Pleshakov. *Inside the Kremlin's Cold War: From Stalin to Khrushchev.* Cambridge: Harvard University Press, 1996.

Zweig, David, and Bi Jianhai. "China's Global Hunt for Energy." *Foreign Affairs* 84, no. 5 (September/October 2005): 25–38.

Index